D1602704

PRACTICAL LESSONS ON THE EXPERIENCE OF LIFE

WITNESS LEE

Living Stream Ministry
Anaheim, CA

© 2001 Living Stream Ministry

First Edition, June 2001.

ISBN 0-7363-1241-2

Published by

Living Stream Ministry
2431 W. La Palma Ave., Anaheim, CA 92801 U.S.A.
P. O. Box 2121, Anaheim, CA 92814 U.S.A.

Printed in the United States of America

01 02 03 04 05 06 07 / 9 8 7 6 5 4 3 2 1

CONTENTS

PREFACE

This book is composed of messages given by Brother Witness Lee in a training in Los Angeles, California from November 1964 to July 1965. These messages were not reviewed by the speaker.

CHAPTER ONE

THE EXPERIENCE OF REGENERATION

(1)

Scripture Reading: Gen. 2:9; Rev. 22:1-2; John 10:10; Col. 3:4; John 3:16, 36; 5:24; 6:47

In this series of messages we shall deal with the experience of life. Here we do not intend to give mere messages and teachings. Rather, we will deal with practice, speaking much about the details of the experiences of the different stages of the Christian life. This will give us much help to learn the lessons of life for ourselves and at the same time to learn how to know people, discern people, and contact people. If we learn to know what stage and condition of life others are in—where they are, what they are, and what their needs are—we will know how to definitely help them to go on according to the experiences of the different stages of life.

GOD'S INTENTION TO BE LIFE TO US

According to the Scriptures, God's intention is to be life to us in His Son, Christ the Lord, and through His Spirit. This is why the tree of life is presented at the very beginning of the Scriptures (Gen. 2:9). Right after God created man, He put him in front of the tree of life. Since that time, the issue related to man is how he deals with the tree of life. If he deals with the tree of life in the right way, he is right in the presence of God. Otherwise, he is wrong. At the end of the Scriptures, in Revelation 22, we again see the tree of life in the very center of the New Jerusalem (vv. 1-2). Throughout the Scriptures, such as in the Psalms, the Gospel of John, and the writings of the apostle Paul, it is clear that God's intention is to make Christ life to us. At least one book, the Gospel of John, clearly tells us that Christ came that we may have life and may have it abundantly (10:10).

CHRIST HIMSELF BEING OUR LIFE

Christ came that we might have not only life but Himself as life. In today's Christianity there is not much teaching about life. If someone comes among us, they may say that we are strange, day by day talking only about life. They may wonder why we do not talk about other things. This shows us that among Christians today there is not much real knowledge of life. To my awareness, there has been only one significant book concerning life in recent times, *The Saving Life of Christ* by Major Ian Thomas. I like this title. However, although I like the term *saving life,* I do not like the term *of Christ.* We cannot find the term *the life of Christ* in the New Testament, because Christ Himself is the life. We should differentiate between the life of Christ and Christ as life. It may be right to speak of the life of Christ, but people may understand that the life of Christ is one matter and Christ is another. This is a wrong understanding of the life of Christ. The life of Christ is nothing other than Christ Himself as our life (Col. 3:4).

OUR NEED FOR TRAINING TO KNOW
THE THINGS OF LIFE IN A DEFINITE WAY

How can we humans receive Christ as our life? Although we have this life, we may not be clear about regeneration as our spiritual birth. This means that we are in a very poor condition with a poor background. This shortage is a problem for our growth in life, and it means that we are not able to help others. We may have heard many messages in a general way, but we may not know how to put these matters into practice. Even though we have been regenerated and can talk about the gospel in a general way, we may not know the definite way to help people to be regenerated. Before I became clear about regeneration, I was in this same poor condition. I could talk with people about Christian teachings, but I did not know how to help people to be saved. Then one day after the

Lord brought me through a crisis, I learned that it is easy to help people to be saved.

Many sisters are able not only to talk about cooking in a general way; they also know the definite way to take a certain amount of flour, sugar, and other items and cook them for a certain time to make a cake. I, on the other hand, can talk about cooking in a general way, but if you ask me to bake a cake, I do not know even how to turn on the fire. I know something in a general way, but I do not know it in a definite way. This is an illustration of the problem with Christians today. Someone may say that the way to be regenerated is to accept Christ or to receive Christ into our heart, but how do we receive Christ? This is like saying that the way to make a cake is to put it in the oven, but what do we put in the oven? Can we put a lump of flour into the oven and get a cake from it? General teachings are not adequate.

HELPING PEOPLE IN A PRACTICAL WAY TO BE REGENERATED

Helping Them to Repent and Believe

In order to contact an unbeliever we must first realize what kind of person he is. We may compare this to fishing: We need to know what kind of fish we are after in order to choose the right kind of bait. If we use the wrong bait, we may scare the fish away, but if we use the right bait, we will attract the fish. If we know what kind of person someone is, we will know in what way to approach him. Then we can give this person a message, a teaching, or a verse for five or ten minutes at the most. This paves the way, clears his understanding, and helps him to realize his need. In other words, it creates his appetite. Then we can point him to the right way. Perhaps we may realize that someone is a moral person, a person who pays much attention to morality. In this case we need to approach him in the highest way, telling him, "In order to have a certain morality, you need a certain kind of life. If you do not have the highest life, you cannot have the highest morality." We may create an appetite in him by illustrating: "If a flower has a poor life, it can never bring forth a better flower. We may be very good, but the life we have is not the highest life. You may be patient to a certain degree, but you do not have the life to be patient to the uttermost. The highest life is Christ as life to us."

We should not give such a person mere doctrine. We must give him something living and "cooked." Many times our talk with people is like giving them uncooked flour to eat. People cannot take this. Rather, we must give them "baked cakes" ready to eat. If we speak in a convincing way, a person will want to know how to receive Christ, but simply to say, "The gospel tells us that we have to repent and believe" is a doctrinal, not a practical, way. We need to speak with people in a practical way. We should say, "To repent means to realize that you are sinful and that you must confess your sins. Christ is holy, and we are sinful. In order to receive Him we must confess. I believe that you are a good person, but in the eyes of God we are all sinful. You need to confess your sins before Christ." This is the practical way to speak about repentance.

After confessing his sins, a person must believe, that is, he must open his heart from the depths of his being to receive Christ into him. If we use the word *spirit,* he may not understand us. We can keep this term for later and simply speak of "the depths of your heart" or "your innermost being." We can continue to tell him to say to the Lord Jesus, "You died on the cross for me. You are the living Savior. I know that You are the very God, the living and omnipresent Lord, so I receive You. I accept You." We should stress to this person that he must have a personal contact with Christ, saying, "Although you cannot see Him, He is here. Wherever you are, He is there. He is so living and real. He is the real God, the divine Spirit. Therefore, you need to open yourself to Him. Tell Him that you receive Him into yourself as your Savior and your life. As the very God, Christ is the Spirit. Just as the only way to contact the air is by breathing, the only way to contact Christ as God, our Savior, the living Spirit, is to pray." If this person asks how he should pray, we can say, "To pray is simply to speak something to Christ from your heart. Do not consider what to speak; there is no need to compose a prayer. Simply speak from your heart." We all must believe that after a person contacts the Lord by prayer, something will happen, either right away or after one or a few days, because this is a real contact in the human spirit with the living Lord.

Helping Them to Be Assured of Their Salvation

After we give a person this kind of instruction, we need to give him some verses from the Scriptures, such as John 3:16. We can help him to read this verse and understand and grasp it. Then we can give him other verses, such as John 3:36, 5:24, and 6:47, reading and stressing the central point to confirm to him that if he confesses his sins and opens to receive Christ, he has eternal life. It is a little complicating to use verses like John 1:12, which speaks of being children of God, and Romans 10:9 and 10, which speak of righteousness and salvation. When we are speaking with an unbeliever, it is best to speak in a concentrated way. Do not give them too many points. Rather, we should hit one point. This is like digging a well in one place until the water comes. If we dig a little here and a little there, we may dig for our whole life without getting any water.

In summary, the way to receive Christ as our life is to repent, realizing that we are sinful and under God's condemnation. Then it is to open our heart and whole being from within to have a living contact with Christ by praying to Him. Then we have the confirmation and assurance of God's salvation by His Word. This assurance is something written. Someone may owe a person a thousand dollars, but if he does not put that into writing, there is no assurance that it will be paid.

We may ask a person who has just received Christ, "Have you believed in Jesus Christ?" If he is not clear, we can say, "You have confessed that you are a sinner. You realized that you need Him, and you opened yourself to Him, prayed to Him, and told Him that you receive Him. This means that you already have believed." This helps him to be clear that he has received the Lord. Then we may ask if he knows that he has the eternal life. Again, if he does not know, we can read John 3:16 and ask him if it says, "Every one who believes into

Him would not perish, but would not know if he has eternal life." We should help him to say, "Every one who believes into Him would not perish, but would have eternal life." He can know he has eternal life because it is written. We should give him two or three passages like this as a definite confirmation that he has the life. To not do this is like wrapping something up but not tying a knot around it; what we wrapped will come loose again. If we speak to someone properly, the Holy Spirit will work, and he will be saved very quickly.

This kind of person may immediately realize that in the past he did many evil things, and he may ask us what he should do about his sins. We need to learn how to help one like this by reading some passages that tell him that his sins have been borne by Christ. This is why we need to learn passages such as 1 Peter 2:24, which says, "Who Himself bore up our sins in His body on the tree." Then we should quickly turn to 1 John 1:9, which says, "If we confess our sins, He is faithful and righteous to forgive us our sins and cleanse us from all unrighteousness." In this way we will cause him to realize that Christ bore all his sins and that God is now willing and ready to forgive him.

HELPING PEOPLE TO HAVE
A CLEARANCE OF THEIR PAST

To help someone to be saved in this way is easy. However, according to the normal, proper experience of Christians, after a person is regenerated, he needs many things. The first thing we should help him to do is to have a clearance of his past. Otherwise, he will not be able to grow well in life. If we help someone to believe and be regenerated, he will trust us. He may approach us, call us *brother,* and speak in an intimate and frank way about his past. Then it will be easy to instruct him. He may confess, for example, that he was wrong with his wife, so we can help him to go to her, confess his failures and faults, and ask her forgiveness. If the new one feels he will lose his face before his wife, we should help him to see that to commit sins and do wrong is to lose our face; to confess and testify how the Lord Jesus has saved us is a heavenly glory. The Holy Spirit will work with the new one, and he will say,

"Hallelujah, praise the Lord! I will do this at any cost." This is one of the many items of the clearance of the past. If a new convert will do this, he will advance very quickly.

There is no need to ask the new one, "Have you ever done something wrong to your parents, or have you ever stolen anything?" Rather, we may testify that we were the same as he. We also did wrong things to our parents and stole things. Perhaps we can tell him that we stole some money and bought a desk and some clothes with it, but after we were saved, we did not have any peace. Whenever we saw those things, we were condemned. It was very hard to sit at that desk to read the Bible or kneel in those clothes to pray. Therefore, we got rid of those things and refunded the stolen money to its owner. If we testify in this way, the Holy Spirit will work in the new one. After one or two illustrations like this, he will be clear. Right away he may realize that there is a radio in his room that was bought with stolen money. This will help him to clear up his past, and the Holy Spirit will continually work within him.

After this, we may say something in a general way, such as, "We are the children of God. God is light, and God is holy. We have to give up everything of darkness, anything that is not holy or righteous. This is to make a clearance of our past life." Then we may pray with him, saying, "Lord, help this brother to clear up his past and to testify to the whole world that he is a true child of the holy God in the light." This is to help someone in a definite way. It is not merely to contact people in a general, impractical way with doctrines. If a new one receives this kind of help, he will be released. He will testify in the meeting, pray, and offer thanks to the Lord. He will be in the heavens.

Many of us may not have had such a clearance of the past. This is not something legal, but the growth in life requires it. Once a person came to F. B. Meyer after a conference meeting and asked him what the proper way is for a Christian to grow. Mr. Meyer asked that person, "When was the last time you made a confession to someone or cleared up your sins with others?" This answer indicates that the more we clear up matters, the more growth we will have. However, after being saved for ten to thirty years, many Christians still do not have a clearance of the past. Therefore, it is hard for them to have the growth in life.

HELPING THEM TO CONSECRATE THEMSELVES

We may then follow up to say, "This is wonderful, brother. Now you have to consecrate yourself to the Lord." The practical way to consecrate ourselves is to go to the Lord to pray. We should tell Him that from now on our right has passed from us to Him. It is better to itemize all that we have and all that we are, including our ability, knowledge, family, wife, children, property, business, job, studies, and our very self, telling the Lord that we offer these things to Him.

Almost all the problems between us and the Lord are related to our consecration. I do not have the confidence that many of us have settled the matter of consecration. For over one year around 1949 Brother Watchman Nee had a training in Shanghai. Week after week he stressed mainly one thing: consecration. Most of the trainees there were full-time co-workers. He dealt with this matter not mainly by giving messages but by asking one person a week to give a testimony about his consecration, the longer the better. Sometimes Brother Nee would say after the testimony, "This is not adequate. Tell us something more." After the testimony, he would critique it. Sometimes he would say, "No, your consecration is false." Over such a long period of time, after many testimonies, only one or two persons' consecrations were proven to be real. He analyzed our consecrations, saying, "Why do I say your consecration is false? I can tell from your word that you have held something back." In this way Brother Nee convinced us about consecration, and we all agreed with him.

HELPING THEM TO
FOLLOW THE INNER CONSCIOUSNESS
AND WALK IN THE SPIRIT

After someone consecrates himself, he must learn to follow the inner consciousness, to follow the Spirit and walk in the Spirit. We can say, "Since you have consecrated yourself to the Lord, from now on you must do the Lord's will. The way to do this is by following the inner feeling, the inner consciousness."

To follow the consciousness deep within us is to walk in the Spirit.

HELPING THEM TO CONTACT THE LORD
THROUGH READING AND PRAYING

We also must help the new ones to contact the Lord by reading the Word and praying. Day by day, preferably early in the morning, they need to have a time to contact the Lord. Here there is much to say and to learn.

HELPING THEM TO EXPERIENCE
THE BAPTISM OF THE HOLY SPIRIT
AND TO BE LIVING MEMBERS IN THE BODY

The foregoing five matters—regeneration, clearance of the past, consecration, following the Spirit according to the inner consciousness, and contacting the Lord in the morning by reading and praying—are very basic. We also should help the newly saved ones to experience the baptism of the Holy Spirit with power and release. To help people with these matters is the best way for them to be regenerated. Following this, we should help them to realize that they are living members in the Body. This means that they must function in the church.

OUR NEED TO TAKE A PRACTICAL WAY
WITHOUT LEGALITY TO HELP PEOPLE

Question: Over what period of time can we cover the foregoing items with an average new believer?

Answer: With a quicker one, we can cover all these six matters within a few weeks. A person can be regenerated right away. Then on the next day we can help him to have a clearance of his past. Following this, we can help him to consecrate himself, to know how to follow the inner consciousness, to start to have a real touch with the Lord by studying and praying, and to experience the outpouring of the Holy Spirit. I do not say this in a legalistic way. In Taiwan we had a large number of new converts, perhaps two hundred, so we would have a series of meetings after their baptism. In one week we would have six or seven meetings in a series in which we stressed these matters for their realization and experience.

However, this does not mean that all new converts can be helped to realize all these items right away. Gradually, most of them will stay in the church meetings and will be helped to experience these things sooner or later, but not later than one year unless they are indifferent or become backsliders. Because of this kind of help, some became elders in the early years in Taiwan after only two or three years.

We must help the new ones in a definite way, not in a general way. I was born and raised in Christianity. I heard many messages and preachings, but not one message told me definitely how to be saved. Many persons were brought into Christianity merely in a general way. If we asked them if they were saved, they would say, "I don't know." If we asked if their sins were dealt with, they would say, "It depends." Everything was general; nothing was definite. This is too poor. We praise the Lord that beginning in 1922 the Lord raised up a testimony in China to make these things very definite and practical. Every light the Lord gave us was very definite concerning certain things. From that time on we could help people in a fast way. We may compare this to cooking. If someone knows the practical way, he can make a cake in a few minutes, and in another few minutes he can make another dish. This is not a general way. If we take a general way, we will have nothing.

Question: Concerning the clearance of our living, there is the need of restitution for things in the past and the clearance of current practices. If we see that a Christian is practicing wrong things, should we try to clear them all up at once?

Answer: Do not do this. Clearance is not a legal matter. We must help people by the working of the Holy Spirit. We do not give people rules. To be a Christian is not a matter of rules but of grace. We help people to realize grace by giving them teaching and instruction. Then the Holy Spirit will work out the matters.

THE NEED FOR THE RECOVERY OF
THE MATTERS OF LIFE

In this series of messages we are emphasizing the main matters of life and how to grow. In a large city we can find many Christian stores and libraries with many books. We can find books on justification, forgiveness, and redemption, but it is hard to find a book dealing with regeneration. Books that seem to be on this subject have little content. The many items in God's salvation, including forgiveness of sins, justification, redemption, cleansing, and sanctification, are not the central item. The very center of God's salvation is regeneration. Forgiveness, justification, cleansing, redemption, and in one aspect, sanctification, are all for regeneration. That is, all these items are for life.

Justification is not the central thought of God. In the garden of Eden after Adam was created, was there the need for justification? There was no need for justification, but Adam still had to receive life, as signified by the tree of life. At that time Adam did not need forgiveness or redemption, because he was not yet fallen and lost, and he did not need cleansing because he was not yet dirty. Yet he still needed to have life. All the other matters—forgiveness, justification, redemption, cleansing, and sanctification in one aspect—are for restoration so that people may be brought back to the position and standing to receive life. However, regeneration as the very center of God's salvation is neglected by Christianity today. Christianity pays much attention to these other items, but there is not the adequate teaching concerning life. This is the subtlety of the enemy. For this reason we believe that the Lord must recover this in these last days. Otherwise, we cannot grow, and if we do not grow, we cannot be built up. Then where is the Body? The Body life depends on the building, the building depends on the growth in life, and the growth in life depends on the true realization of life. Today's Christianity does not have the realization of the matters of life. This is why we must be faithful to the Lord to allow Him to recover these things. If the Lord delays His coming, after a number of years we will see what His way will be. His way will be to recover the matter of life. This is why we are paying our full attention to this.

CHAPTER TWO

THE EXPERIENCE OF REGENERATION

(2)

Scripture Reading: 1 Pet. 1:2; Gal. 3:13; Eph. 1:7; 1 John 1:9;
1 Cor. 6:11; Rom. 5:10-11; 1 Pet. 1:3, 23; John 3:3, 5; 1 John
4:13; 2 Cor. 13:5; Rom. 8:9; John 14:17; 1 John 5:12; John 3:15;
2 Pet. 1:4; Heb. 8:10; Rom. 8:2; 1 John 2:27; 2 Cor. 5:17; John
1:12-13; Eph. 5:30; Rom. 12:5

The spiritual life is of different stages, and each stage has
many spiritual experiences. As we saw in the previous chapter, the first experience in the spiritual life is regeneration.
Many Christians think that they know what God's salvation
is, but most have neglected the aspect of regeneration. God's
salvation has many parts, but the main and central part is
regeneration.

THE SUBSIDIARY ITEMS OF GOD'S SALVATION

The Sprinkling of
the Blood of Jesus Christ

According to the teaching of the New Testament, God's
salvation is first composed of the sprinkling of the blood of
Jesus. After a person repents and believes—repenting before
God, confessing his sins, believing in the Lord Jesus, and
receiving Him as his Savior—the first thing God applies
to him is the "sprinkling of the blood of Jesus Christ." This
phrase is used in 1 Peter 1:2. (In order to help unbelievers
and even young believers, we need to know the experiences of
life and the proper passages from the Scriptures.) God applies
the sprinkling of the blood to us because we are sinners. We
have no ground to receive anything from God; we have no

merit in ourselves. The only ground we have is the blood shed by the Lord Jesus for us. In order to receive or claim anything, we need the proper ground. Without the ground we cannot claim anything. The redeeming blood, which is applied to us, is the ground for all the items of God's salvation. It is the only ground on which we can stand to claim all that God intends to give us.

Redemption from the Curse of the Law

The second item in God's salvation is redemption. After the sprinkling of the blood, we are redeemed. Many people in Christianity speak of being redeemed from sin, from Satan, or from hell, but this is not correct. *To redeem* means "to buy back, to purchase back with a price." God did not need to pay anything to sin, Satan, or hell to buy us back. Rather, He needed to pay something to the requirement of the law. Therefore, we are redeemed from the curse of the law (Gal. 3:13). We were under the condemnation and curse of the law according to its requirements, so God had to pay something to fulfill its requirements. If there were no fall, there would have been no need of redemption. We need to be redeemed because we fell into the condemnation of the law and came under its curse.

Ephesians 1:7 also speaks of redemption through His blood, and 1 Peter 1:18 and 19 say that we were redeemed with the precious blood of Christ. Acts 20:28 and 1 Corinthians 6:20 tell us that we were obtained and bought. To be redeemed is to be bought, to be purchased with a price, which is Christ Himself. When God sprinkles the blood upon us, we are redeemed by that blood.

The Forgiveness of Sins

Third, we have the forgiveness of sins. God can forgive only those people whom He has redeemed; therefore, redemption comes first and then forgiveness. Ephesians 1:7 says, "In whom we have redemption through His blood, the forgiveness of offenses, according to the riches of His grace." Acts 10:43, 1 John 2:12, and Colossians 2:13 also speak of the forgiveness of sins.

The Cleansing of the Stain of Sins

After forgiveness we have cleansing. There is a difference between forgiveness and cleansing. Forgiveness deals with the responsibility of sin. Cleansing, however, deals with the stain of sin. If we damage a shirt, for example, we can be forgiven. Our responsibility is relieved, but the shirt still bears a mark or stain. Therefore, after forgiveness we still need the cleansing of the stain. By the blood of Jesus, God not only forgives us; He also cleanses us. That is, He releases us from responsibility and cleanses us from the stain and mark of our fall. First John 1:9 shows us the order of forgiveness and cleansing. It says, "If we confess our sins, He is faithful and righteous to forgive us our sins and cleanse us from all unrighteousness." After we are forgiven and cleansed of a sin, it is in the eyes of God as if we had never committed the sin.

Sanctification

After we are cleansed, we are sanctified, that is, separated. First Corinthians 6:11 shows us the proper order: "And these things were some of you; but you were washed, but you were sanctified, but you were justified in the name of the Lord Jesus Christ and in the Spirit of our God." According to certain theological teachings, sanctification comes after justification, but this verse says differently. If we are not separated, if we are still in the heap of sinful people, we cannot be justified. We are forgiven, cleansed, and sanctified, and then justified.

First Corinthians 1:2 and Romans 1:7 both say that we are called saints. *Saints* means "sanctified persons." After we receive the Lord Jesus and are sprinkled with the blood, we are sanctified, that is, separated from all the people of the world. We are no longer the same as they are. We are different, separated by the blood.

Justification

After we are sanctified, we are justified. As we have seen, 1 Corinthians 6:11 speaks of justification. To this we may add Romans 5:1. Justification is based on our being sprinkled, redeemed, forgiven, cleansed, and separated. When we have these items, we are qualified to be justified. We are sprinkled with the blood, and by this blood we are redeemed, bought back. Based on this blood we are forgiven, and by this blood we are cleansed and even separated, that is, sanctified. Now further, by this blood we are justified, and we have no problem with God.

Reconciliation

After justification we have reconciliation. We are reconciled with God and have peace. This is mentioned in Romans 5:10 and 11, which say, "For if we, being enemies, were reconciled to God through the death of His Son, much more we will be saved in His life, having been reconciled, and not only so, but also boasting in God through our Lord Jesus Christ, through whom we have now received the reconciliation." (*Reconciliation* in verse 11 is not *atonement,* as it says in the King James Version; *atonement* is an Old Testament word.) To be reconciled to God means that we have nothing contradictory to God. We are at peace with God in a full way.

REGENERATION BEING
THE MAIN ITEM OF GOD'S SALVATION

To be sprinkled, redeemed, forgiven, cleansed, separated, justified, and reconciled is wonderful. Apparently, these items are good enough. However, these seven items are not the central item. They are all subsidiary items. Do not think that I despise the Lord's redemption. I do not. However, all these items are simply the preparation for regeneration. Therefore, the eighth item of God's salvation is regeneration. Here we come back to the very beginning of God's eternal purpose. God's eternal purpose is to work Himself into us as life. We must remember well the first two chapters of the Scriptures. God made man a vessel to contain God Himself (Gen. 2:7). Therefore, after God created man, He put him in front of the tree of life with the intention that man would receive the life signified by that tree, which is the divine life of God Himself (v. 9). Before man received God into him as life, however, Satan came in. Man became fallen, dirty, and condemned by God, so he needed to be sprinkled, redeemed, forgiven, cleansed, sanctified, justified, and reconciled. This shows us that all these items of God's salvation are the procedure to recover fallen man, to bring him to the genuine, proper standing for God to fulfill His purpose to put Himself into man as his life.

The foregoing seven items are not the central and main items. They are the preparation for the main item, which is that man would be reborn. Regardless of whether we are bad or good, we need to be reborn. Many in Christianity have the wrong concept that we need to be reborn because we are sinful, but even if we were not sinful, we would still need to be reborn. If we are not reborn, we cannot have the divine life; we can have only the human life. How can we have the divine life from only our human birth?

Even if Adam had never fallen and had remained in the garden of Eden in a good condition, he still would need to be regenerated. Otherwise, even though he would be a good man, he would have only the created, human life, not the uncreated, divine, eternal life. Therefore, we must be clear that all the subsidiary items of God's salvation are not the central and main items. Regeneration is the central item of God's salvation, and these others are the preparation for regeneration.

First Peter 1:3 and 23 and John 3:3 and 5 speak of regeneration. Regeneration is nothing other than receiving Christ, the very embodiment of God, as the Holy Spirit. It is to receive Christ into our spirit. When we believe in Him and receive Him, He comes into our spirit. By this we have the second life, the divine, eternal life of God, and this life causes us to have the second birth. We had our first birth from our parents, and now we have the second birth by Christ as life as the Holy Spirit coming into our spirit, according to John 3:6b, which says, "That which is born of the Spirit is spirit." In this way, regeneration is the very item that fulfills God's eternal purpose, which is to work Himself in Christ through the Spirit into us that He may be our life in our spirit. That is why we say that the foregoing items of God's salvation are subsidiary, while only the last item—regeneration—is the main and central item.

WHAT WE RECEIVE BY REGENERATION

The Triune God Dwelling in Us

We have been sprinkled, redeemed, forgiven, cleansed, separated, justified, and reconciled. Praise God, all the problems are gone! Now by being regenerated we have received God. God is within us. First John 4:13 says, "In this we know that we abide in Him and He in us, that He has given to us of His Spirit." It is by regeneration that God comes into us to indwell us.

By regeneration Christ lives in us. Second Corinthians 13:5 is the best verse to prove this. It says, "Test yourselves whether you are in the faith; prove yourselves. Or do you not realize about yourselves that Jesus Christ is in you, unless you are disapproved?" As long as we have faith, regardless of how big or little it is, even if it is smaller than a mustard seed, we have Christ dwelling in us.

By regeneration the Holy Spirit also is in us. Romans 8:9 and John 14:17 tell us this. Verse 17 says, "Even the Spirit of reality, whom the world cannot receive, because it does not behold Him or know Him; but you know Him, because He abides with you and shall be in you." This means that we have all three of the Triune God within us. God the Father is in us, God the Son is in us, and God the Spirit is in us. That God is in us means that the greatest One in the entire universe is in us. First John 4:4 says, "Greater is He who is in you than he who is in the world." God is the greatest One, Christ is the strongest, most powerful One (Phil. 4:13), and the Holy Spirit is the most living One. Because the Triune God is in us, we have the greatness, the strength and power, and the living energy.

The Triune God as the Eternal Life

By regeneration we have received life, which is nothing less that the Triune God Himself. We should not think that the divine life is something different from God. It is God Himself in Christ through the Spirit.

First John 5:12 says, "He who has the Son has the life; he who does not have the Son of God does not have the life."

And John 3:15 says, "That every one who believes into Him may have eternal life." *Everlasting life,* as in the King James Version, is an incorrect translation. *Everlasting* refers to time, while *eternal* refers to something more than time. It also refers to the nature and sphere.

The Divine Nature with Its Taste

In addition to the divine life, we have received the divine nature, the nature of God (2 Pet. 1:4). It is hard to define the difference between life and nature. If we have life, we have the ability to live; without life we have no ability to live. Nature is more for the taste of a life. A cat has the taste to eat mice. In the same way, a dog barks because barking is his nature. There is no need to teach a dog to bark; barking suits a dog's taste.

We have the divine life; that is, we have the divine ability to live. Moreover, we have the divine nature as our taste. There is no need for regulations against going to Las Vegas to gamble, because we Christians do not have this taste. We have the heavenly, divine nature, and with the divine nature there is the heavenly taste. According to the nature of a pig, the dirtiest things are tasteful to it. A lamb, however, can fall into something dirty, but that is only an accident; it is not its practice. In the same way, we can fall into gambling, but this is not our practice because we have the divine nature within us. Not only so, to go to the movies does not suit the divine nature in us. There is not such a taste within us.

Life is mostly for ability and energy, while nature is mostly for taste. We have the strength, the ability, to live, and we have the divine nature with a holy, heavenly taste. After sisters go to the department store and buy worldly items, they are not joyful because those things are not sweet to their taste. This is because they have the divine nature.

Recently a friend asked me if I drink, smoke, or go to the movies. When I replied that I do not, he said that was too bad. I said, "No, it is pitiful to you, but it is joyful to me. We have different tastes. To drink, smoke, or go to the movies is a suffering to me. To you, however, it is an enjoyment because you have that kind of nature. I have another nature, the heavenly, divine nature." We have not only the divine life, which is God Himself, but we also have the divine nature. It is an enjoyment for us to have a holy, heavenly living, and it is an enjoyment to walk with God. It is an enjoyment, not a regulation, because this is our taste. We are feasting all the time. If you do not believe this, try to go dancing, to the movies, or to gamble. There will be a factor, the divine nature as your taste, which will constantly trouble you.

The Law of Life with the Power of Life

We also have the law of life. Hebrews 8:10 and Romans 8:2 speak of the inner law, the law of life. Whereas a nature has a taste, a law is for regulating. We have an inner regulation regulating us all the time. By regeneration we have the three of the Triune God and the divine life, divine nature, and the law of life. Because we have the divine life and nature, out from this life with this nature we have the inner law of life.

With every kind of life with its nature there is a certain law. To eat mice is according to the law of the cat life, and to bark is according to the law of the dog life. In the same way, for an apple tree to bear apples is according to its law. An apple tree bears apples and a peach tree bears peaches because they have different lives with different laws. Within the life there is the regulating power. There is no need to regulate an apple tree, saying, "Little tree, you must remember you are an apple tree. You must bear apples, not peaches." Likewise, there is no need to tell a dog, "You must remember you are a dog. Don't forget to bark; that is a dog's duty." In actuality, it is hard to stop a dog from barking because barking is according to its law.

A law is not only a regulation but also a power. The law of gravity, for example, is a power according to the natural law. That a tree brings forth apples is not only according to its law; it is according to its power and energy. If we have a certain law, we have both a regulating and a power within us. Oh, we Christians need our eyes to be opened to see these wonderful matters within us! We have the divine life, the divine nature, and the divine law of life within us. There is no need to throw something up and then worry how it will come down. The more we do something out of worry, the more we may hinder it from coming down. We should keep silent and watch the power of gravity. In the same way, we should keep silent and watch the inner law within us. It is not only a regulating factor; it is also a power. Many Christians think that one day power will come down upon us. They do not realize that they have the inner power. Like the atomic power in small atoms, the real and greatest power is the one within us.

The Anointing as the Moving of the Triune God

By regeneration we also have the anointing (1 John 2:27). This is not only the ointment itself but the anointing as the action, the moving, of the ointment. The anointing is the moving of the Holy Spirit, or we may say, the moving of the Triune God. There is always something moving within us.

When we are regenerated, we immediately have God the Father, God the Son, God the Spirit, the eternal life, the divine nature, the law of life, and the anointing. These seven are actually one. God the Father is in God the Son, the Son is the Spirit, and the Spirit is the very essence of the divine life. The divine life is nothing other than the Triune God, and the divine nature is something of this life. If we have the life, we have the nature; if we do not have the life, we do not have the nature. We cannot separate these two. The law of life comes from the life with the nature, and the anointing is the moving and acting of the Triune God in the Spirit. Therefore, the three of the Triune God are life to us with His nature, so we have the law of life and the anointing as something so living in us.

If we are to know the things of life, we must be clear about these seven items. Otherwise, we will not be able to grow in life in an adequate way. In the early years of my Christian life I was not clear about these matters, so I was not happy at that time. Since I have become clear about these seven items, I have been a happy Christian. I realize that I have God, Christ, and the Spirit in me, and I have the divine life, the divine nature, the law of life, and the anointing. Some men are great, having a high position, high education, and millions of dollars, but inwardly I am greater. I have God, and many of them do not, so they are poor, pitiful people. I have Christ and the Spirit, and they do not. I have the divine life, the divine nature, the law of life, and the anointing, but they do not. All they have is dung, refuse, nothing of any worth. By regeneration the Triune God—the Father in the Son as the Spirit—has wrought Himself into us as our life with the divine nature, so we have a living law within us and the anointing of God Himself. On the one hand, we need to be humble, but on the other hand, we should not look down on ourselves. We must realize that we are big persons, for all the spiritual riches with the fullness of the Godhead are in us.

WHAT WE BECOME BY REGENERATION

The New Creation

After we are regenerated, we become the new creation (2 Cor. 5:17). What is the difference between the old creation and the new creation? In the old creation there is nothing of God's essence, that is, nothing of God Himself. In the new creation, however, there is the very essence of God. The old creation was made by God's hand, but the new creation is something of regeneration with God Himself as life. Moreover, in the old creation we can see the power of God, but the life of God is not in it. God is not mingled with the old creation, while in the new creation God Himself as life is mingled with the creature. Therefore, because God is in the new creation, it is something new. Only God Himself is ever new, and God Himself is newness. Without God in something, that thing is old, but anything with God in it can never be old. The New Jerusalem, the new heaven and new earth, the new man, and the new creation will never be old because God is in them, and God is new and newness. Today we are the new creation.

Children of God

We are also born of God to be the children of God (John 1:12-13). We are not adopted children. Rather, we are born of God with his life in us. The authority and right for us to be God's children is the divine life. If a child is born of someone, he has the life of that person as the right and authority to be that person's child. We have been born of God, so we have the authority to be His children.

Members of the Body of Christ

We are also the members of the Body of Christ (Eph. 5:30; Rom. 12:5). Being members of the Body of Christ means that we are the parts of Christ. You are a part of Christ, and I am a part of Christ.

We are the new creation, God's children, and the members of Christ. Of course, we are many other things, but these three are the most basic ones. As the new creation we have God Himself mingled with us. Therefore, we are no longer only men; we are now God-men. We are also the children of God, born of Him and having Him as our life. Moreover, we are the members and parts of Christ, being one in life with Him. We must be very clear concerning these matters. Then we can go on to grow in a proper way in the spiritual life and develop in what we have received and in what we have become. We need to be developed as the new creation, as the children of God to build up the house of God, and as the members of Christ to build up the Body. The church is the Body built up with the members of Christ, and it is the house, the dwelling place, the habitation, of God built up with His children.

If we spend the time to read these messages with the Scriptures, to study them, pray, and pray-read, we will have an inner realization and understanding, and we will see these things properly. Then we will know that the central point of God's salvation and His eternal purpose is that God is working Himself in His Trinity into us as everything to make us parts of His dwelling place and the members of the Body of Christ, and we will also grow into this stature.

CHAPTER THREE

CONSECRATION

Scripture Reading: Rom. 6:19; 12:1; 1 Cor. 6:19-20; 2 Cor. 5:14-15

Following regeneration a believer needs to have a clearance of the past, and he needs to consecrate himself. The New Testament clearly teaches and deals with our need to consecrate ourselves to the Lord after we are saved. In a local church we must spend a certain amount of time to help the brothers and sisters one by one experience consecration and realize it in a full way. In some places we have spent one or two years, week after week and message after message, stressing that all the believers, the saved ones, need to consecrate themselves, not merely in a doctrinal way but in a very practical way. Some brothers and sisters have even been willing to open themselves and give a testimony of their consecration so that their experience can be checked by others in the church.

In his teachings in the New Testament, the apostle Paul always stresses consecration. In Romans, for example, consecration is mentioned in chapter six and again in chapter twelve. Romans 6 deals with our release from sin by realizing that we have been crucified with Christ. If we read this chapter carefully, however, we will see that the chief point is not only realizing our crucifixion with Christ but that we must offer ourselves, not only consecrating ourselves as a whole but offering our members. Verse 19 says, "I speak in human terms because of the weakness of your flesh. For just as you presented your members as slaves to uncleanness and lawlessness unto lawlessness, so now present your members as slaves to righteousness unto sanctification." To present our members is to present them one by one. If we realize that we have been crucified with Christ and that we are released from sin, we must cooperate with the work the Lord has done by offering our members to Him. Then in chapter twelve, before the apostle begins to say something about the Body life, he advises and exhorts us to present our bodies in a definite way (v. 1).

CONSECRATION BEING THE BASIS
FOR EVERY SPIRITUAL EXPERIENCE
AFTER REGENERATION

From our own experience we can testify that without consecration it is impossible to experience the crucifixion of Christ and even more impossible to realize the Body life. Consecration is the basis for every kind of experience after regeneration. For regeneration alone, there is no need for consecration, but if we do not consecrate ourselves after regeneration, we will be frustrated. We will be outside the gate, having no entrance into further experiences. All spiritual experiences after regeneration depend on the step of consecration.

Many spiritual writings in the past, such as those by Andrew Murray on prayer, the inner life, and abiding in Christ, point out the need for consecration. In many of his writings, Murray points out that in order to experience what he is talking about in that book, we need to take the step of consecration and pass through this crisis. In order to have a prayer life, we must pass through the crisis of consecration. In order to have faith, we must pass through consecration. And in order to abide in Christ, we must offer ourselves to Christ.

In her book entitled *The Christian's Secret of a Happy Life,* Hannah W. Smith also stresses consecration. With the central message of consecration, Mrs. Smith and her husband, among others, began what became the Keswick Convention in England in the second half of the nineteenth century. The Keswick Convention had the sole purpose of helping Christians to realize that they had to pass this crisis, and according to history, the blessing brought in through Keswick was due primarily to consecration. In the early publications of Keswick, the messages spoke much of consecration. It seems that those writers, such as Evan Hopkins, knew nothing but consecration. There is no doubt that at that time, in the latter half of the nineteenth century, consecration was the main item of the Lord's recovery. About that same time, the work of the foreign missions began. This was something of the Lord, because for service in the mission field there is the real need of consecration. According to church history, more people consecrated themselves to the Lord at that time than ever before, most of them helped by the messages of the Keswick Convention.

ENTERING BY THE GATE OF CONSECRATION AND WALKING ON THE WAY OF CONSECRATION

It is entirely right that for any kind of experience we need to consecrate ourselves. Consecration is like the entrance to a building; if we do not pass through the entrance, it is impossible to go anywhere in the building. In order to share in any part of a building, we must pass through the gate. Immediately in front of the first entrance to the tabernacle was the altar. There were many things to experience in the tabernacle. Outside was the laver, and inside were the table of the bread of the Presence, the lampstand, the incense altar, and the ark with its items, but in order to share in those things one had to pass the altar and deal with it. There was no possibility of touching anything within the tabernacle without passing through the altar. With the altar there is the aspect of redemption, but there is also the aspect of consecration. Everything placed on the altar was an offering; this signifies consecration.

The tabernacle is a type both of Christ and of the church. In order to experience the riches of Christ typified by the things in the tabernacle, we need to pass through the crisis of consecration. In addition, in order to experience the church life as God's building and dwelling place, we must pass the altar, that is, the crisis of consecration. In order to have the real Christian life and the real church life, we all must learn day by day to live a life of consecration.

The life of consecration begins with a crisis. Then after the crisis we have the way. The Scriptures speak differently from our common understanding. We often say that we take the way and go through the gate. According to the Scriptures, however, we first go through the gate, and then we have the way. The gate, not the way, comes first, as in Matthew 7:13 and 14. In spiritual matters, if we do not enter the gate, there is no way for us to go on. The gate of the spiritual things related to life is regeneration; for the life within we need the gate of regeneration. After we are regenerated, however, after we receive the life within, we need to have a living, and for our living and daily life the gate is consecration. Many have been regenerated; that is, they have entered the gate of life. However, they do not have the proper living because they have never consecrated themselves to the Lord. They have passed through regeneration, but they have not passed through consecration. Although they are regenerated persons, they do not live as regenerated persons; that is, they have the life but not the living.

The gate for our spiritual living is consecration. Then after we enter the gate of consecration, we go on the way of consecration. Consecration has two aspects: a crisis to pass through and a way to walk on. The crisis is once for all, but the way is not once for all. Many cannot go the way of consecration because they have not entered the gate of consecration. Have you passed through the gate? As I mentioned before, Brother Watchman Nee held a training in Shanghai in 1939 and 1940 mostly for co-workers. For one year's time he stressed almost nothing but consecration. Every week when we came together, he would first ask a person to give his testimony about consecration. Brother Nee would ask us to consider the testimony, and then he himself would critique it. Almost no one passed this examination. We were all subdued by him. He would point out something in each testimony that proved that the consecration was not genuine, absolute, complete, or without reservation.

CHECKING OUR CONSECRATION
AND BEING FAITHFUL TO IT

The way to check whether or not we are faithful and honest in our consecration to the Lord is by our daily life. If we check ourselves, we will see, as Brother Nee pointed out, that in many matters there is a struggle between us and the Lord, and we often win the victory. Whenever there is a struggle, the defeated one is the Lord. It is good to have a struggle with the Lord. If we have no struggle with Him, we are through with the Lord. Especially in this age on this earth there is always the struggle. To not have a struggle means that we are fallen and backslidden. In our struggle, however, who wins the victory, we or the Lord? The way to check whether or not our consecration is complete, genuine, and without reservation is by who wins the struggle. That the Lord is defeated is due to the unfaithfulness of our consecration. We have consecrated ourselves, but we may not be faithful and honest to our consecration. If we Christians would keep our consecration, the Lord will always have the victory.

All our problems today are due to our unfaithfulness in consecration. We may not have a morning watch, for example, because of a problem with our consecration. Many of us have passed the crisis, but we have not continued on the way. Therefore, in order for a church to be built up, the first foundation we must lay is the matter of consecration. We need to check with ourselves and deal with our consecration, and then we need to help others. We need to pray, fellowship, and encourage the brothers and help them one by one to come into the real experience of consecration.

We may say that we do not have much faith. The reason we do not have faith is that we are not faithful to our consecration. When we are faithful to our consecration, we have a living faith. We may say that we do not have power. The reason again is that we are not faithful to our consecration. When we are faithful to our consecration, we have the ground to claim the power, and it is ours. We need to go to the Lord once again to deal with and clear up our consecration. If we do this, we will see the blessings. Then we will have a burden to help others.

ADVANCING STEP BY STEP IN OUR CONSECRATION

We may have consecrated ourselves to the Lord after we were regenerated, but the problem is whether or not we have continued in our consecration. The unfaithfulness to our consecration is the reason why many of us have not grown much and advanced on the Lord's way. We may compare this to someone who walks all the time but does not walk on the right way. We may come to the meetings, fellowship with the saints, and do many things in the Christian life, but we may not be on the proper way. To go on is a matter of consecration. Whenever the Lord points out something to us, we need to say, "Lord, I let You have it." If we do this, we advance by one step, but if we do not let the Lord have the victory, we are not on the way, regardless of how many things we do. To go on the proper Christian way is to take step after step in our consecration.

We have to go on by consecration day by day. A day without consecration is a wasted day. If we have a struggle with the Lord and we win the victory, making the Lord the defeated One, then regardless of how much we do for the Lord we will only waste our time. The measure of our life and going on is our consecration.

If we once again deal with our consecration, we will have a revival. Our outreach to bring people to the Lord and our consecration go together. If we have no real experience of consecration, we have no power to bring people to the Lord. Our power to bring people to the Lord depends on our consecration. If we struggle with the Lord and win, causing the Lord to be defeated, we are weak, and we lose the power to bring people to the Lord. However, if we always take the ground of consecration and go on step by step, we have the power to bring people to the Lord.

THE NEED FOR THE CONTINUAL BURNT OFFERING

As we have said, the crisis of consecration is the key to our other experiences, and it is a life-long, not once-for-all, experience. In the type of the people of Israel, they had to offer the burnt offering day by day, morning and evening (Lev. 6:9, 12-13). The altar was called the altar of burnt offering. The burnt offering was the continual offering, and the fire for the burnt offering was not supposed to cease; it had to stay burning day and night. This type shows us that we have to have a life of the burnt offering, a life with fire burning on the altar all day long. It is entirely right that as Christians we should consecrate ourselves every morning and again in the evening after the day's duties. We may think that this is too much, that we already have offered ourselves to the Lord for many years, but we still need to offer ourselves for each morning and each evening. In addition, although it is not legal, it is right that we should offer ourselves specifically for the Lord's Day and for the service and worship on that day.

THE WAY TO HELP OTHERS TO BE CONSECRATED

By Being a Consecrated Person

In order to help others by bringing them to the Lord as new converts or by helping the younger ones to go on, we need the real experience of consecration. Then when we help someone, we should first determine whether or not he is regenerated. If he is not, we need to find a way to help him to experience regeneration. If he is a regenerated person, however, the most important thing is to help him one way or another to consecrate himself. A person may pray to the Lord, seek His mercy, and obtain His mercy, but if he is not consecrated, these are not the real experiences of life. The genuine experience of Christ depends entirely on consecration.

In order to help someone to be consecrated, we must first be a consecrated person. If we are not a consecrated person, we cannot help others to be. We must also have a consecrated living. If we live in our consecration, it will be easy to help others to consecrate themselves, because there will be an atmosphere and a power of life with us. When we contact people and fellowship with them, we will have an influence on them. This must not be something in word only; this must be something we practice.

By Praying for Them

In order to help someone in this way, we must pray for him to find one way or another to bring him through the crisis of consecration.

By Fellowshipping with Them

Giving a Testimony of Consecration

Then after we have a certain amount of prayer, we should

fellowship with that person. Here we need the proper techniques. Of course, the way we take depends on the Lord's leading at the time, but our fellowship will usually be in one of several ways. One way is to give him a testimony of consecration. We may give our own testimony, but to present someone else's testimony can also be effective.

Having a Fresh Sense of the Lord's Loveliness

A second way is to help him to realize the Lord's love and how lovable He is. This is not easy to do. Many ministers realize that the most difficult message to give is one on the loveliness of the Lord. To speak of the Lord being faithful, great, or marvelous is easy, but some brothers may not be able to speak for five minutes on the loveliness of the Lord. To say something about the loveliness of the Lord requires that we have the fresh sense of His love. Someone may have love for a brother, for example, but after working with him for a year he no longer has a fresh sense of love. Even a husband and wife can lose the fresh sense of love. If we do not have a fresh sense, it is hard to speak about love. We may talk about love, but we may not have the power of inspiration.

The most effective way to help people to consecrate is to help them to realize the loveliness of the Lord. I have heard the testimony of a certain co-working sister many times. Every time she speaks of the Lord's loveliness, she speaks with tears. With her there is always the freshness of the sense of His loveliness. I have never heard her testimony when I did not see many people weeping. She has caused thousands of people to consecrate themselves to the Lord.

Using the Proper Verses of the Scriptures

The third way to fellowship with someone is to use the proper verses of the Scriptures. One of the best passages is 2 Corinthians 5:14 and 15, which say, "For the love of Christ constrains us because we have judged this, that One died for all, therefore all died; and He died for all that those who live may no longer live to themselves but to Him who died for them and has been raised." Another good passage is 1 Corinthians 6:19 and 20, which says, "Or do you not know that your body is a temple of the Holy Spirit within you, whom you have from God, and you are not your own? For you have been bought with a price. So then glorify God in your body." As we have seen, Romans 12:1 also speaks of presenting our bodies.

By Helping Them to Pray

A further way to lead someone to consecrate himself is to help him to pray with us. When we help people, we should not talk too much. When we bind something with a cord, we tie a knot in it. To talk too much with someone is to loosen the knot. Before praying, many people do not have the sincerity to consecrate themselves, but after they pray, their consecration becomes real. After we talk with someone, we must find a way to help him to offer himself in prayer to the Lord. This is the same as in our gospel preaching. When we speak with people about the gospel, at a certain point we need to ask them to pray. The Lord is very willing and ready to hear and answer a prayer of consecration.

We need to help people to pray in a definite way. This very much depends on our own experience. If we have the experience of consecrating ourselves in a real and full way, we will know how to help someone. We will be able to help him to realize that he must offer to the Lord in a definite way whatever he is, whatever he has, and whatever he can do. We must believe that when a person prays in this way, he is having a real contact with the Lord.

Even if a person is not sincere, the Lord is faithful. In the types we can see that whether or not a person was sincere in offering something on the altar, the Lord accepted it. Anything offered on the altar could not be taken back, even if it was offered without sincerity. We can make a deal with a man and then cancel it, but we cannot cancel our deal with the Lord. We cannot say, "Lord, I gave You something wrongly, so I take it back." We may agree with that, but the Lord will never agree. Some brothers and sisters were not sincere before they prayed, but after they prayed they became sincere, consecrated ones. Someone may even say, "A brother asked me to pray to offer myself to the Lord, so I just prayed. It did not cost me much." However, his prayer is still accepted. He may cancel it, but the Lord will not. He may "break the engagement," but with the Lord there is no divorce. There is no account in the Scriptures in which a person brought something to the altar, then repented, and the thing came back to him. There is no repentance for anything offered at the altar. Regardless of what kind of person one is, if he offers anything at the altar, the matter is settled.

Therefore, we should not talk too much. At a certain point we should help someone to pray, to go to the altar and lay himself on the altar. Then we will see the result. I have heard genuine testimonies to this effect. Someone may still remember the place, the time, and the persons he was with when he offered himself to the Lord. He may testify that for many years he did not keep his word, yet he could not forget it. Even after twenty years that word still remained with him, and he had no peace until the Lord caused him to keep his word of consecration. If we know many Christians, we can present many testimonies like this. Let us help people in a practical way. We should not merely give them a message. We must help them to "tie the knot" by making a definite decision in prayer.

THE ISSUES OF A PERSON'S CONSECRATION

Helping Others to Stand on Their Consecration and Not Doubt It

After a certain time we should fellowship again with the new ones to check the outcome of their consecration. We mostly find one of three issues. First, after consecrating themselves, some genuine ones doubt whether or not they have truly consecrated. They may not feel they were sincere. We must help them to realize that this doubt comes from God's enemy. We should help this kind of person believe that he has truly consecrated himself. We should not say, "If you do not feel that you have truly offered yourself, do it again." If we help someone in this way, we open the back door for the enemy to come in. Then if we come to that person a third time, we will find that he is still doubtful. Rather, we should say, "Brother, there is no need for you to pray in this way. You have already offered yourself. The only way you should pray now is to say, 'Lord, I stand on the ground of my consecration, and I continue to offer myself more and more.'" To pray in this way is right.

I once heard of a brother who offered himself to the Lord, after which the enemy came in to fool him and cause him to doubt. He was a farmer who tilled the soil. When he was at one end of the field, he offered himself to the Lord, but by the time he reached the other end he already doubted it, so he offered himself again. However, by the time he turned around and reached the first end of the field, he doubted his consecration again. He did this many times, falling into the snare of the enemy. Finally, he realized what he was doing. He put a stake in the ground and said, "Satan, this marks the spot on which I truly consecrated myself to the Lord. Do not speak any further word of doubt to me." After that he had the peace to go on. If we are not sure that we have consecrated ourselves to the Lord, it is hard to have the peace to go on. This is why the enemy, Satan, always does his best to cause us to doubt our sincerity and doubt whether we have truly consecrated ourselves to the Lord. We must learn this lesson of how to help people.

Calling on the Highest Authority for a Person

A second issue of a person's consecration is that he may have offered himself in a shallow way. After his consecration, he neglected it. The best way to help him is to pray, not in a general way but by calling on the Lord as the highest authority to deal with this person. We may pray, "Lord, this is a brother who prayed in Your name. You have to honor Your name, raise up Your name, and claim this person." Many times this kind of prayer is prevailing. We should not pray this way in our self, because many times the Lord will do something such as bring a certain kind of hardship to that person. He will answer this call to the highest authority and come in to intervene and deal with the person for whom we pray. Then something may happen to him, and he will come to us for help. It is not like this every time, but this is a principle.

Being Defeated by the Lord
and Following the Inner Anointing

The third issue of a person's consecration is that it is real and normal without any doubt. This is wonderful, but we still must know how to help such persons, not legally but according to the principles of the spiritual life. We should tell them that consecration is not a once-for-all matter. It is not only a crisis to pass through but a way to go on. Day by day we must keep our consecration real, living, and available. This means that day by day we need to consecrate ourselves. Then after we consecrate ourselves to the Lord, there will always be some struggle between us and the Lord. Whenever this happens, we must be defeated by the Lord; we must never defeat Him. Always let Him win the victory, and be willing to be defeated. We should pray, "Lord, I want to be defeated by You. I do not want to defeat You."

We should also help such a person to realize that his inner consciousness, the anointing of the indwelling Holy Spirit, will now be very living and keen. All day long he must walk, live, and do things in the way of caring for this inner consciousness. As long as we care for the inner consciousness, we will keep a living fellowship with the Lord. Strictly speaking, therefore, the next experience after consecration is the sense of the inner anointing. It is a great thing to help the brothers and sisters pass through a crisis of consecration and enter into the stage of the inner sense of the anointing.

OUR NEED FOR TRAINING WITH DEFINITE TEACHING
CONCERNING THE EXPERIENCES OF LIFE

Too often we help the brothers in the church only in a general way. This is why I tell the co-workers that the proper way to learn something is in courses. The proper way to learn mathematics, for example, is by completing one course and moving on to another. If we do not learn by courses, we can study for our whole life and never learn much. In the church we may have message after message every week, but some brothers have been listening to messages for fifty years without learning much because the teaching is too general. The writings of the apostles, especially of the apostle Paul, are not general; they are very definite. Today in the church we need definite teachings. This is why we need trainings. It is right to take a certain period of time in a local church to deal with the stages of spiritual experience. We may need six months to deal with the real experience of regeneration, helping people to be clear what regeneration is and how they can know its experience. We need another period of time to deal with consecration. We need period after period in this way for a number of years. Then we will see a local church built up with a group of believers who have the real experiences. They know what regeneration is, they have experienced it, and they know how to help people with it. Likewise, they know what consecration is, they have this experience, they live in it, and they know how to help new converts to go on. The believers will have not merely a certain desire or love but the experience of life, the genuine learning, the discipline, and the practice. Such a church is a proper church.

CHAPTER FOUR

THE FELLOWSHIP OF LIFE

Scripture Reading: 1 John 1:1-9; 2:27-28a; Acts 2:42

A FURTHER WORD
CONCERNING CONSECRATION

Many people say that consecration is for the purpose of being used by God to do a work for God. To some extent this is a wrong understanding. If we come back to the Scriptures, we will find that consecration is actually for life, not for work. We consecrate ourselves to the Lord not to work for Him but for Him to work in us. To do something for the Lord is a matter of work, but to be wrought on by the Lord is a matter of life. What we mainly need is to be worked on by the Lord. We are not the workers but the workmanship in the hand of the Lord (Eph. 2:10). For the Lord to work on us requires our cooperation. If we do not cooperate with Him, He cannot work on us. In order to put something in a bottle, there is no need to ask the bottle to cooperate, because the bottle has no life, no mind, no will, no emotion, and no desire. To put something in the bottle is an easy, one-sided matter. To give medicine to a child, however, is to put something into a living "bottle." This is hard to do because it requires the child's cooperation. If a child is not willing to cooperate, the parent may need to open his mouth and force the medicine into him. God has many things to put into us and many things to remove, but this requires our cooperation, which is our consecration. We need to consecrate ourselves to the Lord, saying, "Lord, I am here. I accept what You accept and refuse what You refuse."

The human concept is that the Lord is waiting to use us. However, if we are not wrought on by the Lord, we cannot be used by Him. Work comes out of life; it is the outflow of the inner life. How much we can be used by the Lord in His hands depends on how much we have been wrought upon by Him. His work through us and on us depends on our cooperation, that is, our consecration. We always have to consecrate ourselves to the Lord for His work upon us. We should not have the concept that we consecrate ourselves because the Lord needs us to work for Him. We are not tools in the Lord's hand. Rather, we are vessels to contain Him (Rom. 9:21-23).

On the negative side, many things need to be taken out of us. We have been filled up with many things other than the Lord. On the positive side, however, many things of the Lord—all the riches of Christ—must be wrought into us. On the one hand we are dirty, while on the other hand we are empty. Therefore, we need the Lord's work to clean us out and remove the many things other than Christ, and we need Him to put Christ into us more and more. This is the work of the Lord upon us, which always requires our consecration.

As we said in the last chapter, after we consecrate ourselves to the Lord, we must try never to defeat Him. Always be willing to be defeated by Him. If we are persons consecrating ourselves to the Lord, there will often be a struggle between us and Him. This is because the Lord wants to take some things out of us. If we say, "Lord, don't take it," there will be a struggle, but in this struggle we must learn never to defeat the Lord but rather to be defeated by Him. Then the Lord will have the opportunity to work something into us. This requires our genuine consecration, which is for life, not for our work.

After I have spoken here about consecration, I will not continue by speaking about how to work for the Lord and be used by Him. Rather, my intention is to speak about life. Consecration is for life. Consider the type of the tabernacle. After passing the altar, we come to the laver, and after the laver we come into the Holy Place. If we understand the correct meaning of the types, we can see that there is not much work here. Instead, there is much enjoyment. This indicates that after our consecration, our main need is not to work for the Lord but to grow in life. We need to be worked on by the Lord. To work for the Lord is not even secondary; it may be the eleventh item of importance, because there may be ten other things the Lord needs to do in us before He uses us to do something for Him. We need to leave the thought of working for the Lord and pay our full attention to life.

In the Gospel of John, the Lord told us to do almost nothing but believe in Him, love Him, and abide in Him. Then we will bear fruit. Our work is to bear fruit. This is a not a work apart from life. Fruit-bearing is the out-working of life.

KNOWING LIFE IN OUR EXPERIENCE

After our consecration there are three basic matters of life that we need to know: the fellowship of life, the consciousness of life, and the law of life. To a greater or lesser degree, these matters are neglected in today's Christianity. I have no intention to condemn others, but I must speak the truth. I have read many books and have listened to messages, and I am sorry for the situation of Christianity today. Here and there in various groups of Christians, people talk about life, but *life* is often just a term or an "-ology." A brother once testified that when he came among us, he found that we always talk about life; almost all the messages in our conferences and trainings concentrated on life. He asked himself, "Why do these people always say 'life.' Why don't they say 'the Spirit?'" Later, however, the Lord opened his eyes to see the meaning of *life* and the meaning of *Spirit*.

If we do not know the three basic matters mentioned above, we will not be able to know what life is. In theology, in terminology, and in teaching we may know life, but we will not know life in our experience, and we will not be on the line of life. However, if we do know the fellowship of life, the sense or taste of life, and the law of life, then we know what life is in our experience.

LIFE PRODUCING THE FELLOWSHIP OF LIFE
IN TWO DIRECTIONS

The scriptural basis for the fellowship of life is 1 John 1. The Gospel of John is a book on life, showing how to have and receive life, while the First Epistle of John is on the fellowship of life. After we receive the eternal life in Christ, that is,

Christ as our life, we need to pay attention to the fellowship of life. That is why the Epistle of John comes after the Gospel of John.

First John 1 is one of the greatest chapters in the entire Scriptures. Because it is one of the few chapters on the fellowship of life, it holds an extraordinary position. Other passages speak of the fellowship of the Spirit, such as 2 Corinthians 13:14, but John speaks of the fellowship of life. The first two verses of 1 John 1 say, "That which was from the beginning, which we have heard, which we have seen with our eyes, which we beheld and our hands handled, concerning the Word of life (and the life was manifested, and we have seen and testify and report to you the eternal life, which was with the Father and was manifested to us)." While verse 1 speaks of the Word of life, verse 2 simply says *life*. The life which was with the Father and was manifested to us is the Son of God, Christ Himself.

Verse 3 continues, "That which we have seen and heard we report also to you that you also may have fellowship with us, and indeed our fellowship is with the Father and with His Son Jesus Christ." The apostles ministered life to the believers in a practical and real way. As a result, the believers had fellowship. Since fellowship comes from life, we call it the fellowship of life. Moreover, this fellowship is "with us," the apostles. The apostles saw life, and they ministered this life that we may have fellowship with them. In addition, our fellowship is with the Father and His Son. Here is a fellowship in two directions, vertical and horizontal. Horizontally we fellowship with one another, and vertically we fellowship with the Father and with His Son Jesus Christ. From life we have fellowship, and this fellowship is with the saints and with the Triune God.

THE FELLOWSHIP OF LIFE BEING UNIQUE

Verse 3 speaks of the fellowship with the apostles. The fellowship in the Body is the fellowship of the apostles. Acts 2:42 says, "And they continued steadfastly in the teaching and the fellowship of the apostles, in the breaking of bread and the prayers." Four things are mentioned here, but according to the grammatical construction, only two things are of the apostles. The teaching and fellowship are of the apostles, while the breaking of bread and the prayers are not. We can have no other teaching than that of the apostles. Any teaching other than the apostles' is heresy. Likewise, we cannot have any fellowship other than the apostles' fellowship. Among the saints there is only one fellowship because there is only one life, one source of life, one Lord of life, Christ Himself. The Lord Christ is the unique source of this unique life, so from this unique life we have the unique fellowship. We cannot say that the saints in the ancient time had one fellowship while we have another. Neither can we say that the brothers in the Far East have one fellowship, but here we have another. In the universe, among all the saints—east and west, ancient and modern—we have only one fellowship, the fellowship that comes from the unique life which is Christ Himself.

THE FELLOWSHIP OF LIFE
BEING THE FLOW OF LIFE WITHIN US

We know that life is Christ Himself, but for many years I considered what the fellowship of life might be. I believe we now have the right words to describe and define the fellowship of life. It is the current, or flow, of life. We may compare it to the flow of blood in our body. There is one life in our body. The finger does not have one life, the nose another life, and the ears a third life. There are many members in our body, yet they have one life, and in that one life the entire body has one fellowship. Among all the members in the physical body there is the fellowship of life, which is the flow of the blood. The blood circles in our body very quickly. While I am still speaking, the blood already may have made one or two complete circuits. We may also compare the fellowship of life to the current of electricity. If we go to the electric meter, we can see that the current is flowing. If the current stops, the lights go out.

The flow of the blood in our body is the blood itself, just as the current of electricity is the electricity itself. If the electricity is stationary, there is no current, but when it moves, it is the current. In the same way, the fellowship of life is the flowing, the current, of life within us; it is life itself flowing. Since we were saved, there has been something flowing in us. The life which we received in Christ is a flowing life, and when it flows, it becomes the fellowship of life. In this fellowship, you fellowship with me, I fellowship with you, we fellowship with the other saints, and we all fellowship with the Lord. There is something living and flowing within us all the time. Therefore, after we consecrate ourselves to the Lord, we must care for this inner flowing, because consecration is for life. Consecration is for us to be worked on by the Lord, and the Lord works in us by the flow of life.

The flow of blood within us does much work for the physical body. It supplies the nourishment the body needs, and it carries away discharges. It molds the body and strengthens its functions. This is a good illustration of the fellowship of life. What the Lord works in us, upon us, and into us depends entirely on the flowing of life. When we have the flow, the fellowship, of life, this flow kills the germs of death within us and carries them away, and it also nourishes us with a supply and molds us into a certain shape. We cannot be molded by teachings. Teachings help, but what type of Christian we are mostly depends on the inner molding by the flow of life.

THE FELLOWSHIP OF LIFE
PRODUCING OUR INNER FUNCTION

In addition, our function comes from the inner flow of the fellowship of life. In Christianity today there are many different practices, such as the formal practice, the fundamental practice, the Pentecostal practice, and the Brethren, Methodist, Baptist, and Presbyterian practices. Which of these is prevailing? It seems that none is prevailing, because for the most part Christians neglect the function that comes out of the inner flow of life, thinking that their function is something that comes from outside of them. I may be the best dentist, but if I take teeth from outside of you and put them into you, they will not function as real teeth. In the same way, an eye specialist can put two new eyes into you, but they will not work. The function of the members must come from within. Consider a baby. He is born without even one tooth, but if we feed him properly, the blood within him will constantly flow, and the more it flows, the more the teeth will come. The kind of teeth that come from the flow of life function properly, but teeth inserted from the outside do not work. In a similar way, seminaries have "teeth experts," but the "teeth" they put into people do not work.

Some believe that 1 Corinthians tells us that when we have the gifts, we have the function. In more than forty years I have never observed that the baptism or outpouring of the Holy Spirit develops the inner function. It is only when we have the inner function that the outpouring, the baptism, helps. The proper function of all the members of the Body comes from within, not from the outside. Is there a function in any member of our body that comes from the outside? Rather, all the members' function comes from within. Therefore, we must have a strong, pure current of blood flowing all day long. Whatever we should not have, it will carry away, and whatever we need, it will supply. It will afford the function we need, and it will build us up into the right shape or mold. Our shape and mold all depend upon the inner flowing. If we stop the current, everything in us will stop.

Today what we need is the flowing of life within. All the precious experiences of Romans 6, 8, and 12 depend on the flowing of life within, that is, on the fellowship of life. The problem in the church is a problem related to the inner fellowship of life, and the problems of all the saints are also problems related to the inner fellowship of life. Therefore, we must pay our full attention to this inner life, to the inner flowing, the fellowship of life. We have received Christ as life, and with this life within there is the flowing, the current. This flowing is the fellowship of life.

BEING IN THE LIGHT AND
BEING CLEANSED BY THE BLOOD OF JESUS

First John 1:5 and 6 say, "And this is the message which we have heard from Him and announce to you, that God is light and in Him is no darkness at all. If we say that we have fellowship with Him and yet walk in the darkness, we lie and are not practicing the truth." After fellowship we have light. If we are in the fellowship, we must be in the light, because the fellowship brings us into the presence of God who is light. That is why if we are still in darkness but say we are in the fellowship, we are lying.

Verse 7 continues, "But if we walk in the light as He is in the light, we have fellowship with one another, and the blood of Jesus His Son cleanses us from every sin." Light is God Himself with whom we fellowship. When we are in the light, we need one thing: the blood. The word *cleanses* here is in the present tense. Regardless of how much we have grown, as long as we are in this old nature and as long as we are on this earth, there is always some defiling touch. When we are in the fellowship and the fellowship brings us into the presence of God, who is light, we are in the light. Then at this time we realize that we need the cleansing. Because we are under the light and in the light, the light exposes us and we see that we are dirty. Therefore, right away we sense the need of the blood; we need the cleansing of the blood. Consider your own experiences. If we do not neglect the inner fellowship, in the light of God we will always realize and sense that we are dirty, sinful, wrong with something, and wrong with someone. For this reason, as long as we are in the light we sense the need of the cleansing of the blood.

Here we have four items: life, fellowship, light, and blood. We receive the life, and the life brings us into the fellowship, the current, the flowing of life. This fellowship brings us into the light, and in the light we sense the need of the blood. Many times when I hear brothers and sisters praying, they do not definitely and strongly mention that they need the cleansing of the blood. I doubt a little that they are truly in the fellowship. To be in the fellowship means that they are in the light. Why then do they not realize their need of the cleansing of the blood? If we are truly in the light, we will have the real sense, the real realization, that we need the cleansing of the blood, because we are still in this old nature and we are still on this earth. Regardless of how careful we are, we are still dirty. Can we be so careful for a whole week that we do not need to wash our face and hands? Regardless of how careful we are, we still have to wash. I am not careless, but I still need to wash my hands five, six, or seven times a day. If I do not wash, I have a certain kind of feeling. I may not see that I am dirty, but I still need to wash. Then after washing, I feel refreshed and cleansed. Even while we sleep at night, some dirt comes upon our face. There is no need to touch the dirt; the dirt comes to visit us. This is a dirty universe and earth, so we need the cleansing.

THE ANOINTING FOLLOWING
THE SPRINKLING OF THE BLOOD

In type, after the sprinkling of the blood there is the anointing. The anointing of the oil always follows the sprinkling of the blood. According to type, these two items are the very means to keep us in fellowship with God. Whether it is an item of furniture or a person that is brought into the presence of God, that item or person needs the sprinkling of the blood, and after the sprinkling and upon the sprinkling it is anointed. There is not one person who can come into the presence of God without being sprinkled and anointed. If a person comes into the presence of God without the sprinkling and the anointing, he will die immediately. He needs the sprinkling of the blood, and upon the sprinkling of the blood he needs the anointing. Then by the sprinkling of the blood and the anointing of the ointment, this person or this item of furniture is acceptable to God. This means that these two things—the sprinkling of the blood and the anointing of the ointment—bring people into the presence and fellowship of God.

In chapter one of the First Epistle of John there is the cleansing and sprinkling of the blood, and in the very next chapter there is the anointing. Verses 27 and 28 of chapter two tell us that we need to abide in the Lord according to this anointing. Verse 27 says, "The anointing...abides in you...and even as it has taught you, abide in Him." This abiding is the very fellowship; to abide in the Lord is to fellowship with the Lord. According to typology, this inner anointing comes to us based on the sprinkling of the blood; that is, the anointing follows the blood. Exodus and Leviticus clearly tell us that all the items and persons that come into the presence of God had to be sprinkled with the redeeming blood and anointed with the ointment. We must realize that we always need the blood on the negative side to cleanse us and the ointment, the Holy Spirit within us, on the positive side to anoint us. This kind of anointing brings us into life. The more anointing we enjoy, the more life we have; the more life we have the stronger the fellowship we are in; the stronger the fellowship we are in, the more light we have; and the more light we have, the more cleansing of the blood we need. Then more cleansing of the blood brings us into more anointing, and the more anointing we enjoy, the more we have life. This is a cycle. When we have life, we are in the fellowship, in the fellowship we are in the light, as we are in the light, we sense the need of the cleansing, under the cleansing we enjoy the anointing, and the anointing brings us more life.

**THE FLOW OF LIFE
SOLVING ALL OUR PROBLEMS**

This is the real flow of life, and the more flow of life we have, the more our problems are solved. When I was younger, I was active to help people solve their problems. I would say, "This is easy; let me help you. Just do this and that—one, two, three, four—and your problem will be solved." Eventually I found that this does not work. "One, two, three, four" is good in mathematics, but in the matters of life it does not work. Only the inner fellowship, the current within us flowing all the time, can solve our problems. No one and no teaching can do this. If a brother has a problem with his wife, I may advise, warn, beg, and entreat him. I may say, "Brother, you must do this and that for the Lord's glory." But regardless of how much I speak in this way, although it may seem that he receives the help, in actuality he does not. One day, however, he may consecrate himself to the Lord, saying, "Lord, I love You, and I consecrate myself to You for You to work on me." Then as he allows the inner flowing to flow, this flowing will solve his problems. If not for this, Christianity would be like the many religions. Religions always try to solve problems by teaching and instructing people. The proper way, strictly speaking, is different. It is something within that is living and flowing.

THE INNER FLOWING
REQUIRING OUR CONSECRATION

If we still have problems, either with God or with man, we are wrong concerning the fellowship. Probably the flowing within us is stopped. At least it is not fresh, living, strong, and adequate; it may be weak and nearly dead. At this time we need to experience our consecration. In order for the inner flowing to be stronger, we need to refresh and renew our consecration. The more we consecrate ourselves, not to work for the Lord but to be worked on by the Lord, the stronger the inner flowing will be, and when it flows strongly, it solves our problems.

We cannot help people to avoid even the sin of a little pride. We may say, "Brother, I realize that you are a proud person. Because you love the Lord and I love you, I want to tell you frankly that you must learn to be humble. Don't be proud!" This, however, does not work. I did this kind of work many times when I was young, but now I never do this foolish work. I do not like to do this kind of foolish and useless work. It would be better for me to go to sleep. We should let such a brother be proud; it is better for him to be proud. To advise him to be humble is falsehood; that is not the real humility. He will merely be acting. What this brother needs is the inner flowing of the inner life. When he truly loves the Lord and consecrates himself to Him, does not struggle with the Lord, and never defeats the Lord, he will have a strong flowing within him. This will solve the problem of his pride. It will be something within, life swallowing up death. It will not be an outward adjustment, correction, or improvement, which is the work of religion, and not the working of the inner life. The working of the inner life is the constant flowing. In order to know life and in order to describe what life is in the way of experience, we must describe it in the way of fellowship.

CHAPTER FIVE

THE INNER SENSE OF LIFE

Scripture Reading: Eph. 4:17-24; Rom. 8:6; John 8:12; Heb. 8:10; Rom. 8:2; 1 John 2:27-28a; Gal. 2:20; Phil. 2:13

CARING FOR THE INNER SENSE OF LIFE

Ephesians 4:17 through 24 speak concerning the consciousness of the inner life, the sense or feeling of life. Verse 17 says, "This therefore I say and testify in the Lord, that you no longer walk as the Gentiles also walk in the vanity of their mind." This verse mentions the vanity of the mind. Whatever is in the mind of the unbelievers is vain, an emptiness and vanity, in the eyes of God. Even the best thing that they think and consider in their minds is vain. It is a vanity of vanities. They walk in the vanity of their mind because in their mind they do not have God; they do not have Christ who is the reality.

Verse 18 says, "Being darkened in their understanding, alienated from the life of God because of the ignorance which is in them, because of the hardness of their heart." After speaking of the mind, this portion speaks of the understanding. When the mind is filled with vanity, the understanding is darkened. That they are alienated from the life of God means that they do not have the life of God; they are cut off from the life of God. This means that they do not have the sense of the life of God, the consciousness from the life of God. This verse also mentions ignorance. This ignorance, this foolishness without knowledge, is due to the hardness of the heart. In these verses we have the mind with vanity, the darkened understanding, and the hardened heart. We should pay attention to the order here. First the mind is full of vanity; then the understanding is darkened because of the hardness of the heart. This proves that they have nothing to do with the life of God. They are alienated, cut off, from the life of God.

We need one or two messages for each of these matters, which are all related to the inner life. In order to learn the inner life, we must know all these things. If I had the time, I would like to sit with you once or twice a day to talk about all these matters from the New Testament teachings. These things have been lost in today's Christianity. We may have been Christians for many years and may have listened to many messages from the pulpit, but we may not have heard a message about these matters. What is the vanity of the mind? What is the darkened understanding? And what is alienation from the life of God due to the hardness of the heart? I am sorry to say that in today's Christianity no one stands up to teach the Lord's people about these things.

Verse 19 begins, "Who, being past feeling." This verse speaks of feeling. Do not think that the feeling, or consciousness, of life is a term invented by us. No, this is something we have discovered in the Word of God. Darby's New Translation renders this phrase as "having cast off all feeling," while the Interlinear Greek-English New Testament renders it as "having ceased to care." Those who have vanity in their mind, whose understanding is darkened, and whose heart is fully hardened have cast off all feeling, and they no longer care. They give up all care for the feeling.

Verse 19 continues, "Have given themselves over to lasciviousness to work all uncleanness in greediness." Because they cast off all feeling, they give themselves over. In Ephesians Paul exhausted his vocabulary, using all the words he could use. We should pay attention, however, to the matter of the feeling. The Gentiles' minds are full of vanity, their understanding is darkened, and their heart is hardened because they cast off all feeling; they do not care for the feeling.

This is the description of the Gentiles. However, verse 20 says, "But you did not so learn Christ." We have learned Christ not in the way of casting off all feeling but in the way of caring for all feeling. Then verses 21 through 23 say, "If indeed you have heard Him and have been taught in Him as the reality is in Jesus, that you put off, as regards your former manner of life, the old man, which is being corrupted according to the lusts of the deceit, and that you be renewed in the spirit of your mind." Verse 24 goes on to speak of putting on the new man. Putting off the old man and putting on the new man depend on the spirit of the mind. What then is the spirit of the mind, and how can we know the spirit of our mind? By all these verses we must conclude that in order to know the spirit of our mind we must know the inner consciousness of life. It is by the inner consciousness of life, the inner, deeper feeling of life, that we know the spirit of our mind. Without this inner feeling, consciousness, and sense of life, how can we know the spirit of our mind? If we read these verses carefully, we will conclude from the context that there must be a consciousness, a feeling, a deeper sense within us by which we are able to know the spirit of our mind.

This passage presents a contrast between the Gentiles and the Christians. The Gentiles cast off all feeling, but as Christians we take care of the inner feeling. It is by this inner feeling that we know the spirit of our mind. Then we are able to realize the putting off of the old man and the putting on of the new man.

THE INNER SENSE BEING RELATED TO LIFE

Romans 8:6 says, "For the mind set on the flesh is death, but the mind set on the spirit is life and peace." This verse speaks both of death and of life and peace. It does not use the words *feeling, sense,* or *consciousness,* but consciousness is here in fact. We would all agree that *peace* refers to a certain feeling within us, something within that can be sensed, of which we have a consciousness. Therefore, this verse speaks of having peace in our sense, in our inner feeling. If peace were not a matter of feeling or consciousness, how could we know we have it? We know we have peace because we sense it. When we go along with the spirit and set our mind on the spirit, we have peace within. How do we know we have peace? We sense it; we feel it and have the consciousness of it.

As we know, we have three parts—spirit, soul, and body. In our body we have five physical senses to sense the physical world. In the soul we have the psychological sense, the self-sense. Then in the spirit we have the spiritual sense to sense the things of God, the things of the spirit. When we speak of the sense of life, we mean this spiritual sense. The spiritual sense is the very sense of life. However, we speak of the sense of life rather than the spiritual sense because this sense is one hundred percent related to life. If a man is physically dead, if his life is gone, all the senses of his body disappear. This proves that senses are related to life. The sense is in the life. If we have life, we have the sense; if we do not have life, we do not have the sense. We have a sense in our spirit because in our spirit we have the divine life.

With any kind of life there is a certain kind of sense. There is no animal without a sense. Even a little fly has a sense because it has life. However, the principle is that the higher the life is, the higher the sense is. If we have the highest life, we have the highest sense. Sense goes along with life. In our body we have the physical life, in our soul we have the psychological, soulish life, and now in our spirit we have the divine life, which is the life of God. This is not merely the higher life but the highest life. In our spirit we have the highest life, the life of God, that is, God Himself. With this highest life we have the highest sense, the highest feeling, the highest consciousness. Many of us have been in Christianity for many years, but sorry to say, all these precious matters have been lost and buried there.

SPIRITUAL KNOWLEDGE
BEING THE SENSE OF LIFE WITHIN

We often speak of spiritual knowledge, or we may say, "Spiritually I have seen something," or "I have seen something in the spirit." What is this seeing, this knowledge, in the spirit? The seeing or knowledge in the spirit is nothing other than a certain kind of feeling. Spiritual seeing, spiritual knowledge, and spiritual understanding are the spiritual sense, the spiritual feeling. When I was about sixteen years old, I was invited to a feast. On the table there were two bowls of white granules, one of salt and the other of sugar. It is hard to discern what is salt and what is sugar. The color, the shape, and the appearance are about the same. As we were eating something which needed a lot of sugar, I took the wrong bowl, the one full of salt. I put salt on my food, supposing that it was sugar, and I put it into my mouth. I needed no dictionary, teacher, tutor, professor, preacher, or minister to tell me I was wrong. Right away I sensed that I was wrong because it was too salty. This was a matter not of knowledge but of the sense of life.

Even a new baby will spit out something salty, but if you give him something sweet, he will swallow it. This is not knowledge; it is not something taught. It is the very sense of life. If someone is dead, however, he will have no reaction to whatever you put in his mouth. This is because when the life is gone, the sense is gone. This illustrates that there is such a thing as the sense of life. If we have the life of God, we have the divine sense. Because this life is the highest life, with this life there is the highest sense.

A young brother who had just been saved came to me once, saying, "I don't know why last night I had much happiness, but this morning I lost it." I answered him, "Brother, I am sure you do not know why in your mentality, but you know the reason deep within." He said he could not understand this, so I replied, "I know you cannot understand, but please tell me: What do you sense within you?" He simply said that he had no happiness and that he had come to me to learn the reason. Still I said, "I would ask you to tell me the reason." Eventually I found out that he had done something wrong; he had lied to some people. In his understanding he thought that was not wrong, but in his spirit his sense was damaged. To tell a lie damages the sense of life.

If instead of coming to the meeting you go dancing, what will happen? The faster an unbeliever walks to the place of dancing, the happier he is. He is truly happy to go dancing. But what about you as a reborn believer? Will you be happier the faster you go? We all know that it is just the opposite. The sense you have is not happiness but bitterness. This is the sense of life. The secret of the Christian walk after we are saved is to take care of this sense of life.

THE INNER SENSE BEING THE LIGHT OF LIFE

We need to know this inner sense in a full way. This inner sense comes out of five main items within us. The first is the light of life. Since we have the life from the Lord, we have the light of life. John 1:4 speaks of the light, but it does not mention "the light of life." This phrase is in 8:12, which says, "Again therefore Jesus spoke to them, saying, I am the light of the world; he who follows Me shall by no means walk in darkness, but shall have the light of life." Strictly speaking and according to our experience, the light of life is the sense of life. When we received the Lord Jesus, He came into our spirit as life to dwell and work there. By His dwelling, working, and living there is this sense, and this sense is the enlightening. When we have the life of the Lord Jesus within us, this life enlightens us. We know this because we sense it; we have the feeling and consciousness of it. If a believer, a reborn young man, goes dancing, as he is going, there is the inner sense within him. That is the light of life. To have this sense means that we are not in darkness but in the light. The faster the unbelievers go to dance, the happier they are, because they are in darkness. They do not have this inner sense to tell them that they are wrong. It is needless to speak of going dancing; sometimes when we have only a wrong or impure motive, right away there is the sense of condemnation in us. This sense of condemnation is the light of life. Now you can understand that the light of life is simply the inner sense in the spirit. When we have the inner sense in the spirit, we have the light of life.

How do we know we are wrong? We may say we feel or we sense we are wrong. This sense within us is the enlightening; at least it comes out of the enlightening of the inner life. The inner life, which is the Lord Jesus Himself, enlightens us within, and by this enlightening we have the inner sense. There is no need for anyone to tell us that we are wrong. Many times we argue that we are right. Some things seem right as long as we argue for them, but when we stop arguing, we see that we are not right. According to our argument we are right, but in fact we know that we are not right. If we were truly right, there would be no need for argument. Many times a wife may argue with her husband, insisting that she is right. She may be right in word, but she is not right in her spirit and in life. When her words stop, she realizes she is wrong. We know this because we sense it, and we sense it because we have the life of the Lord Jesus shining within us. Therefore, we are in the light and not in darkness.

Many times when a brother argues with me, I am happy, because I know that behind his speaking is a sense of condemnation as the light of life. The more he argues, the more I am clear that he is in the light. When such a person argues, I often do not say much. I may say, "Perhaps you are right," although he is right only in argument. In actuality, he is in the light; he has light within. This light is not from knowledge or teaching. This is the light of life. "In Him was life, and the life was the light of men" (John 1:4).

If we have Christ within us as our life, this very life is the shining light within us. We simply have a sense within us which we cannot escape. We cannot escape from this shining. Young men especially always like to be right. When I was young, however, I went to people perhaps ten times a day to confess. I might say, "Brother, excuse me. I am wrong. This morning I argued with you, but now I am clear. To tell the truth, I am clear not only now, but even this morning I was already clear. While I was arguing with you, I was clear that I was wrong, but I would not lose my face. Now by the Lord's mercy I know that I have to confess to you." This means that I was in the light. These experiences prove that we have something living within us, because we have the life of Christ. This life within us is the light of men and the light of life. Please keep this in mind: The light of life gives us the inner sense while it enlightens. We can never separate the sense of life from the enlightening of the light of life.

THE INNER SENSE BEING
THE REGULATING OF THE LAW OF LIFE

Second, we have the law of life in us (Heb. 8:10). Romans 8:2 speaks of the law of the Spirit of life. The law of life and the law of the Spirit of life are one item, that is, the inner regulating. We know we have the inner regulation because we sense it. We realize the inner regulating by the inner sense. Strictly speaking, the inner law is the inner sense, or at least we can say that the inner sense comes from the inner regulating. When the inner law regulates, it gives us the inner sense. Why do we have the inner sense of life? It is because we have the inner law of life. Within us there is not only the light of life shining, but there is the law of life regulating. From the shining of the light we have a sense; from the regulating of the law we also have a sense.

When the law regulates, we sense it; it gives us an inner consciousness. This is especially the case when we are about to do something wrong. When we are going to do something right, we may not sense the regulating, but when we are wrong, we sense it. We may compare this to our stomach; if there is no trouble in our stomach, we do not sense our digestion, but when we are sick in our stomach, we sense it. As Christians, when we walk rightly in the presence of God, we may not have much sense. When we come to a meeting, for example, we may not have any sense. But if we try to go to a movie, the regulating sense comes. When we read the Bible, we do not have the sense we are right, but if we try to read novels or look at the pictures in the newspaper, we do not have peace. Something within us is regulating. The regulating sense is very obvious and clear when we do wrong things. On the one hand, this is the regulating of the inner law, but on the other hand, it is the inner sense of life. The inner sense of life comes from the regulating of the inner law. We have the inner sense because we have the inner law.

THE INNER SENSE COMING FROM THE ANOINTING

Third, we have the anointing (1 John 2:27). *Anointing* is a gerund, ending in *-ing*. It is a moving, an action, within us. This moving and action is the working of the Holy Spirit. When the Holy Spirit works within us, His working is the anointing. When the anointing works, it anoints; it is the ointment moving and acting. To be sure, this motion gives us a feeling. If a part of our body is alive and proper, it has a feeling when it moves; the feeling comes from the moving. The anointing within us is constantly moving. This is the work of the Holy Spirit, and this work never stops, regardless of what we are or where we are. However, we must be a little quiet to sense it. If I put my hand on a brother when he is arguing with someone, he may not feel it. In the same way, we often do not have the sense of the inner anointing because we are too active. If we would quiet ourselves a little, right away we will sense the inner anointing. If a brother argues that he is right, we should not argue with him. The more he argues, the more he will not sense that he is wrong. We should simply keep quiet and help him to be cool and quiet. When he is silent, he will sense that he is wrong. In quietness we sense the inner anointing, the inner moving of the Holy Spirit.

THE SENSE OF LIFE
COMING FROM CHRIST LIVING IN US

The fourth item is that Christ not only is life in us, but He is living in us (Gal. 2:20). Christ is living and acting within us. We cannot say that a chair lives in a room. We only say that a person lives in a room. To live is to act, move, work, and do things. If a person lives in a room but does not do things, he is either sleeping or sick. However, Christ is never sleeping. He is always working, moving, acting, and living within us, and from this living and acting there is a sense. The sense of life comes from the living Christ within us.

THE SENSE OF LIFE
COMING FROM GOD OPERATING IN US

Fifth, Philippians 2:13 tells us that God operates in us both the willing and the working for His good pleasure. The word *operate* is a strong word. In Greek it is the word from which we have *energize*. For God to operate in us means that God energizes in us. This is to work not in an ordinary way but in an extraordinary way. To be sure, this involves some feeling. It is impossible for a brother to be energized but have no feeling of it.

Verse 12 says, "So then, my beloved, even as you have always obeyed, not as in my presence only but now much rather in my absence, work out your own salvation with fear and trembling." We have received salvation, which strictly speaking is God and Christ Himself in us. Now we need to work out the salvation that we have already received, which means to live it out, by obedience with fear and trembling. What is it that we obey? Verse 13 continues, "For it is God who operates in you both the willing and the working for His good pleasure." The word *for* indicates that verse 13 is an explanation of verse 12. The thing that we obey is the working of God within us. We must be obedient not merely to outward teachings and doctrines but to the working of God within us both to will and to do. Learn to obey the inner working of God. It is by this obedience to the inner working of God that we work out, live out, the salvation that we have received.

THE ABOVE CRUCIAL MATTERS BEING
THE MARK OF GOD'S ECONOMY

I hope you will do some homework to read the passages of Scriptures concerning the above five matters: the light of life, the law of life, the anointing of the Holy Spirit, Christ living in us, and God operating in us. We must consider these teachings not only in the meetings. We should spend some time to read all the related passages, meditate, and pray about them. I would especially ask the young brothers and sisters to practice these matters much and to remember them. Even while you sleep, you may repeat, "The light of life, the law of life, the anointing, Christ lives in me, God operates in me." This is truly helpful. If I had ten lives, I would spend them all to teach people about these very matters. Nothing is more important than this today. This is the mark of God's economy. How pitiful it is among God's people today! No one helps them to know these things. They talk about many other things that do not help much. It means little whether or not you know those other things. But the sense of life is one thing that is truly meaningful. If we know this, we are alive; if we do not know it, we are dead. This is a matter of life and death. Therefore, I beg you young brothers and sisters to learn to know these matters—the light of life, the law of life, the inner anointing, the living of Christ in us, and the operating of God—in your experience. The inner sense, the inner consciousness, always comes from these five items. The more we are conscious of the inner sense, the more we are healthy spiritually. If you do not have the inner sense, I am afraid that you are wrong.

THE NEED OF OUR OBEDIENCE
TO THE INNER SENSE

Since we know these matters, we must take care of our obedience to them. As obedient Christians we must learn to obey the inner working of God, the inner sense, all the day long. We must take care of the inner sense and obey it. The true obedient child of God is one who truly obeys the inner sense. We may obey many teachings, but we may be rebellious to the inner sense. People may admire that we are so obedient to all the teachings and doctrines, yet we ourselves may know that we are always very rebellious to God according to the inner sense. We need to learn to obey God in the inner sense. This is the true meaning of walking according to the spirit. Romans 8 and Galatians 5 both speak of walking according to the spirit or walking by the Spirit. To walk according to the spirit is simply to take care of the inner sense deep within us. When we take care of the inner sense, we are walking according to, or in, the spirit. Thus, to obey the inner sense and walk according to the spirit are one thing.

It is by this obedience that we are able to abide in the Lord. First John 2:27 and 28 tell us to abide in the Lord according to the anointing. This is to abide in the Lord according to the inner sense, the inner consciousness. To have something wrong in our inner consciousness means that we are not abiding in the Lord.

The result of taking care of the inner sense is that we keep the fellowship with the Lord, we know the Lord in a living way, we grow in life, we are built up in the Body, and we have not merely outward power but the inner might in life. By being obedient to the inner consciousness we realize all good things in the spiritual life. This is the secret and the key, but this has been lost by so many Christians. From now on we must consecrate ourselves to the Lord for this: "Lord, now I know that I have the light of life, the law of life, the anointing of the Holy Spirit, Christ living in me, and God operating within me. I have all these wonderful, divine things that are so active, alive, and living in me. For this purpose I consecrate myself to You, Lord. I hand myself over to You." By this you can see that to consecrate ourselves does not mean that we work for the Lord. Rather, it means that we cooperate with Him. We must consecrate ourselves to Him for this, and after our consecration we simply must take care of the inner sense, going along with it not only in great matters but also in small matters in our daily walk and even our family life. In all our daily life and walk we must take care of the inner consciousness.

We must consecrate ourselves once again, read all the related passages of the Scriptures, put ourselves on the test, and practice these things. If the dear brothers and sisters truly put this into practice, there will be a great change among us. We must strictly take care of the inner sense of life, the inner consciousness.

As we have seen, 1 John shows us that our fellowship comes from life; thus, it is the fellowship of life. This fellowship is maintained, on the negative side, by the cleansing of the blood and, on the positive side, by the anointing of the Spirit. The blood is mentioned in chapter one, and the anointing is in chapter two. In the Old Testament type, anything or anyone brought into the presence of God needed to be sprinkled with the blood and anointed. We must learn how to apply the blood of Christ and how to take care of the anointing, the inner consciousness. The sense, the consciousness, of life has very much to do with the fellowship of life. The fellowship of life depends on the consciousness of life. If we are careless with the consciousness of life, we will lose the fellowship of life.

This fellowship comes from life and brings us into light. Fellowship brings light to us because fellowship brings us into the presence of God, who is light. To fellowship with Him means that we are in the light. Experientially, the light gives us the inner consciousness. All these things are related. When we fellowship with God, we are in the light, and when we are in the light, we are full of the inner consciousness and we are clear in the inner sense. Then if anything is wrong, we can apply the blood for cleansing. Following the cleansing of the blood we enjoy the anointing of the Holy Spirit, and by the anointing of the Holy Spirit we have the inner sense, the inner consciousness. It is by all these things that we go on in life. Therefore, I hope that you will learn to take care of all these matters. Then you will know the way for the growth in life.

Again I would ask you to do some homework on these points. If you do, you will receive a double portion. Otherwise, you eventually will not have much benefit from what you have heard. Look into all these points, read all the passages, pray about them, meditate a little, and put them into practice. Then you will learn these things, and you will be able to help others. Among the Lord's children there is the real need of these matters of the inner life.

CHAPTER SIX

THE LAW OF LIFE

(1)

Scripture Reading: Heb. 8:10-11

After we receive the Lord Jesus as our life, we have three main things: the fellowship of life, the sense of life, and the law of life. In order to know the inner life, that is, to know and experience Christ as our life in a very practical way, we need to know these three related matters. According to the teaching of the New Testament, the law of life is even more important than the other two. Hebrews 8:10 and 11 say, "For this is the covenant which I will covenant with the house of Israel after those days, says the Lord: I will impart My laws into their mind, and on their hearts I will inscribe them; and I will be God to them, and they will be a people to Me. And they shall by no means each teach his fellow citizen and each his brother, saying, Know the Lord; for all will know Me from the little one to the great one among them." Verse 10 is a quotation of Jeremiah 31:33, but in Jeremiah *law* is single in number, while in Hebrews it is not one law but *laws*. In addition, Jeremiah 31 says that God will put His law "within them," that is, in their inward parts, while Hebrews says that God puts His laws "into their mind." The inward parts spoken of in Jeremiah must refer to all the parts of the soul—the mind, emotion, and will.

THE LAW BEING THE TESTIMONY OF GOD AS THE REGULATION OF THE LIFE OF HIS PEOPLE

When Christians today speak of the law, we mostly have a bad impression. We may say of a certain matter, "That is just the law!" It seems that the law is something bad. This is wrong. Here we are speaking of the law not according to the human way, thought, and understanding but according to the scriptural meaning. It is hard to define what the law is in the Bible. To say that the law is simply the commandments from Moses is too common. This is what a child in Sunday School would say. In the ancient time God had Israel as His people. As a people, there was the need for regulation in their life and walk. If there is no law, there is no regulation for living. The law, therefore, is the regulation of the life of God's people. This is the basic definition of the law.

Today, just as the people of Israel in the ancient time, the believers are the people of God, who need to be regulated. By what are we regulated? It is not by Moses but by God Himself. As the people of God, we must be regulated by God in our life, our walk, and our daily living. God must be our law. Do not think that the law in the Scriptures is something bad. According to the proper understanding, the law is God Himself, or using the scriptural term, the law is the testimony of God. In the Old Testament the ark was called the Ark of the Testimony, and the tabernacle was called the Tabernacle of the Testimony (Exo. 25:21-22; Num. 1:50, 53). The ark was the testimony because within it were the two tablets of the law. As a Christian for many years I tried to find out why the law is the testimony of God, but no one could tell me. I was not able to understand this until one day God Himself opened my eyes. According to human words, the testimony of God is the description of God. The purpose of the law is to testify, define, and describe God. As the people of God, our walk, living, conduct, and entire being must correspond to this very God.

What kind of God do we have, and what are His attributes? This is the purpose of the law. The law was given to tell us what kind of God we have. We may compare it to a document that describes a certain person, telling us his size, hair color, and other features. Such a document would be the testimony of this person. In the same way, the law is the description and definition of God, so it is His testimony. We as His people must be regulated in our walk and living by this description, this testimony. We may also compare the law to a photograph. If I take a picture of a young man, the picture becomes his testimony. We may say that it is the photograph of the man, or we may even say that the photograph is the man. Because the law is the testimony, description, and "photograph" of God, we can say that the law is God Himself.

The Ten Commandments described God to the people of Israel (Exo. 20:3-17). Many of us can recite the Ten Commandments, but we still may not know what kind of God the commandments describe. First, God is a jealous God. It seems that *jealous* is not a good word, but God is jealous because He is holy, separate, and not common. If He were common He would not be jealous. He is the holy God. Therefore, the first attribute described by the Ten Commandments of the law is the holiness of God. Second, God is righteous. Of course, we do not have the words *holy* and *righteous* in the Ten Commandments, but if we know the spirit of the commandments, we realize that they describe the holiness and righteousness of God. The Ten Commandments also describe God as a God of love, which includes mercy and grace. Fourth, the Ten Commandments show us that God is a God in light. He is a God of holiness, righteousness, love, and light. We should write these four words as a heading over Exodus 20. Then as we read these commandments again and again, we will see their true meaning. The Ten Commandments describe the very God who is holy, righteous, of love, and in light.

God is also omnipresent, transcendent, and great, but these attributes are not the regulation of the walk of God's people. There is no need to be regulated by God's transcendence or greatness, so these attributes are not found in the Ten Commandments. Rather, the walk of God's people must be regulated by four attributes of God—holiness, righteousness, love, and light. These are the very elements that regulate the walk of God's people.

On the one hand, knowledge alone does not mean much, but on the other hand, we need the knowledge of the law. We need to know the law given by God as His very testimony. A particular kind of person will make a particular kind of law. A lazy person, for example, will make a regulation that breakfast is at 9:30 A.M. There is no need for a second commandment, for just by this one commandment we can realize that the maker, the legislator, of this law is a lazy person. If we read the Constitution made by the founding fathers of America, we can see what kind of people they were. When I read the Constitution, I realized that those persons at least had the fear and reverence of God. It is different from certain Chinese and Japanese laws, from which we realize that they were worshippers of idols. The law made by God is a description, definition, and testimony of God Himself, testifying what kind of God He is. He is the God of holiness, of righteousness, of love, and in light. In order to be the people of God, our walk and daily living must be regulated by and correspond to these four attributes. Our walk must be holy, righteous, of love, and in light. In principle, the law is God Himself being the regulation of the walk of His people.

GOD WITHIN US BEING THE LIVING LAW

The law of the Old Testament was the law of letters outside of the people of God. On the one hand, the law testified and described God, but on the other hand, it also demanded the people to correspond to God's attributes. As to God, it testified, but as to the people, it demanded and eventually condemned. If one was able to correspond to God's law, the law was only a demand, but if one could not correspond with the demand, the law was a condemnation. This is the old law, the law in letter.

The new law is still the law; in this sense it is the same. The law in letter was the testimony of God, and the law in life is still the testimony of God. However, this same law is now not in letter but in life. The law within us today is the very living God. This living God who is holy, righteous, of love, and in light, who in the ancient times was described by the written law, has come into us as the new law. Today God Himself is the law. We may prefer the old way of the law, because the new way is too bothersome. The old way is simply to write down all the commandments, and if we act according to them, we are all right. The new way, however, is a living Person. There is no written commandment. Whatever we do, we must go to Him. We always need to contact Him and see His face. If there is a law that says that breakfast in a brothers' house is at 7:30 A.M., everyone knows when breakfast is. But if we have to come to a certain brother to ask him when breakfast is, he may change the time each day. This is the way of the living law. This is why the New Testament does not have commandments in the old way. There is not even one such commandment. Rather, there is one God within us. This very God, who was described by the written law, has come into us as the living law. Therefore, the law is God Himself within us, regulating us by Himself. He is within us as the regulating element. Whatever we do, speak, or accomplish must correspond to this very God within us.

GOD AS THE LAW BECOMING OUR TASTE

This very God in us becomes our taste. We do not like to eat bitter things because they taste bad. We were not taught this; rather, we have a taste of life within us. The holy, righteous God of love and in light is our taste, and this taste is the regulating factor and power. If we do something in the nature of hatred, we can taste it within. But if we do something in the nature of love, light, holiness, and righteousness we have the taste from God that consents and agrees with us. The Lord told us that we have to love our enemy. When I was young, even after I was saved, I shook my head when I read that. I said, "Lord, I cannot keep this word. I cannot love my enemy." Later, however, I experienced that if I even had the thought of hating, the taste within me would not go along. This taste is the law, and the law is God Himself. He is the very God of love; He is not a God of hate. With Him there is no hate. Hatred is one hundred percent against His nature. His nature is a nature of love, and His nature is love. This nature becomes our taste. Regardless of whether we are willing to love or willing to hate, the taste within us is a taste of love. When we love, the taste corresponds with us. Otherwise, the taste within us protests.

We have a taste within us. If we simply go along with the taste, it is easy. Because of our taste, it is easier to eat something sweet than to eat something bitter. As humans we also like to sleep because it "tastes" good. Praise the Lord, we have the taste within us! Now it is so easy for me to love, and it is very hard to hate even my enemy. If I am about to hate my enemy, something within tastes bitter. The taste works within me. If, on the other hand, I love my enemy, the taste within encourages, confirms, and strengthens me to love. This is the living law.

To be a Christian is a matter of taste and not outward regulation or religion. We like to serve others because it tastes good. We like to sacrifice, even to sacrifice our life for others. To them it seems that we suffer a lot, but to us it is a taste. When I sacrifice, I taste. This taste is the very law. Taste regulates. If we put something bitter into the mouth of even a small baby, he will spit it out, but if you put chocolate in his mouth, he will find it delicious. There is no need to teach him this because he has a taste. The taste is the regulating, and the regulating is the law. Today God within us is the very law giving us a taste and regulating us by this taste. Whatever corresponds with Him gives us a good taste, but if there is anything against His nature, the taste protests. To take care of the taste is to take care of the inner law. This inner law is the divine life, and the divine life is God Himself.

Since God put Himself into us as the law, giving us a taste and regulating us in all things, there is no need for anyone to teach us. Teaching is mere outward knowledge, but we have an inward taste. By this inward taste we have the inward knowledge. In Hebrews 8:11 there are two Greek words for *know*. Verse 11 begins, "And they shall by no means each teach his fellow citizen and each his brother, saying, Know the Lord." This *know* is one word. The verse continues, "For all will know Me from the little one to the great one among them." This second *know* is another Greek word. Darby's New Translation translates this as "know...in themselves." A note for that verse tells us that this *know* denotes the inner realization of certain things, the consciousness in oneself, the internal, inner knowledge. Teachings are outward knowledge, but the taste is the inner knowledge. By this inner knowledge we taste, we sense, what corresponds to God and what does not.

GOD BEING OUR GOD BY THE INNER LAW

Hebrews 8:10 says, "I will be God to them, and they will be a people to Me." God is God to us according to the inner law, and we are the people of God according to this law. In the ancient times God was God to the people of Israel, and they were a people to Him, according to the Ten Commandments. Although David the king did many good things, he killed a man and took his wife. At that time God was not God to Him, and he was not a person of God, because he acted against the law of God. That was why he needed atonement and reconciliation to God. Without atonement it was not possible for him to be a person of God nor for God to be God to him. One had to be a person according to the law of God, and God was God to him according to His law. Today it is the same in principle. The living law within us gives us the sense to love our enemy, but we may not be willing to go along with it. Instead, we may try to do many good things for others. In this case we will not have a right relationship with God. We may say, "Others bring one person to the Lord in one year, but I have brought two persons just this month." However, God may say, "I do not reckon that. I only reckon one thing—the inner law. I am God to you not according to all the good things you do but according to the inner law." We have to be a people to God according to the inner law, and this inner law is the living God.

Again I say, Christianity today has missed the mark. What is the mark? It is that God Himself, the living Spirit within us, is the very law. God can be God to us and we a people to God only according to this law, not according to the good things we do. Suppose that the inner, living law within me energizes and moves in me, giving me the taste or the sense that I must humble myself before a brother because I offended him. This law may give me the sense, the consciousness, that I have to come to him and make a confession. However, I may not want to lose my face. Rather, I tell the Lord, "Lord, I will do many things for You. I will shine everyone's shoes and clean the dining hall." Regardless of how many good things I do, the Lord may say, "No, I only demand one thing. Go to the brother, bow your head, tell him that you are wrong, and ask him to forgive you." Still I may say, "Lord, I will do anything, but not this." This means that I am still doing good things but breaking the regulation of the inner law. Many, many times we act in this way. I know many stories like this. It is especially this way with some wives. For a wife to make a confession to her husband is not easy. She may do many things, but she would not say, "I'm wrong; excuse me." God can be God to us only according to His law, and we can be a people to Him only according to this law.

Where is this law? It is in us. And what is this law? It is God Himself. He Himself is the living law. He is holy, righteous, of love, and in light. Therefore, whatever we do, speak, or think, and however we act or walk, must be one hundred percent in correspondence with the very God who not only is holy but holiness, who not only is righteous but righteousness, and who is love and light. If we do this, we will have a sweet taste; otherwise, we will have a bitter taste. It is a matter of taste, and this taste is the very regulating element of the inner law that is God Himself. The law, which is God Himself, is within us as our life, nature, taste, and regulating element.

HAVING NO NEED FOR OTHERS TO TEACH US

If we mean business and pay our full attention to this inner law, there is no need of teaching. We need a certain kind of teaching simply because we are not faithful and honest to this inner law. We do not pay our full attention to this inner law, so we need the teachings to help us. This is a poor situation. If we mean business and pay our full attention to this inner law, that will be glorious. Many times when people ask us a question, we point out, "Brother, you know the answer within yourself. There is no need for you to ask me. You know within." Sometimes the brothers say, "Yes, I know, but I would like you to give me a confirmation." To this I say, "Rather, I like to be confirmed by your inner feeling. I am not the confirmation; your inner sense is the confirmation. You know within."

THE INNER LAW BEING FOR REGULATION, AND THE ANOINTING BEING FOR GUIDANCE

In the New Testament there are two passages that tell us that there is no need for others to teach us. Hebrews 8:11 is one, speaking of the inner law. The other is 1 John 2:27, which speaks of the inner anointing. In the Old Testament times there were the law and the prophets. The Jews themselves referred to the Old Testament as "the law and the prophets." This means that in the ancient times the people of God had two factors to guide them. The law was the first factor, and the prophets were the second. There was a difference between the regulation of the law and the guidance of the prophets. The regulation of the law was according to the attributes of God. Therefore, it could not change. For any person it was the same, and in any place and time it was the same. You have to love others, and everyone else has to love others also. In the morning you have to love, and at night you have to love; yesterday you had to love, and today you still have to love. Both in this city and in another city you still have to love. There is no need to seek the Lord's guidance as to whether or not we should love a person, because this is something according to God's nature. This is the regulation of the law.

The function of the prophets, however, was for guidance. From the regulation of the law we cannot know whether or not to marry a certain person, unless, of course, the marriage breaks the law; then the regulation comes. Again, we cannot find in the regulation of the law whether or not to go to a certain place and do certain things. Therefore, the law was for regulation, and the prophets were for guidance. In the same way, we have the law of life within as the regulation, and we also have the anointing of the Holy Spirit within as the guidance.

There is no need, for example, to seek guidance whether or not to cut our hair in a peculiar way, because the nature of God, the holiness of God, within us regulates us. We know that it is not right for a child of God to cut his hair in a peculiar way. There is no need to seek guidance, because of the inner regulation. But as to which barber shop to go to, or whether to let a brother cut our hair, is a matter of the inner anointing, not something of the inner law. The inner regulating law does not work in this matter. The law is the regulation according to the unchangeable nature and attributes of God, while the anointing is the guidance according to the move of God, which is very changeable. The move of God may let Peter go to a certain place but will not let Paul go to that place. The attributes of God never change, but the moving of God changes all the time. Therefore, as far as the attributes of God are concerned, we need the regulation, but as far as the move of God is concerned, we need the guidance. The regulation comes from the inner law, and the guidance comes from the inner anointing.

Whether or not a sister should go shopping is a matter of the guidance of the inner anointing. However, when she gets to a department store and tries to choose a dress, the inner regulating may come to her. Just as the people in the ancient times had the law in letters and the prophets, we have the inner anointing as the prophet and the inner regulating, the law of life, as the law. Again I say, the law relates to what God is, and the anointing relates to what God does. The law relates to God's nature, while the anointing relates to God's moving, God's actions. With God's move and actions, we need the guidance; there is no certain regulation. But with God's nature and attributes, there is never any change; therefore, we have the regulation.

KNOWING LIFE IN A PRACTICAL WAY

The three things we have spoken about—the fellowship of life, the sense of life, and the law of life—are matters of the spiritual life. This spiritual life is in our spirit. In our spirit there are three functions—fellowship, intuition, and the conscience. The three matters of life correspond with the three functions of our spirit. The fellowship of life, of course, is a matter of fellowship, and it is related to the fellowship of the spirit. The sense of life is a matter of the inner knowledge, and this inner knowledge is related to the intuition of the spirit. The law of life is a matter of regulation, and this regulation is related to the conscience of the spirit. We need to learn these things in a practical way in our experience. Then we will know life in a practical way, and we will be able to help people to experience Christ as life in the spirit.

After we are saved, we have an inner sense from the light of life, the law of life, the anointing of the Holy Spirit, Christ living within us, and God working and energizing within us. The life within us enlightens us as the light, the life regulates us as the law, the Holy Spirit anoints us, Christ lives in us, and God works within us. These five items always give us a certain inner consciousness, a certain feeling. Moreover, the fellowship of life, the sense of life, and the law of life are related one to another. In order to keep the fellowship with the Lord, we have to take care of the inner sense, and in order to take care of the inner sense, to be sure, we must go along with the inner law. To break the law of life means that we cast off the sense of life, and to cast off the sense of life means that we damage the fellowship of life. The main thing is to take care of the law of life. It is when we take care of the law of life that we have harmony with the sense of life, and when we have harmony with the sense of life, we keep the fellowship with the Lord. Then everything with us is right in the presence of God.

The main point is the law of life. The whole Christian life and walk hinges on the law of life, the inner regulating. Oh, this is so important! I am afraid that not many Christians walk day by day by being regulated within. We have to learn to be regulated by the inner law. Then God will be God to us, and we will be a people to Him. We will have fellowship with God in harmony with our inner sense, because we are always going along with the law of life. I hope you will do some homework concerning these matters and fellowship with two or three others. Then you can put them into practice and learn more, and you will know the way of life. Many times when I hear people talking about the inner life, I shake my head, realizing that it is just talk; they do not know what the inner life means. If we do not know the law of life, the sense of life, and the fellowship of life, we do not know the inner life. We may know it in terms, in letter, in word, on paper, and in knowledge and teaching, but we do not know it in practicality. In practicality we need to know the law of life with the sense of life and the fellowship of life. This is very important, but we are not used to these things, so we need more practice.

CHAPTER SEVEN

THE LAW OF LIFE

(2)

Scripture Reading: Jer. 31:33; Heb. 8:10; 10:16

I still feel that we need to see something more clearly concerning the law of life. Jeremiah 31:33a says, "But this is the covenant which I will make with the house of Israel after those days, declares Jehovah: I will put My law within them and write it upon their hearts." I would ask you to pay attention to the phrase *within them,* or *in their inward parts,* as in the King James Version. Most Christians do not understand what is meant by *within them.* For many years as a Christian I never heard a message or read something concerning the inward parts. It is only in the last few years that the Lord has guided us to pay attention to this term, which also appears in Psalm 51:6. In the new covenant God promises to put His law in our inward parts and write it in our hearts. In Jeremiah *law* is singular, not *laws.* Moreover, He first puts His law within us, and then He writes it upon our hearts. This is the order in this verse.

In Hebrews the apostle quoted this verse twice. The first time is in 8:10a, which says, "For this is the covenant which I will covenant with the house of Israel after those days, says the Lord: I will impart My laws into their mind." We have to learn the way to study the Word. The best way to study is to compare related passages. Then we can see the differences, and by the differences we can know something deeper. In the quotation of Jeremiah 31:33, *law* becomes *laws.* Here there is no longer only one law. Something else also changes. *Within them,* or *in their inward parts,* becomes *into their mind.* By this we can realize that *inward parts* refers to the parts of the soul, because the mind is one part of the soul. There is no passage in the Bible that tells us what the parts of the soul are, but if we read the entire Scriptures and pay attention to this matter, we will find adequate proofs to confirm that within the soul there are at least three parts. The leading part is the mind, and there are also the emotion and the will. By comparing Hebrews 8:10 with Jeremiah 31:33, we realize that the inward parts are the parts of the soul, of which the mind is the leading part. Hebrews 8:10 continues, "And on their hearts I will inscribe them." *Them* is plural, referring to the laws.

Hebrews 10:16 is the second quotation of Jeremiah 31. This verse says, "This is the covenant which I will covenant with them after those days, says the Lord: I will impart My laws upon their hearts, and upon their mind I will inscribe them." There is a difference between Jeremiah 31, Hebrews 8, and Hebrews 10. I do not think the apostle made a mistake. There is a real purpose in his making a change. In Jeremiah there is the singular law, while in Hebrews there are the plural laws. This is the first difference. Then in Jeremiah there is the inward parts, while in Hebrews there is the mind. This is the second difference. Then even between the two quotations in Hebrews there are changes. In chapter eight the mind is first and then the heart, but in chapter ten the heart is first and then the mind.

However, there is one consistency in all three passages, in the original and in the two quotations. They all use *put* or *impart* first, and then they use *write* or *inscribe*. The King James Version uses the word *write* in Hebrews, but the Greek Interlinear version uses the word *inscribe,* and the Amplified Bible uses *engrave* in 8:10. Both *inscribe* and *engrave* mean something deeper than *write*. To engrave is to write by cutting or carving, and to inscribe is to cut in, to write not with an ink pen but with a knife. To put or impart, however, is very general. To put the law somewhere is general, but to inscribe it somewhere means much more. For me to put a composition on you is easy, but to inscribe it on you may require a whole year. Moreover, you must cooperate with the inscribing. Sometimes because you feel the pain you may stop cooperating, and I can do nothing. The writing is here, but I will not be able to inscribe it on you.

According to the lexicon, to put or impart means to give or to pass on. To impart His laws into our mind is to give His laws to us in our mind. After this giving, however, there is the need for engraving. To inscribe or engrave is much deeper than giving. This is why these passages refer first to imparting and then to inscribing.

GOD'S ECONOMY IN HIS DIVINE TRINITY
BEING TO WORK HIMSELF INTO US AS LIFE

God's economy, God's eternal purpose, and God's intention are to work Himself into us by being life to us. This is a basic word, the foundation, which we should not forget. God can work Himself into us only by being life to us. If He could not be life to us, He can never be worked into us. The only possibility for God to work Himself into us and be mingled with us is to be life within us. Even with physical things, the only way for something to be worked into us is that we take it as our life supply. How can a big cow be worked into us? The only way is for the cow to become our life supply. Through a kind of death and resurrection, the cow must be taken, eaten, swallowed, and digested by us. Then the cow becomes us. By being life to us, the cow mingles itself with us and becomes us.

In order to know the Scriptures, we must know the central thought of God's economy. Without comprehending this central thought, we can never understand the Bible; we will not know what this book is talking about. The entire Scripture reveals to us this one thing, that God is always working Himself into us as our life. And what is life? Life is nothing less than God Himself in three Persons. We must always remember the economy of the three Persons of the Godhead—the Father, the Son, and the Spirit. I am not asking you to learn the doctrine and theology of the Trinity. I would ask you to forget mere doctrine and theology. Rather, I am speaking of the economy of the Persons of the Godhead: the Father as the source, the Son as the course, and the Spirit as the flow. This Triune God comes into us; that is, the Father is in the Son, the Son is the Spirit, and the Spirit with the Son and the Father comes into us as life. Never consider that the Holy Spirit is someone other than God Himself. That is wrong. If you have the Spirit, you have the Son, and if you have the Son, you have the Father. I long that I could have the adequate time to speak this very thing to the Lord's children.

The Triune God comes into us as our life. If we apprehend and grasp this in our understanding, the entire Bible will be new and gloriously open to us, and we will understand it in a heavenly way; we will know what it is talking about. We have this wonderful life, which is nothing less than the Triune God in the Spirit dwelling in our spirit.

THE FELLOWSHIP OF LIFE, THE SENSE OF LIFE, AND THE LAW OF LIFE

There are three main things we must know concerning this life. First is the fellowship of life, second is the sense of life, and third is the law of life. Why must we know these particular three aspects of the divine life in us? It is because they match the three functions of our spirit. The spirit is the organ for us to fellowship with God; this is the first function of the spirit. There is also a deeper function, which is the intuition, the direct sense within our spirit, for us to sense something of God. Third, in our spirit there is the conscience. The fellowship of life is related to the fellowship in our spirit; the sense of life, the consciousness of life, the inner feeling, is related to the intuition; and the law of life is related to our conscience. In order to know the inner life, that is, God as life to us, we must know all these things. This is the spiritual "medical science," and we are learning to be the spiritual "medical doctors." Without knowing the science of eating, we do not know our physical body. In the same way, if we do not know the above matters in detail, we simply do not know the way to experience the inner life; we do not have the spiritual science of the inner life.

The fellowship of life comes from life. When life comes into us, there is the flow, the current, of life, which is the fellowship. By this flowing, the fellowship of life, we constantly have the inner sense, the inner feeling, the inner consciousness, which is the sense of life. Then this sense helps us to realize the law of life regulating within us all the time. If the fellowship is broken, that is, the inner current is stopped and frustrated, then the sense of life is gone, and the regulating of the inner law seems to no longer work. In this case we become dull, we are in darkness, and we cast off all feeling, becoming a person without regulation (Eph. 4:18-19). This is dangerous. Many Christians are like this. Today, however, we have been taught that the Triune God has come into us to dwell in our spirit as life. With this life there is the constant flowing and current, which is the fellowship of life, and by this flowing of life there is always the bountiful sense of life, the rich consciousness of life, the richness of the inner feeling. Then by this inner sense the law of life regulates in everything all day long. What I am saying here is not mere knowledge; it is based on experience. Your own experience confirms this.

Again I say, if the fellowship of life is frustrated, stopped, and broken, the inner sense will be lost, and the regulating will not work. In this case, we are outside of life. We may still be very good and moral, but we are merely keeping the moral laws; there is no inner regulation of life. We Christians should not be regulated merely by outward moral regulations. We are persons who are regulated by the inner regulation of the inner law, the law of life. This is the big difference between the people in the world and Christians. The worldly, moral persons act only according to outward regulations, but we Christians walk according to the inward regulation. Why do I not do certain things? It is not because of outward regulations but because of the inner regulation. Something within me is regulating, so I cannot do those things, I cannot say certain things, and I cannot go to certain places. Others can go because they do not have the inner regulating. But I have it, so I cannot go. Strictly speaking, a Christian is a person who lives, acts, and does things from within. Whatever he does must be something of life, something as the working out of the inner life, not merely an outward behavior.

THE LAW BEING GOD HIMSELF LIVING AND WORKING WITHIN US

In principle, the law is the regulating of the being of God's people by God Himself, or rather, by what God is. We as the people of God must be regulated by what God is. We must live, move, and have our being according to what He is and corresponding to what He is. If God were a God of hatred and murder, we would have to live in the way of hatred and murder people day by day. In this way our moving and acting would be corresponding to God. But, as we know, our God is a God not of hatred but of love. Therefore, we must live according to His love, being regulated by what He is.

There are two ways to have God as our law, our regulation. One way is to paint a picture of God, that is, to write down a description of what He is, and put it before us. Then we may read it and see what kind of God He is. This is the way of the Ten Commandments. The Ten Commandments are a description, a picture, of God. This outward way does not work well. To be regulated outwardly by a description of even a small person is not easy. We would have to walk as he walks, stand as he stands, and pronounce our words with his accent. This is not easy.

The other way is that God Himself—the living law, not the written law; the real person, not the picture—comes into us. If a living person comes into us to be the law within us, there is no need of an outward description. This is the difference between the old law, the law of letters, and the new law, the law of life. The old law was a picture, a photograph, a description of God presented to us outwardly, according to which we should live, walk, and do things. This does not work. The new law, the law of life, is God Himself coming into us to be the law. He comes into us to be a person, so there is no need only to have His picture. The person Himself is within us, living and working in us as the living law.

GOD INSCRIBING HIS LAW
INTO OUR MIND, EMOTION, AND WILL

God within us is the unique law. Therefore Jeremiah 31:33 speaks of the law in the singular number: "I will put My law within them." We may illustrate this from our experience. Before we were saved, we understood and considered things in a certain way. But from the first day we were saved, there was a change in our understanding, our thinking, and our way to consider things. There was also a change in our emotion and will. We may say that this is due to God's salvation, but beyond that we must realize that this was the putting of the law into us, into our inward parts, the parts of our soul. The tripartite man has a human spirit as his center, a soul surrounding it, and a body as the environment for it. At the time we were saved, God came into our spirit as our life. By this, there was an influence in our mind, will, and emotion. We may call this an influence from God being life in our spirit, but God calls it the putting of His law within us. God put His law into our mind, our will, and our emotion.

However, the putting of His law within us is general; it is not very deep. After this putting, God works on us to engrave, to inscribe, to do something deeper within us. If, after we are saved, we cooperate with God by going along with the sense of life from the fellowship of life, day by day God's inscribing hand works on us to inscribe Himself into our mind, will, and emotion. The more we fellowship with Him, and the more we live, move, and have our being according to the inner sense in the fellowship, the more God has the opportunity to engrave and inscribe. Then the law put into us will become a law not only written on us but inscribed in us. This is the real transforming work. When God's law is inscribed on our mind, our mind is transformed. The more God's law is increased in our mind, the more our mind is renewed and transformed. Ten years ago our mind may have been awful, wild, ugly, earthly, sinful, and even satanic, but today our mind has been improved and refined by the inward regulating, and if we cooperate with God in a fuller way over the years, our mind will even be wonderful. It is the same with our emotion and our will. We often speak of the growth in life, or we may say that a brother has had some improvement. In actuality, the growth and improvement in life are the inscribing of the law in our inner parts.

Too many real Christians are still wild in their thinking. Their minds have never been refined and renewed because their minds have never been regulated by God's inscribing. Similarly, many sisters are dear, but their emotions are poor, peculiar, and ugly. I have been ministering for more than thirty-five years, and I do know the problem in the church with the sisters. Their problem is their emotions. I do not like to contact many sisters because of their troublesome emotions. If the emotions of the sisters could be dealt with, the church would be spiritual and truly in the heavens. If the sisters and even the brothers would simply cooperate with God and let Him inscribe on their emotions, let Him put the regulating of the inner law in a deeper way into their emotions, then their emotions will be renewed. The building of the church has been very much frustrated by the emotions of the brothers and sisters. The building cannot proceed in a successful way simply because the emotions of the dear saints have not been dealt with and renewed by God. God needs a full and thorough cooperation so that He can inscribe His law upon our emotions. What is the growth in life? It is the constant inscribing of God's hand in us.

It is the same with our will. The natural will of some people is wild, stubborn, stiffened, and hard. Others, however, are so soft that it seems they have no will at all. Some brothers among us are like this. If you say the earth is heaven, they will say, "Yes, it is heaven," but if you say it is the earth, they will say, "Yes, it is the earth." Whatever you say is right, because they have no direction, goal, or will. In the so-called churches in Christianity today, people admire this kind of person. They say, "Look how nice he is. Whatever you say, he just goes along with you." However, there is no possibility for a person with such a soft will to be coordinated in the church. We can build a building with solid stones, but we cannot build with mud.

On the other hand, there are many in the church that if you say, "This is the earth," they will say, "No, it is heaven," and if you say "It is heaven," they will immediately say, "It is the earth!" This is a stubborn will. A good number of brothers like this never go along with others. When they initiate something, they feel it is right, but if others initiate it, they say no to it, even if it is the same thing. If such a brother is driving, he may say, "Let us go on Beverly Street," but if someone else is driving and takes Beverly Street, he will say, "No, go on

Third Street." We do not realize how fallen our will is. This is why it is hard to build the church. I have learned this, and I am still learning. In my early days, even thirty years ago, I caused trouble with the brothers and sisters, because at that time I did not know the secret. Today if someone says, "Go on Beverly," I go on Beverly, and if they say, "Go on Third," I go on Third.

The problem is that for many years after we were saved, we did not cooperate with God to let Him inscribe His law on our mind and will. If we cooperate with Him and let Him inscribe His law on our will, we will have the renewing of our will; a real transformation will be worked on our will. Our will, in this case, will be good and adequate for the building of the church. If the brothers' mind, emotion, and will have been renewed by God's inscribing, we will see the real growth in them.

ONE LAW BECOMING MANY LAWS
IN OUR INWARD PARTS

I like the phrase *God's inscribing*. God inscribes Himself as the law on our mind, emotion, and will. Then this law is not only put into, but inscribed upon us. The law is written by inscribing. At this point the one law becomes many laws: a law in the mind, a law in the emotion, and a law in the will. One law becomes many laws, just as the one river in Genesis 2:10 was parted into four streams in four directions. The one law in our spirit becomes many laws in our many inward parts.

Christianity with its teachings today is too shallow. Many Christians are deep in the doctrinal letter, but they do not know much about the inner life. Many seek victory over sin and the overcoming of their besetting sin. However, if we learn the lesson to cooperate with God to let Him inscribe on our mind, will, and emotion, there is no need to seek victory over sin. There will be something deeper within us. Then we will see transformation, an inner change. Even only two years after being saved, a brother may have a great change, not merely in his outward behavior and conduct, but in his way of thinking, of loving and hating things, and of making decisions.

Such a brother has growth and a real improvement, and within him we can see a measure of Christ. Our measure of Christ depends on how much God inscribes on our mind, will, and emotion, how much God works Himself into us. First He puts Himself into us, and after this He starts inscribing all the time. This inscribing is the regulating, and this regulating is the work of the inner law. The regulating depends on the inner sense, and the inner sense comes from the fellowship of life. This is very practical.

THE INSCRIBING OF THE INNER LAW
BEING TRANSFORMATION INTO THE IMAGE OF GOD

Someone may say, "I praise the Lord I am saved. Now I do not do anything sinful. It is good that some brothers pray early in the morning, but I don't like to do that. Rather, on Sundays I come to the church meeting." This is a rough, careless, outward Christian, one not walking by the inner sense and regulated by the inner law. If we are persons who truly cooperate with God, there is no other way but to love Him, and if we mean business to love Him, we will realize the flow within. We must love Him without any other intention, aim, or goal; we love Him simply because of who He is. We should say, "Lord, I love You. I have no motive; I just love You." If we do this, the flow within us will be vigorous and powerful. This flow is the fellowship of life, and this fellowship will operate. How much the fellowship operates depends on how much we love Him. The more we love Him, the more it works. This flow, this inner fellowship, brings us a sense and consciousness. The more we have the fellowship of life, the more we will have the sense of life, and the sense will be deeper. This inner sense then helps the regulating of the inner law. This means that God is inscribing His law upon our mind, will, and emotion to renew, saturate, permeate, and take possession of all our inward parts, that is, to transform us into His image.

The more God inscribes on us, the more He transforms us into His image, the more we will be like Him and have His likeness. What God inscribes on us is the image of Himself. Originally, we had only an outward picture of God, but now we have an inward image inscribed by God within us. This is the work of transformation.

THE REGULATING OF THE LAW OF LIFE COMING BEFORE THE GUIDANCE OF THE ANOINTING

The Old Testament is called the law and the prophets. The law and the prophets are the two elements of the Old Testament. As we have seen, the law is fixed principles that never change. To honor our parents is a law, a fixed principle, and no one can change this. To love our neighbor is also a fixed principle. There is no need to seek guidance as to whether or not we should love our neighbor and honor our parents, because a principle has been set up in the law. The law also says that we should not make an image of God and worship it, so there is also no need to seek guidance about the worship of images. No one can change the principle; everyone has to take it and be regulated by it.

It is different, however, with the prophets. With the prophets there is guidance. We cannot find in the regulation of the law whether or not to visit a certain place. There is no regulation of the law as to whether one should stay in Nazareth or go to Bethlehem. For these matters we need the guidance. Since there was no prophet to help Joseph, the husband of Mary, an angel of the Lord appeared to him in a dream and said, "Flee to Egypt." In principle, that was the ministry of the prophets. This is guidance, not regulation. Again, we may illustrate this with shopping. Whether to go to one department store or another is a matter of guidance. However, once I go to the store, there is the need for regulation in the things I buy. Some things I as a Christian should not and cannot buy, because that would be against the inner law, the inner regulating. I cannot, for example, go to a bookstore and buy a book all about movies; this would be against the nature of God and the inner regulation. This is a matter of regulation, not of guidance. As a Christian walking in the presence of God and living by Christ, can we say something dirty and evil with our mouth? No, because that is against God's nature and the inner regulating. When we contact people and speak for the Lord, however, what we say is not a matter of regulating but a matter of guidance.

In the Old Testament there are the law and the prophets, but in the New Testament the law of life replaces the law of letters, and the inner anointing replaces the ministry of the prophets. The inner anointing is not the law but the guidance. Today we do not need the law of Moses because we have the law of life within, and we do not need the ministry of the prophets because we have the inner anointing. When we have the law of life and the anointing, we have the regulating and the guidance.

The regulating is a narrow realm, while the guidance is a very broad realm. We may compare the regulating to Washington D.C. and the guidance to the whole of the United States. If Washington D.C. is in order, the whole of the U.S.A. will be in order, but if Washington D.C. is upside down, the condition of the fifty states will be terrible. In the same way, if we are not clear about the inner regulation, we can never be clear about the inner guidance. Many Christians do not know the guidance of the Lord simply because they do not take care of the regulating. The law comes first and then the prophets. Even in the Old Testament the first part is the law and the latter part is the prophets. Therefore, we must learn to take care of the inner regulating; then we have to learn to take care of the anointing.

First John 2:27 tells us that since the anointing abides in us and teaches us concerning all things, we have no need that anyone teach us. Similarly, Hebrews 8:11 tells us that since the law of life regulates within us, there is no need to teach our brother to know the Lord. Verse 10 also tells us that God is God to us by this inner regulating, and we are a people to God also according to the inner regulating. The relationship between us and God can be maintained only by this inner regulating. Whenever we neglect the inner regulating, the relationship between God and us as His children is a mess. Therefore, we all must learn how to take care of this inner regulating. Then by this inner regulating we will be helped to realize the inner anointing. When we are under the regulating, we will have the guidance in all things.

CHAPTER EIGHT

THE ANOINTING

Scripture Reading: Luke 4:18; Heb. 1:9; 1 John 2:27

As we saw in the previous chapters, in order to be a proper, typical, normal Christian, walking in the spirit and following the Lord all the way, we must take care of the inner life. The way to do this is in three aspects: We must know the fellowship of life, the sense of life, and the law of life. I say again, these important matters concerning the Lord Himself, the indwelling Spirit, and the inner life have been very much neglected by today's Christianity. There are not many messages in Christianity on the fellowship of life, the sense of life, and the law of life. These three items are all related to the inner life, and this inner life is nothing other than the Lord Himself.

God's economy is to dispense Himself into us. This is why the one, unique God is in three persons. The Trinity is not a mere theology. The Trinity is for our experience of God's economy, God's dispensing. In God's economy He dispenses Himself into us. What we mean by God's economy is that God the Father works in the Son, and the Son comes into us as the Spirit. When we say that the Spirit dwells in us today, we mean that the three persons of the one Godhead work together within us as life. God mingles with us by being our life. He must be our inner life, and this inner life is nothing less than God Himself.

As we have seen, this life within us is in three main aspects. If we do not know the fellowship of life, the sense of life, and the law of life, the inner life is merely a term to us; we do not know how to deal with the inner life. One brother among us studied and worked in the United States. After he was saved, he sought the Lord very much. When he heard about the Lord's move in Taiwan, he went there purposely to get the help. After he arrived there, however, he was very bothered. So many of the messages he heard among us stressed the matter of life. He had never heard or spoken much concerning life. But after he stayed with us for a period of time, the Lord helped him to realize that our real need today is life.

In the beginning of the Scriptures there is the tree of life. Immediately after God created man, He put him in front of the tree of life (Gen. 2:7-9). At the end of the Scriptures there is the tree of life again (Rev. 22:2). The tree of life is the beginning, and it is also the end. God has only this one intention: to work Himself into us as life. Now in order to know this inner life, we must realize that life is God Himself in three persons, mainly in the fellowship of life, the sense of life, and the law of life.

God is life to us in our human spirit, and in our spirit there are three functions: the fellowship, the intuition, and the conscience. The fellowship of life corresponds to the fellowship in our spirit; the sense of life corresponds with the intuition of the spirit, because the intuition is the function that gives us a direct sense; and the law of life corresponds to the conscience. The law tells us what to do and what not to do, and the conscience checks us concerning what is right and what is wrong. To deal with these matters in detail will take years. In addition, we must also put them into practice in our daily life.

THE ANOINTING BEING GOD HIMSELF
MOVING AND WORKING WITHIN US

It is hard to find a message in today's Christianity about the inner anointing. We do have this term, and we do realize that Christ's name means *the Anointed One,* but the inner anointing has been almost entirely neglected. What is the inner anointing? Just as the inner life is God Himself within us as life, the inner anointing is God Himself moving, working, operating, and adding Himself within us. *The anointing* is an inclusive term, because it is God Himself. As we have pointed out, the Old Testament was called the law and the prophets, because at that time there were these two main ministries. The ministry of the prophets covered more than the ministry of the law, because the prophets' ministry included the law. If a person went to a prophet, many times the prophet would tell him something according to the law and condemn or justify him according to the law. The law, however, did not include the prophets. The sphere of the law was narrow, while the sphere of the prophets was wide, including everything. In the same way, the sphere of God as the law of life is narrow, but the sphere of God Himself working, moving, and operating within us as the inner anointing is very broad, including everything. Because the anointing is so inclusive, we must use many words to describe it: *operating, working, moving, acting,* and *energizing.*

Why does the Holy Spirit in the New Testament refer to the operating of God within us as *the anointing?* Grammatically speaking, this word is a gerund, a verbal noun. It is not just *anoint* but *anointing,* denoting an action, as in mov*ing,* add*ing,* and operat*ing.* The main element of the anointing is the oil. In type, when a person was to become a priest or king, he had to be anointed with the anointing oil. Not only persons used by God, but the tabernacle itself and all the furniture and utensils in it, which were brought into the presence of God, had to be anointed. The operation to anoint persons and items was the anointing.

The ointment typifies the Holy Spirit of God. Luke 4:18a, as a quotation from Isaiah 61:1 says, "The Spirit of the Lord is upon Me, because He has anointed Me." From this we can see that the ointment is the Spirit, with which God anointed Christ. In addition, Hebrews 1:9, quoting Psalm 45:7, says, "God, Your God, has anointed You with the oil of exultant joy above Your partners." This means that God gave the Spirit to the Son. On the day Christ was anointed by God, the Spirit of God descended like a dove and came upon Him, not in part but as a whole (Matt. 3:16). You and I enjoy the Spirit in part, but Christ enjoyed the Holy Spirit in full, as a whole. By all these verses, we are clear that in typology the oil, or ointment, typifies the Holy Spirit.

The Holy Spirit is the third person in the economy of the Godhead. Without the Spirit, God the Father and God the Son could not reach us, because the Spirit is the final person in the Godhead. We may illustrate this by the way I touch a brother not with my shoulder or hand directly, but with my fingers. My fingers are a part of me, so for my fingers to touch the brother is for me to touch him. The Father is in the Son, the Son is the Spirit, and the Spirit comes to us. Who is the Holy Spirit? The Holy Spirit is the very God who reaches us. For God the Father to reach us, He has to reach us in the Spirit, and for God the Son to reach us, He has to reach us as the Spirit. Without the Spirit, there is no direct relationship between us and the Father and the Son. It is in the Spirit, through the Spirit, with the Spirit, and by the Spirit that the Father in the Son reaches us. Therefore, the ointment is the very Triune God, and the anointing is this Triune God, who is life to us, moving, working, acting, operating, and energizing within us.

If I anoint a brother with ointment, the ointment becomes a part of him and is one with him. If the ointment is red, for example, the brother will be all red after I anoint him. If the ointment has a sweet smell, the brother will be the sweetest smelling person in the room. Within you and me there is an anointing work. This anointing is like painting. If I paint someone, he becomes a painted person, full of paint. His color will be the color of the paint, and his smell will be the smell of the paint. He becomes a painted man, a man mingled with the paint. Who is the "paint?" God Himself is the paint, and He is also the painter. His work is a work of painting. God paints us with Himself.

As we have said, the more I come to someone and do the work of painting him, the more paint he will have. He will be a painted person, a person mingled with paint. He and the paint become one. Originally the paint was in a can, but now the paint is on him and mingled with him. Many of the furnishings in the tabernacle were overlaid with gold. That overlaying was a kind of anointing, with gold as the "paint." God's painting, however, is to paint us not outwardly but inwardly. God is the paint, and He is the painter. He paints us with Himself.

The basic principle of God's economy and His work is to mingle Himself with us. On the one hand, He is life within us; on the other hand, He is the paint, the ointment within and without. When God paints us, anoints us, with Himself, whatever He is becomes our element, and His essence and substance become our essence and substance.

THE ANOINTING TEACHING US CONCERNING ALL THINGS

Christians today often speak of doing God's will. Thirty-five years ago I also spoke in this way, but now I say that to speak of God's will in this way is not accurate. We may illustrate God's will in this way: If someone comes to me and asks me what my will is, I may reply, "Do you really mean business about doing my will? If so, here is my will," and I will begin to paint him. My will is to make him a painted person. Similarly, if a brother asks me, "What color do you want me to have?", I will indicate what color I want by painting it on him. By my painting, he knows what color I want. In the same way, if we ask the Lord what His will is about getting married, He will paint us. By this painting we will know His will about marriage.

First John 2:27 says, "And as for you, the anointing which you have received from Him abides in you, and you have no need that anyone teach you; but as His anointing teaches you concerning all things and is true and is not a lie, and even as it has taught you, abide in Him." What does it mean that the anointing teaches us? It means that the painting teaches us. We are such foolish people. We always think that God is in the heavens, far from us. We may foolishly pray, "Should I go to college in San Francisco or in Los Angeles? O Lord, tell me and prove it to me by the outward environment." I prayed in this way when I was young. Whenever I prayed to seek the Lord's will, I prostrated myself on the ground. I was so humble and said, "Lord, You are so high, and I am so low." This is the natural way to pray without any revelation. Today when I seek the Lord's will, there is no need to bow down, kneel, or prostrate myself. Whenever I say, "Lord, what must I do?", He paints me, that is, He anoints me with Himself. A brother may ask, "Tell me whether or not I should get married. Tell me in plain English words." This is foolish. Rather, the Lord will answer this prayer neither in English nor in Chinese, but with "paint"; He will simply paint him. By this anointing he knows what the Lord wants him to do. The next day he may ask, "Should I eat Chinese food or American food?" or "Should I buy a suit and shoes?" Again the answer will come by painting. The Lord's teaching and His speaking are the painting, the anointing. Read 1 John 2:27 again; it says that His anointing teaches us. After a month's time the brother will be full of the anointing. He will be a "painted" person, full of "paint." This is exactly the meaning of this portion of the Word. When we ask the Lord what to do, He simply says, "Let Me anoint you." After this kind of painting, knowing what to do is secondary; the primary thing is that we have more paint.

GOD'S INTENTION BEING
TO ANOINT US WITH HIMSELF

Many times when I was young, I was bothered that we are not very obedient to the Lord. Many times we know the Lord's will, but we are not willing to obey Him. Later though, I was happy. I said, "Lord, whether I obey or disobey, as long as You anoint me, I have the ointment." If we ask about the Lord's will concerning marriage, He will paint us. After this painting, whether or not we agree with Him, we have been painted. If we obey, we are painted, and if we do not obey, we are still painted. Our aim is to do something, but His aim is the painting. Our aim and intention are to know God's will, but His intention is to anoint us with Himself. We may disobey His will, but as long as He anoints us, He is happy. God's intention is not for us to obey His will and do something for Him. God's intention is to anoint us with Himself.

I know many real stories along this line. A young man was saved and began to love the Lord. Then one day he wanted to go to the movies again. He prayed, "Lord, is it right for me to go to the movies?" We cannot find the word *movie* in the Bible. In a peculiar way, we may dream about whether or not to go to the movies, but God may never tell us His will concerning movies. Rather, since we seek the Lord's will, He may say, "Do you wish to know My will about movies? All right, I will simply paint you. I will anoint you within." This young man had a certain anointing within him, and this anointing, this moving within, gave him the understanding that it was not right to go to the movies. However, he eventually went. He disobeyed, so he became sorrowful, and he came and confessed. I told him, "Praise the Lord, brother, I am so happy that you disobeyed. That you disobeyed means that you knew God's will. How did you know God's will? Did you find *movie* in the Bible? Rather, you sensed it. As long as you sensed it, that is good. This means God anointed you. Regardless of whether you obeyed or disobeyed, the painting was accomplished." What is the painting? It is the imparting, the applying, of God to us. Therefore, I told the young brother, "Brother, I am very happy. I believe that after this you will have more of God in you. Before yesterday you may have had only a little of the element of God within you, but this morning I realize that there is more of God's element within you. I don't care whether you obeyed or disobeyed. I just care whether or not God has been painted in you." The brother asked, "Then what about the next time?" I said, "Brother, do not worry about next time; just go on."

God's intention is to paint us with Himself as the paint. It is rather hard for God to speak to us. Sometimes we say that God speaks to us. That is right, but we all know that this kind of speaking is not in clear words, neither in Chinese nor English, nor in letters. In what way does God speak to us? It is by painting us with Himself—by moving, acting, working, and operating within us. In this sense, the Lord does not care whether or not we obey His word. As long as we come to Him and seek His will, He will paint us; that is good enough. He cares not for our marriage or schooling but for this painting. He wants to make us painted persons, full of paint. Whether or not we marry is not what matters. One day in the New Jerusalem the Lord will not see our wife or our BA, MA, or

Ph.D.; He will see only His painting. He cares about this one thing, that is, that He paints us with Himself.

GOD TEACHING US NOT BY A CLEAR WORD, BUT BY ANOINTING

The anointing that abides in us teaches us concerning all things. God's teaching, God's revealing, is by His anointing, not by a clear word. This anointing is God Himself, and it is God's work by Himself and with Himself. The result of the anointing is that God is mingled with us. The more God anoints us, the more His element is mingled with us. After a month of being anointed, the problem that troubles a brother is gone, and the anointing is mingled with him. He becomes a painted man. The paint is still the paint with its color and odor, but now the paint is in the form of a man. God's glory, splendor, and His divine "color" and "odor" still remain divine, but now they are in a human form. If we study the books written by the apostle Paul, we can see that they are full of the divine color, odor, and splendor but in a human form, that is, in the Pauline form. It is the same with the writings of Peter. There is the same divine splendor, glory, essence, nature, color, and odor, but it is in a Petrine form.

By the mercy of the Lord, I want to impress you with this word: *The anointing teaches you.* The anointing is the teaching. If I can impress you with this, it will change your Christian life. God teaches not by a clear word, strictly speaking, but by anointing. If we say that God does teach by speaking, it must be that this speaking is actually the anointing. Today God's teaching and speaking are the anointing. In your experience have you ever heard a clear word from the Lord in English letters, using the ABCs? I have been a Christian for more than forty years, but I never heard such a speaking. Some may say that they have heard this kind of word, but that is dangerous. To hear a clear word like one from someone outside of us is very dangerous, and to hear a clear voice inside of us may mean that we are mentally ill. I know at least four persons who told me that for a long time they heard a voice within speak certain clear words and names. I told them that this may mean they are mentally troubled. God does not speak to people in this way, especially today in the New Testament time.

In 1922 or 1923, a brother said that whenever he prayed in his room, there was a voice in the corner of the ceiling speaking to him. He was not the only one who heard this; a number of Christians went there and also heard it, including a medical doctor with whom I stayed for many years in Manila. One of these brothers came to Brother Watchman Nee with this account. Brother Nee told him that according to 1 John 4, we should not believe every spirit, but prove the spirits. Brother Nee instructed them to ask the spirit that was speaking whether or not he confessed that Jesus Christ is the very Son of God who came in incarnation. The next time the voice came, they asked the spirit if he confessed that Jesus Christ came in the flesh. The spirit replied by telling them to read 1 Corinthians 13 concerning love. The brothers were happy and referred this again to Brother Nee. However, he reminded them that the Lord said, "But let your word be, Yes, yes; No, no; for anything more than these is of the evil one" (Matt. 5:37). He told them to go back to ask the spirit definitely, not in a neutral way. The next time they asked the spirit, the spirit said that Jesus is accursed. That was the last time; from that time on, the spirit never came again. Just by this one event, many young ones learned the lesson and received the help. At that time there was the tendency to be influenced by the Pentecostal movement, but this event was the main reason why the young brothers from the very start were delivered from this influence. They became frightened, at least careful, concerning these things, and they learned to prove the spirits.

The New Testament principle is that God's speaking to us is not in clear words but by painting. The inner anointing is the teaching. Read 1 John 2:27 again and underline *His anointing teaches you concerning all things*. This verse is not the ministry of God's word at the beginning of the New Testament. John's ministry was the mending ministry, the recovering ministry. Something had gone too far, to an extreme, and it needed recovery. In the recovery, in the mending, the main item is the fellowship of life and the anointing of God within us. We all must learn the anointing, the spiritual, divine painting within us. God speaks, teaches, and reveals by painting.

In the Scriptures do we have the words *Los Angeles, San Francisco, UCLA, USC,* and *MIT?* These are not in the Scriptures. In this sense, the anointing teaches more than the Scriptures. If God spoke all these things in the way of clear letters, we would need a whole library to store our Bible. There would be thousands of volumes in the Scriptures. However, we have just what is in the Bible. That is good enough, because today God speaks by the anointing; He reveals by painting. If we ask concerning red or yellow, God will simply paint, and we may see that He actually likes green. We see this not in English letters or in Chinese characters but by the "color." This is the way of God's anointing.

THE PURPOSE OF THE ANOINTING BEING NOT OBEYING BUT ABIDING

Many Christians today neglect this matter, yet we do experience it day by day. I cannot tell you how many times I experience this daily. If you obey God's painting twenty times out of one hundred, you may be the best Christian on the earth. I must be faithful to say that many times I have not obeyed this painting, but praise the Lord, regardless of whether I obey or disobey, I am painted. Day by day God paints me. Therefore, I am happy. As far as things are concerned, I have done things wrongly and committed many blunders, but as far as God is concerned, I am painted; I am full of paint. We all need to learn this.

First John 2:27 says, "And as for you, the anointing which you have received from Him abides in you, and you have no need that anyone teach you; but as His anointing teaches you concerning all things and is true and is not a lie, and even as it has taught you, abide in Him." This verse does not say, "Even as it has taught you, you shall obey." The purpose of the anointing is not that we obey but that we abide. One day the Lord spoke to me, "Child, I do not care whether you obey Me or disobey Me. I only care that after I anoint you, you will abide in Me." If I put paint on a brother, whether he takes my word or disobeys me, he still abides in the paint. The young brother who went to the movies, to whom I referred earlier, later told me, "Brother Lee, I cannot tell you how much God has given Himself to me just by my one failure." I said, "To you that was a failure, but to God it was not a failure. To God that was a success. God painted you, and from that time on, more or less, you abode in God."

Read verse 27 again. To our opinion, since it speaks of teaching, it should also speak of obeying. It is so strange, however, that the word *obey* is not there. *Obey* comes from the natural man. We speak so much about obeying. We have a good hymn that says, "Trust and obey." I liked that hymn, but not now. Verse 27 says, "Even as it has taught you, abide in Him." The purpose of the anointing is not obeying but abiding. This is the main point, which we must stress.

Some may say that my teaching is dangerous, that I encourage people to be disobedient. I do not have the intention to encourage you in this way. If you can be disobedient, then be disobedient. To stand is easy, but to fall is hard. Try it. How many times have you fallen down? It is not easy to fall, but it is easy to stand. Let us learn to say this. Change your mind. Do not be deceived by the enemy, saying, "Oh, it is so easy for me to fall." It is easy only for dead persons to fall; in fact, they are fallen already. But it is not easy for living ones to fall. As long as you are living, it is hard to fall.

For more than three years, I have never fallen, physically speaking. Rather, I always stand. If I were dead, however, there would be no need to fall; all day long I would already be fallen. Are you dead or living? Some may answer by saying, "I am not talking about being dead or living. I am talking about being disobedient or obedient." We must realize what the difference between religion and life is. Disobedience and obedience are the teaching of religion. Here we are speaking about the matter of life, so I do not want to teach you to obey or disobey. Forget about that. Learn to realize that you are living because He is living. He is living in you, so you are living. Praise the Lord, He is always anointing. Therefore, if you can be disobedient, then do it. Try, and see if you can. This is outside of the realm of God's teaching. God's teaching is of life, while religion's teaching is of disobedience or obedience.

More than thirty years ago I received the light to see something about the anointing, but at that time I did not see that the purpose, the result, of the anointing is not obeying but abiding. However, in 1953 in a training in Taiwan, I came to see that the anointing within us is for abiding. I had seen the first part of 1 John 2:27, but until that time I had not seen the last part. It says, "Even as it has taught you, abide in Him." "Even as it has taught you, obey Him" is wrong; that is the religious thought. Learn to abide according to His anointing.

It is hard to understand this passage until we have the experience. Without the experience, we cannot know what is taught here. The New Testament principle is that God does not speak to us in plain words, in speech, but by anointing, by painting. Moreover, the purpose of this anointing is not for us to do things rightly or wrongly, but for us to be painted by God, to be anointed by God that we may abide in Him.

CHAPTER NINE

DEALING WITH THE HEART

Scripture Reading: Jer. 31:33; Psa. 51:6; Prov. 4:23; Rom. 10:10;
Ezek. 36:26; 2 Cor. 3:15-16; 1 Kings 3:9; Mark 12:30; Matt. 5:8

The inner life is nothing other than the Lord Himself as
life within us to be mingled with us. I would ask you to pay
your full attention to this brief word. Not all Christians are
clear about this. As we have pointed out many times, God's
purpose, God's economy, is to work Himself into us to make
Himself one with us. This is the main and central item. God's
way to make Himself one with us is to be life within us, so
that we may take Him and experience Him as our life. Concerning life, there are three necessary matters: the fellowship
of life, the sense of life, and the law of life, which correspond
with the three functions of the human spirit—the fellowship,
the intuition, and the conscience as the representative of the
divine law. These matters should not be merely lessons that
we speak about; I would ask you to put all these matters into
practice in your daily life. It is too easy merely to bring
our two ears to listen to messages and grasp them with our
understanding. This helps, but it does not work out these
matters. When you put what you have heard into practice,
you will truly learn it, and it will be so practical and living
to you. Try to practice how to have the fellowship of life in the
spirit; try to exercise your spirit to sense God's intention, will,
and mind; and try to exercise the conscience to realize and
cooperate with the law of life.

We have also seen that God Himself, the Triune God—the
Father in the Son and the Son as the Spirit—is working,
moving, acting, operating, and energizing within us. In the
New Testament, this working is called the anointing. The

anointing is the very work of the Triune God. God Himself as the Father, the Son, and the Spirit is working by anointing us. Previously we used the illustration of painting. God's anointing within us is just like a painter painting us. I have the assurance that even in one week's time you have experienced something of this painting. We have been painted by the Lord many times. He Himself is the painter, He Himself is the paint, and His working within us is the painting work. God paints us with Himself as the paint. Eventually, the issue is that God has been painted into us.

KNOWING OUR INNER PARTS

Thus far we have seen three matters of the inner life and one matter concerning working. These three plus one, however, are on God's side. No doubt, the fellowship of life, the sense of life, the law of life, and the anointing within us are very subjective. Yet these four matters that are so vital and necessary to the inner life are still somewhat objective because they are on God's side; they are not on our side. Because they are within us, they are subjective, but in themselves they are objective. The things that are subjective, as far as we ourselves are concerned, are our inner organs, or inner parts. We have to know all these inner parts.

All good drivers agree that in order to drive well, you must know the inner parts of a car. Every smart, experienced driver knows the inner parts. I do not drive, but for a long time I was with Brother Watchman Nee, who had a car. He told me, "There is no need to look inside the car. When you drive, you just listen to the sound of the car. Then you will know if it is right or not, and if you are an expert, you can realize what part is wrong just by listening to the sound." Recently when I listened to someone start my car, I could tell by the sound that she did it incorrectly. I begged her to ask her driving instructor the right way to start the car. She answered by complaining that I just had a poor car. However, when another brother drove my car, it started very smoothly and softly, like music. After that, the first person learned the secret to starting the car. If the starter in the car is something fine, not rough, we should treat it finely. This illustrates that we need to know the inward parts.

In the same way, medical doctors study the whole body with all the inward parts. If one does not know the inward parts of the entire body, he cannot be a good doctor. Even for our own health, we must know our members and inward parts. Otherwise, we may feel that something is wrong in our head or feet and say there is a problem with our kidneys. This may seem laughable, but many Christians are like this with their spiritual life. Some things people say are nonsense, because they do not know the inner parts of the person; they do not know what they have within them. Learn to know the inner parts.

THE MAIN PART RELATED TO
THE INNER LIFE BEING THE HEART

The inward parts are not a concept we invented. This term is mentioned in the Scriptures, specifically in Jeremiah 31:33 (King James Version) and Psalm 51:6. Within our body we have a spirit and a soul; these are the two main parts. However, the main part related to the inner life is neither the spirit nor the soul but the heart. The relationship between us and God does not depend firstly on our spirit or our soul but on our heart. The heart is neither the spirit nor the soul, nor is it separate from the spirit or the soul. Rather, the heart is a composition of the three parts of the soul and one of the functions of the spirit: the mind, will, and emotion plus the conscience. Therefore, the heart is almost a composition of the spirit and the soul, but not exactly. All three parts of the soul are in the heart, and one part of the spirit is also in the heart.

The relationship we have with God first depends on the heart, because the heart is the very organ by which we express ourselves and by which we make decisions to receive or reject things. The heart controls these things, so the heart is the guard to the being, the person. The main entrance of a building is its guard, controlling what should remain outside or what should come in. In the same way, our heart is our guard. It is the entrance into ourselves. Whatever goes out or comes in does so through our heart. There is at least one verse in the

Scriptures that tells us this. Proverbs 4:23 says, "Keep your heart with all vigilance, / For from it are the issues of life." This can also be translated as, "Guard your heart." The issues of life are the flowing out of life. By this verse we can realize that the heart is the entrance, the guard, of our whole being. We believe in the Lord Jesus, but by what organ do we believe? It is by the heart (Rom. 10:10), because the heart is the organ we use to make a decision, to reject or receive something.

The heart, I say again, is our guard. Ezekiel 36:26 says that at the time of our conversion, God renewed our heart. In God's salvation, in His way of conversion, the first part within us He recovered and touched was not the spirit but the heart; then the spirit follows. In verse 26 there is first the heart and then the spirit. The heart is the first thing God must deal with and touch. The first thing we touch when we come to a building is the entrance; we have to find a way to get through the entrance. In the same way, God must deal with us to open an entrance to Himself. What is the entrance? It is the heart. When God comes to deal with us, it is first to deal with our heart.

THE FOUR STEPS OF GOD'S DEALING WITH THE HEART

First, God Touching the Mind

As we have seen, the heart is of four parts: the mind, will, emotion, and conscience. When God comes to deal with us in our heart, what part does He touch first? The first message, the first word of the gospel of the New Testament, is "repent" (Matt. 3:2; 4:17). In Greek, repent is metanoeo, meaning to change the mind. You have to change your mind. In God's dealing with us, the first thing within us that He touches is the mind. He enlightens the mind. This is why we need to preach the gospel. Second Corinthians 4:4 says, "In whom the god of this age has blinded the thoughts of the unbelievers that the illumination of the gospel of the glory of Christ, who is the image of God, might not shine on them." The god of this age has blinded not the will, emotion, or conscience, but the thoughts, the mind. Then verse 6 says, "Because the God who said, Out of darkness light shall shine, is the One who shined in our hearts to illuminate the knowledge of the glory of God in the face of Jesus Christ." By these two verses we know that God shines in our heart through our mind. We may compare ourselves to a camera, our mind to the lens, and our heart to the film; in addition, Christ is the figure before the camera and God is the light. The light from the figure (Christ) comes to the film (our heart) firstly through the lens (our mind). Once when I traveled on a train, I took some pictures with a camera. However, I did not get anything because I was hurried and did not take the cover off the lens. This illustrates how Satan blinds the mind.

The mind is the first thing God touches. That is why we have to preach the gospel. To preach the gospel is to give knowledge to the minds of people, to enlighten their minds. If someone is in darkness, he cannot turn to God and he cannot be touched by God. We must be brought under the knowledge of God by the preaching of the gospel.

Second, God Touching the Emotion

Without exception, God first comes to touch our mind. Second, God touches our emotion. If people had no emotion, no one could be saved. To be saved is truly an emotional matter. We can preach the gospel to a chair, but it cannot be saved because it has no emotion. Whenever God touches our mind, He always follows to touch our emotion. Therefore, the best way to preach the gospel is first to bring a little knowledge about God and Christ and then to tell people about God's love and mercy. This touches people's emotions. Do not argue too much. I observed a brother who is an expert in gospel preaching. He never argues with people. He tells people, "Friend, you have to know God. You need Jesus." If someone argues, the brother simply says, "Oh, God loves you. The Lord Jesus loves you and is waiting for you." The first few words touch the person's mind; then all the following words touch his emotion. Sometimes there is no need to touch people's mind purposely. You can simply preach about God's love. This one "stone" will kill two "birds." Eventually, people's minds will be touched, and their emotions will be stirred up. The mind is first, and the emotions are second.

Third, God Touching the Conscience

Third, God touches the conscience. In order to know how to deal with people in God's way, we have to learn this. After we say something about God's love, when people's emotions are stirred up by our preaching, we need to say something about God's law and people's sins. This hits the conscience, causing people to condemn themselves. The two easiest ways to preach the gospel are to preach concerning God's love and to preach concerning people's sins.

Lastly, God Touching the Will

Then when the mind is enlightened, the emotions are stirred up, and the conscience is convicted, a person makes the decision to believe. This decision is the exercise of the will, which is the last step. However, I know many persons who, after listening to the gospel, were enlightened by God in their mind, touched in their emotion, and convicted in their conscience. Eventually, however, their will would not cooperate. They hardened their will like Pharaoh. Exodus says many times that Pharaoh hardened his heart and even God hardened his heart for a purpose. When the heart is hardened, what part of it is hardened? It is the will. To harden the heart is to be stubborn in the will. We need these four steps: the mind enlightened, the emotion stirred up, the conscience convicted, and the will submissive. Then we can deal with God in a good way.

These four steps of God's dealing are good not only for unbelievers but also for His dealing with us. This is why the New Testament tells us that after we are saved, our mind must be transformed by renewing. To be renewed is simply to be enlightened. First, our mind must be enlightened. Then the New Testament tells us many times that we have to love the Lord. The first steps of God's dealing with us as believers are that our mind is renewed and our emotion is stirred up to love Him. Then our conscience always needs to be convicted. We need to be convicted that we are wrong, we are short of

God's glory, and we are disobedient to God. We need this kind of conscience. Eventually, we have to make the decision by our will to seek God. Our mind must be enlightened, renewed, and transformed; our emotion must be stirred up and encouraged; our conscience must be convicted; and our will must be soft and submissive to make decisions. These are the steps in God's dealing.

HAVING A PROPER HEART

Having an Understanding Mind

We all have to learn that for God's dealing our mind must be as clear as possible. In order to take a good picture with a camera, the lens must be very clear. Our mind must be very clear. The minds of many brothers and sisters are not clear concerning God. They are still covered under a veil. The veil has not been taken away (2 Cor. 3:15-16). This is why we have to come to the meetings, listen to messages, read the Word, and read spiritual books. This will help us to clear up the mind. The enemy Satan always tries his best to keep people away from the proper knowledge. To be without knowledge is to be under a cover. What our mind needs is to be clear. We must have an understanding mind.

The Scriptures speak of an understanding heart. In 1 Kings 3:9 Solomon asks, "Give therefore to Your servant an understanding heart to judge Your people and to discern between good and evil." In the parable of the sower in Matthew 13, the seed is sown in the heart, but if someone does not understand the word, Satan snatches it away (v. 19). For the heart to be understanding means that the mind of the heart is in a good condition. Because the mind is the "lens" of the whole person, it must be clear. We must have a clear understanding, a clear mind concerning God. However, the minds of too many Christians are not clear. It is hard to speak the things of God to them. They are under darkness; their mind is blinded, and they are "darkened in their understanding" (Eph. 4:18).

Having a Loving Emotion

In addition, our emotion must be loving. We need to love

the Lord from our whole heart (Mark 12:30), that is, from the emotional part of our heart. Our emotion should be loving, not toward something else but toward God Himself. Some Christians have a clear mind, but they are short of a loving heart. They do not love the Lord with their emotions. Their treasure is not the Lord Himself. The Lord Jesus said, "For where your treasure is, there will your heart be also" (Matt. 6:21). If our treasure is the Lord Himself, then our emotion toward Him is loving; we will love Him in our emotion. Some may say, "Don't be too emotional. You are too emotional toward the Lord." We are not emotional enough; we need to be more emotional. I wish that every one of you would weep for the Lord each day. We need to be emotional. A person can never be spiritual if he is not emotional. In order to be spiritual, we have to be emotional.

Having a Right Conscience

Our conscience must also be right. It must not be wrong. We have to be right with God, right with others, and right with everything in our conscience. In our conscience we must be right toward everyone and everything.

Having a Soft and Submissive Will

Moreover, our will must be soft and submissive. To be soft is one hundred percent different from being weak. Our will must be strong but not hard or stiff.

Our mind must be clear before the Lord; our emotion must be loving; our conscience must be completely right with the Lord, being wrong in nothing; and our will must be soft and submissive. If we put these four things together, we have a proper heart. We need to deal with these four matters. We should check whether or not our mind is clear. If not, then our heart can never be right, because our mind is darkened. Then we should check, do we love the Lord? Are we right according to our conscience with God, man, and everything? Is our will soft and submissive?

THE NEED FOR OUR COOPERATION

We have the fellowship of life, the sense of life, and the law of life within, and we have the anointing of the Triune God within us. However, this requires our cooperation, and our cooperation depends first on the heart. We speak much about the exercise of the spirit. This is good, but before we learn how to exercise our spirit, we must learn how to deal with our heart—to be renewed in our mind, to have a loving emotion, to be right in our conscience, and to have a soft will.

I hate to see that the dear brothers come simply to listen to messages. If we do not put all these things into practice, the messages will not help much. If we deal with our mind, emotion, conscience, and will, we will have a proper heart, and it will be a useful entrance for God. We will have a good dealing with the Lord, and we will allow Him to have the ground and the way to deal with us in a proper way. Then we will have the Triune God within us as life and the anointing. This requires our cooperation. Therefore, I ask you, especially the young brothers and sisters, to put all this into practice. Practice to be clear in your mind, love the Lord with your emotion, have a right conscience, and be softened in your will. The only way to do this is by praying. We need to go to the Lord to pray, "Lord, give me a clear mind, an understanding heart." The prayer in Song of Songs 1:4, "Draw me; we will run after you," is a prayer for a loving heart. We also have to pray, "Lord, give me a loving heart toward You and emotions that love only You." We also must pray for this, and also pray for our conscience to be right. Then when we pray, we will see that our will is not only hardened but stubborn, so we need to pray for our will to be softened.

If we do not deal with these things, we can never have the proper growth in the inner life. The proper growth of the inner life depends on dealing with the heart. That is why in the New Testament there are many teachings concerning the renewing of the mind, the understanding of the heart, loving the Lord, how the conscience must be good, pure, and without offense, and concerning the will. All the New Testament teachings concerning life stress these matters. Many Christians today read these words in the New Testament, but they do not know why there is so much stress on these four matters. It is simply because these are the things related to our heart. If our heart is not ready and right with God, there is no way for God to deal with us, and there is no way for us to grow.

If we deal with our heart, we will have a pure heart. Matthew 5:8 says, "Blessed are the pure in heart, for they shall see God." What does it mean for a person to have a pure heart? It is these four matters—the mind is clear, the emotion is loving, the conscience is right, and the will is soft. This kind of heart is a pure and right heart. It is a proper heart. We all need to deal with our heart in this way. We need such a heart, so we must pray for this.

CHAPTER TEN

DEALING WITH THE CONSCIENCE

(1)

Scripture Reading: Acts 24:16; 1 Tim. 1:5, 19; 3:9; 4:2; 2 Tim. 1:3; Rom. 9:1; 2 Cor. 1:12; Heb. 13:18; Eph. 4:19

In the previous chapter we saw a full sketch concerning the heart. The heart is a composition of four things: the mind, the emotion, the will, and the conscience. In order for the heart to be proper, the mind must be clear, enlightened, and transformed; it must be as crystal, transparent and not opaque. Then the emotion must be loving and caring toward the Lord. In addition, the will must not be weak but strong, yet not stubborn but soft and pliable. Then the conscience must be right; it must be a good and pure conscience, a conscience without any offense. With these four together we have a proper heart. If the mind is transparent, the emotion loving toward the Lord, the will pliable, and the conscience good, pure, and without offense, then the heart is proper. Now we must see something more concerning the conscience. There are many things spoken in the Scriptures concerning the conscience, which is very important, not only to the heart but also to the spirit.

THE SOURCE OF THE CONSCIENCE

It is hard to find a verse that tells us what the source of the conscience is, where it came from, and how it came into function. Before the fall of Adam, man was innocent. To be innocent means that there was no need for the function of the conscience. If there were the function of the conscience, it would mean that man was not innocent. However, we do not dare say that there was no conscience, because the conscience is a part of the created human being. In God's creation the conscience was there already, but its function was not there; before the fall of man its function was not yet developed. We may compare this to certain functions of our body. The medical doctors can tell us that when we were born of our parents, we had everything in our body, but certain functions still needed to be developed.

Bible students agree that the first of the so-called seven dispensations was the dispensation of innocence, the dispensation without sin. The second dispensation was the dispensation of the conscience. This is because before the fall man had no sin, so there was no need for the function of the conscience, but after the fall man was in sin. From that time, therefore, man began to need his conscience. This dispensation was the period of man living under the government of the conscience. The conscience was created by God, but the function of the conscience was developed after the fall of man.

THE POSITION OF THE CONSCIENCE

In order to know the position of the conscience, we need to know the whole human being. A person is of three parts—spirit, soul, and body. The three parts of the soul are the mind, the emotion, and the will, and the spirit has the three functions of the conscience, the fellowship, and the intuition. Then as we have seen, the heart comprises all three parts of the soul and one function of the spirit, the conscience. By this we can see the position of the conscience. The conscience is the very means to control the spirit and the heart. It is the most important part of the spirit as well as of the heart. When our conscience is wrong, our heart is wrong, and our spirit is also wrong. Both our heart and our spirit depend on the conscience.

A Contrite Heart and a Contrite Spirit Being Related to the Conscience

Psalm 51:17 speaks of a contrite heart, and Isaiah 57:15 and 66:2 speak of a contrite spirit. In what inner part are we contrite? To be contrite is to exercise our conscience. Both the contrite heart and the contrite spirit are related to the conscience. When we exercise our conscience to confess our sins, our heart is contrite and our spirit is also contrite. As we have seen, repentance is something in the mind; in Greek *repentance* means a change of mind. We have to have a change in mind and turn our mind to the Lord. Then after we repent, our confession follows. Whereas repentance is in our mind, confession is a matter of our conscience. Therefore, when we confess, we have both a contrite heart and a contrite spirit, because the conscience is a part both of the heart and of the spirit.

Our Conscience Being at the Gateway to Our Spirit

According to the Scriptures, the Lord comes into our spirit, but our spirit is enclosed within our heart. The heart is the gateway—the entrance and exit—of the spirit. Our heart must be open to the Lord in order for Him to come into our spirit. How can we open our heart? We must repent and continue to repent in order to exercise our conscience. Not only did we need to repent at the time we heard the gospel, but even after we are saved we have to repent continually. In the seven epistles in Revelation 2 and 3 the Lord demands that we repent (2:5, 16; 3:3, 19). To repent is to turn our mind, which is one door of the gateway of our heart. When we turn our mind and our mind is open, our confession follows. This is the exercise and opening of the conscience. Then when we have true repentance and real confession, our emotion and will follow to make a decision for the Lord. In this way, the whole heart is exercised and open, and the Lord comes in through our heart into our spirit.

However, many times after we are saved, we close our heart again and imprison the Lord in our spirit. Therefore, we must repent again. We must exercise to turn our mind even more and then follow to exercise our conscience by confessing. Then our emotion will be for the Lord, and our will follows to make a decision for the Lord. In this way the entire heart opens, and the way is paved for the Spirit to come in to fill us in our spirit. This shows us that the conscience is a very central matter, having very much to do with the heart and the spirit.

According to the New Testament, a Christian's conscience is very important. The apostle Paul said that he exercised himself to always have a conscience without offense toward God and men (Acts 24:16). He lived in a good conscience before God all the time. He also said that the Christian life is a life of love out of a pure heart and out of a good conscience and out of unfeigned faith (1 Tim. 1:5). Both love and faith depend on a pure conscience. Without a pure conscience it is hard to have love and faith. Moreover, he said that if we thrust away a good conscience, we will become shipwrecked regarding the faith (v. 19). By this we can see how important the conscience is.

THE GOVERNMENT OF THE CONSCIENCE

Before the fall man lived in the presence of God and was directly under the government of God, so there was no need for the conscience. After the fall, however, man fell out of the presence of God into himself, and in losing the presence of God, he lost the government of God Himself. Therefore, man began to need his conscience as a government, a control. This is why the conscience came into function so manifestly after the fall. By the fall the conscience was developed very much, and it stepped in to govern human beings. This is why Bible students say that after the fall the second dispensation, the dispensation of the conscience, began. After the fall man was under the control, the government, the rule, of the conscience. This was a self-government.

This, however, was not the end of the fall of man. Following this was a second step, in which man fell from self-government. Genesis 9:6 says, "Whoever sheds man's blood, / By man shall his blood be shed." This indicates that since man was lawless, God put man under human government. After the second fall humans needed to be governed by others. Consider today's Los Angeles; if we were to take the police and courts away, what kind of city would this be? The entire fallen race of man is under human government. In school and at home there is a human government. I am ashamed to say that many in the church today still need a kind of human government. This is because man has fallen again and again.

After the third dispensation, the dispensation of human government, came the dispensation of promise. God promised to come in to deliver people back. At that time, however, men could not understand what God meant by His promise, so He gave them the law. Therefore, this was the dispensation of the law, which proved to man how much he needed God's salvation. After this came the dispensation of grace. Grace came to fulfill the promise.

Being Brought Back
to the Rule of the Conscience

If we are fallen under human government, still needing others to govern us at school, at home, and in our city, we are fallen to the uttermost. God's salvation comes to deliver us from human government to self government. A genuine Christian should not need this kind of human government. If a student still needs the government of the school, he is either not saved or not saved properly and adequately. If one has been saved adequately, there is no need for this kind of human government, because he has been saved back to his conscience. From the West Coast to the East Coast everyone is afraid of getting a ticket from the police. Do we Christians need to be patrolled by the police? We should not, because we have been delivered from human government back to the conscience. There should be no need for human government to rule us, because we are under the government of the conscience.

The Conscience Being the Bridge
to the Presence of God

I believe that now you can see the importance of the conscience. However, we must realize that the conscience is not the ultimate goal. The conscience is only a bridge to the ultimate goal, which is the presence of God. We need to get on the bridge and pass through to reach the other side. We cannot believe that a brother who does not have a proper conscience can be governed by the Lord directly. If we are not pure in our conscience, if our conscience is not void of offense, it is very hard to live in the presence of God. If we have an offense on our conscience, a certain kind of accusation, how can we be in the presence of God? If this is our case, we must get back into the presence of God through our conscience. To be in the presence of God we must be right in our conscience. Our conscience must be pure, good, and without offense.

If, for example, I habitually lie, there will be an offense, a certain accusation, in my conscience. With such an offense, can I be in the presence of the Lord? No, I have to pass through the conscience. The conscience has to approve. I tell you again, the conscience is the bridge. We must pass the bridge to reach the other side.

God's salvation is to bring us back from human government to the conscience and then through the conscience into His presence. This is why the apostle Paul told us that we must have a good conscience. If we lose a good conscience, we lose the presence of God. It is through the conscience that we are brought back into the presence of God.

THE FUNCTION OF THE CONSCIENCE

The function of the conscience is threefold: to know what is right and wrong, to justify or to accuse, and to govern for God. Just as the police govern people for society, the conscience within us constantly governs us for God. After the fall, God governs us through the conscience that man may know what is right and wrong. Man has such an organ to justify him or to accuse and condemn him.

THE FEELING OF THE CONSCIENCE

The conscience has a consciousness, a feeling, or a sense. The function of the conscience depends on this consciousness. Ephesians 4:19 says, "Who, being past feeling, have given themselves over to lasciviousness to work all uncleanness in greediness." In Darby's New Translation, this verse says, "Having cast off all feeling." The unbelieving sinners cast off their feeling. *Feeling* here mostly refers to the feeling of the conscience.

Nine Factors That Affect the Feeling
of Our Conscience

The experience of all spiritual persons proves that the conscience is like the window to a building. A window itself does not give light; the light comes from the sunshine. Similarly, the conscience derives its consciousness through other factors. First, the conscience functions through the mind. When the mind is darkened, the conscience is also darkened. It is hard for the conscience to have a sense when the mind is darkened. This is why we must preach the gospel to the unbelievers. The gospel enlightens their darkened mind. Through the enlightened mind the light will shine upon the conscience. Then there will be the consciousness and feeling, and the conscience will function.

In the same way, the conscience has much to do with the emotions. A person full of love has a tender conscience, but a person full of hatred has a hardened conscience. The feeling of the conscience has much to do with the tenderness of the emotions. If there is tenderness in our emotion, our conscience will also be tender.

Likewise, if our will is stubborn and hardened, the conscience will also be hardened. The conscience of some people does not function because their will is hardened. If our will is pliable and soft before God, the conscience will function in a proper way.

Moreover, if we have fellowship with the Lord, our conscience will be even more enlightened. Then the more our conscience is enlightened, the more it will function, and the deeper the feeling in our conscience is, the deeper the fellowship we will have with the Lord. In addition, the conscience has something to do with the intuition, and it also relates to the Holy Spirit and the divine life, because in any kind of life there is a sense, or feeling.

The conscience of proper Christians is much more tender than that of the unbelievers. Their mind is darkened, but our mind is enlightened. Their emotion is not proper, but our emotion must be proper. Their will is stubborn and hardened, but ours must be pliable. Their fellowship is killed and their intuition is deadened, but our fellowship and intuition have been made alive. Moreover, they do not have the Holy Spirit and the divine life, but we do. All these things added together give us a deeper, even the deepest, feeling in our conscience.

The function and degree of the consciousness of the conscience depend on two more matters. The first is the growth in life. The more we grow in the divine life, the more feeling we have in our conscience. Perhaps two years ago our conscience did not have a feeling about certain things, but today our conscience does have a feeling about them, because we have grown a little in these two years. When the growth of life increases, the feeling of the conscience also increases.

The last item is the increase of spiritual knowledge. The conscience functions according to the degree of our spiritual knowledge. The more spiritual knowledge we have, the more feeling our conscience will have. With certain things, however, there is no need for education. Even if we train children to steal, for example, they eventually will feel that stealing is wrong.

In summary, the nine factors related to the function of the conscience are the mind, the emotion, the will, the fellowship, the intuition, the Holy Spirit, the divine life, the growth of life, and our spiritual knowledge. Our intention in knowing about our conscience is this: If we do not have a pure and good conscience, if there is an offense in our conscience, our Christian life is bankrupt, we cannot go on, and we are shipwrecked.

Three Categories of the Feeling of the Conscience

The feeling of the conscience can be classified into three categories. The first is the consciousness of sins. When we commit a sin, there is a feeling about it in our conscience. Second, there is the consciousness of worldliness. If we love something worldly, our conscience feels an accusation from the Lord. Our conscience senses the worldliness in our life. Third, there are times that we have neither sins nor worldliness, but our conscience still tells us something. We still have some feeling that we are wrong before God. To be under the government of the conscience is mostly to be governed to know what is right and wrong. To be governed by the presence of the Lord, however, is to be governed not according to right and wrong but according to something deeper. If we tell a lie, for example, the conscience will govern us. This is to be under the government of the conscience, but to be under the government of God Himself is different. We may speak something that is true, but the Lord may govern us by saying, "Don't say that. You have said enough." This proves that we are not only under the government of the conscience but under the government of the Lord Himself. However, we still have to pass through the conscience to get into the Lord's presence.

The feeling concerning matters other than sin and worldliness is the government in the presence of the Lord. As we are speaking, the government of the Lord's presence may tell us not to speak, but we may still speak. This is a kind of disobedience, but it is different from sins and worldliness. This can even include matters of our character. We are those who are learning to live in the presence of the Lord by building up a proper character. Therefore, for us to throw our coat down is neither sin nor worldliness; it relates to our character. If we do not learn to deal with our conscience, we will not care, but if we do learn the lesson to deal with our conscience, it will give us the feeling to be more careful. Then we will pick up the coat and either put it on or hang it up. To throw down a coat is not sinful or worldly, but the conscience will give us a feeling about it.

The conscience is a great matter and a great subject. We will say more about it in the next message. If we intend to know the inner life and we mean business to live in the inner life, we must know the conscience. If we note how many times the apostle Paul stressed this in his writings, we will see its importance.

CHAPTER ELEVEN

DEALING WITH THE CONSCIENCE

(2)

Scripture Reading: Acts 24:16; 1 Cor. 8:7; 1 John 1:9

A REVIEW OF THE POSITION
OF THE CONSCIENCE

As we have seen previously, a human being is of three parts—spirit, soul, and body. In our body there are many members. In our soul there are three parts—the mind for knowing, the emotion for feeling, and the will for choosing. In our spirit there are also three functions—the conscience to know what is right and wrong and to justify or to condemn, the fellowship for us to commune with and contact God, and the intuition for us to sense the will of God directly. Thus, our inward being has six parts, including the mind, emotion, will, conscience, fellowship, and intuition. Of these, the conscience is at the center. This is the position of the conscience in our human being.

All our inward parts are related to the conscience. Therefore, the consciousness, the sense, of the conscience is related to these parts. If the other five inward parts are strong, right, and normal, our conscience is strong, right, and normal. But if these five parts are wrong and abnormal, the conscience is wrong and abnormal, because the condition of the conscience is related to these five parts. In order to have a proper conscience, our mind must be renewed, enlightened, and clear; our emotion must be loving toward the Lord; and our will must be pliable, soft but not weak, strong but not stubborn. Moreover, our fellowship must not be broken or frustrated, we must have a thorough and continuing fellowship, and our intuition must be transparent and keen. Then we will have a proper conscience, and we will know the consciousness of our conscience.

The purpose of these messages is not only for you to know and understand these things, but also to help you to help others. We all have to know how to help others. In the next few months some new converts may be brought in, and we will have to care for them. We should help them to know all these matters. This is not mere knowledge; this is an understanding of our being, of ourselves. If we have a typewriter or a camera, we have to know how to use it. Even until today I do not know how to use a portable radio or a camera. Today I may learn, but by tomorrow I will forget because I do not practice using these things. If I learn in a fast way, I will forget in a fast way. In the same way, we need an understanding of how to operate our "spiritual machine" to contact the Lord. We need to practice and be impressed with these matters. Those who often drive can do it very easily. In the same way, I do not boast, but it is as if I can speak about our inward parts in my sleep, because I am practiced in these matters.

A REVIEW OF THE GOVERNMENT
OF THE CONSCIENCE

As we have also seen, there are three kinds of government: the divine government, the government of the conscience, and the human government. God is a God of order, a God of law in the positive sense. God is not lawless; He is lawful. With Him there is a government. Whether or not one recognizes that there is a God, he is still under the government of God, either directly through his conscience or indirectly through some human authority. We have no right to be free. The United States is called a free land, but we cannot be as free as we imagine. For example, we do not have the freedom to drive as we like. When I came to this country I discovered that the best discipline for people is to come here and drive; their careless character will be adjusted. Recently a brother drove me to get a vaccination, and when we came out of the hospital there was a ticket on his car for parking in the wrong place.

We have to learn the lesson to be ruled. This is a free land, yet how many regulations there are! We need this. I have traveled in many countries, and I would say that the United States has the best order. The regulations, rules, and laws are some of the reasons I like this country.

We must realize that this universe is neither yours nor mine; it is God's, and God has His regulations. Whether or not we recognize Him, we are under His government. Whether unconsciously or unwillingly, we are under either the divine government, the conscience, or human government. In the garden of Eden before man was fallen, he was under the divine government in the presence of God. There was no need for anyone other than God to rule, reign, and govern. Man was governed by God Himself. Bible students call this the first dispensation, the dispensation of innocence. However, man fell from the presence of God, so he lost the divine government of God. Still, God is sovereign, so at that time the function of the conscience developed. The conscience functions for God to govern us. This was the second government, in the second dispensation, the dispensation of the conscience. God's way in this dispensation was to have the conscience govern man.

At that time people were under the control, the government, of the conscience. However, the human race had a second step of the fall. By this, we fell from the conscience into the government under the human hand. This is the reason that we have human government. If we did not have Washington, D. C., city hall, the law court, and the police station, what kind of country would this be? The fallen race is under the human government. Praise the Lord, the salvation of God came to bring us back from human government to the conscience, and if we enjoy more and more of God's salvation, then we are brought back even to God Himself through the conscience.

Both for the fall and for the deliverance, the conscience is the bridge. That is why in order to know God in a living way, we must know this conscience. It is very important. We can never be adequate or normal in the spiritual life if we neglect the conscience. This is why there are many verses in the New Testament dealing with the conscience. All the verses related to the conscience are important, strong, and serious. We need to know the conscience.

THE CONDEMNATION OF THE CONSCIENCE

Whenever there is something wrong either with God, with man, or even with ourselves, our conscience condemns us. If, for example, I tell a lie to a brother, immediately there will be a condemnation in my conscience. The condemnation of the conscience must be dealt with right away; otherwise, it becomes an offense. Condemnation is right temporarily; it is normal in a negative sense. However, we should not have condemnation in our conscience all the time. If we do, it becomes an offense, a blame, or a charge in the legal sense. Therefore, whenever we have condemnation, we must deal with it by confessing and by applying the cleansing of the redeeming blood. We must say, "Lord, forgive me." When we deal with that wrongdoing by applying the blood, the condemnation is dealt with, and it is over. If, however, we do not deal with the condemnation but rather live in it, it will become an offense and a blame within us. This will hinder, frustrate, and even damage our spiritual life.

As long as we are in the old nature walking on this earth, we are not perfect. Therefore, to have some condemnation is normal, in a negative sense. However, we should have no offense. We must have a conscience void and clear of offense. If we do not deal with condemnation right away, our conscience will be spoiled. We will not have a conscience void of offense; rather, we will have a conscience with offense. I say again, this will damage our spiritual life.

THE KEENNESS OF THE CONSCIENCE

Concerning the conscience, there is a difference between sensitivity and keenness. You may say that I am splitting hairs, but some times we have to split hairs. If the nuclear scientists did not split something smaller than a hair, we would not have nuclear power. Keenness is right; with the conscience there should be keenness, not sensitivity. Sensitivity is abnormal, while keenness is normal. I do not want to be a sensitive person, but I would like to be a keen person. To say that a sister is sensitive is not a good description, but for a brother to be keen is a good qualification.

The consciousness of our conscience must be keen, but it may become too much so. When it becomes too much, the conscience is sensitive. To be keen is at a normal level, but to be sensitive is over the level. When we seek the Lord, deal with our conscience, and are faithful to the consciousness of our conscience, our conscience will be keen and tender. This is right; we all need a keen and tender conscience. However, we must be careful not to go too far, or our conscience will become sensitive.

The worldly people and even the Christians who do not seek the Lord and walk in spirit are careless in their feeling. Even if they tell a lie, they do not care; they have no feeling. Many times they are even happy when they lie, because they can do it successfully. After we are saved in a proper way, however, there is the consciousness in our conscience that we cannot tell lies. When we tell a lie, right away there is a sense in our conscience. Then the more we go on with the Lord, the more we have a consciousness in our conscience. Right after we are saved, we know not to tell lies, but we may still have some freedom to speak certain other things. But after we love the Lord, seek Him, and learn to walk in the spirit, the ruling, reigning, and governing in our conscience becomes stricter. Then we not only do not have the freedom to tell lies, but we also do not have the freedom to speak whatever we want to speak. We have to go along with the inner sense not to speak. If we do not go along with the inner sense and speak something against the inner sense, even if what we speak is true and is good, we will be under condemnation.

The more we walk with the Lord and follow Him in the spirit, the keener our conscience will be. This is right and good. At this point, however, there is the possibility that our conscience will become sensitive. It may seem that we have to say something, but we may have the sense to be careful, that to say something is wrong, so we do not say it. When we do not say it, however, we may still have the sense that we need to say it; to not say it is also wrong. Then we do not know what to do. If we speak, there is condemnation, and if we do not speak, there is accusation. This is beyond the proper level. This is sensitivity, and it is abnormal. When a brother or a sister stands in the meeting, we may sense that he or she has learned the lesson of dealing with the conscience but has become too sensitive. A brother may say, "I'm afraid I am going to say something wrong, but I'm afraid if I do not say it, I will also be wrong. I don't know whether or not I should speak." This kind of sensitivity bothers us very much.

If a radio is too sensitive, it does not work. Similarly, our spirit is very delicate, like the filament in a lightbulb. If it is only a little wrong, it will not work. The conscience is more delicate than the fellowship and the intuition. It is easy to have a conscience too dull or too sensitive, but it is rather hard to keep our conscience always so keen. If we do keep it keen, it will operate like a good radio.

THE WEAKNESS OF THE CONSCIENCE

First Corinthians 8:7 speaks of a weak conscience. A weak conscience is similar to a sensitive conscience, but it is somewhat different. In 1 Corinthians 8, the apostle deals with the problem of eating the sacrifices offered to idols. The mature saints are grown in life, so they have the adequate knowledge and understanding of these things. They realize that for something to be offered to idols means nothing because the idols are nothing; rather, the food that is offered was created by God for us to eat. Those saints are not affected by the idols, and they have the confidence that it is right to eat. The new and young believers, however, are not grown in life, and they do not have the adequate knowledge. They have the thought that the idols are awful and that we should not have anything to do with the things associated with the idols. This is right, in a sense, but this is the conscience of the younger believers. It is a kind of weak conscience. The conscience is weak because their life is young and their knowledge is inadequate. Therefore, the apostle Paul told us that for some believers to eat the things offered to idols is right, but for others to eat the same things is wrong. If one person does it, it is right because he is strong, but if another person does it, it is wrong. The one person is grown and has adequate knowledge, so he has a strong conscience, but the other person is still young.

When I was first saved, I realized that the Lord was truly with me; I had the grace of the Lord and I loved Him. Therefore, whenever I prayed, I had to sit in a proper way, and mostly I had to kneel in a proper way. Otherwise, there was condemnation in my conscience. I can never forget the first time I saw a brother praying sitting on a sofa. That really bothered my conscience. I said to myself, "No, you cannot pray that way. You are too loose. If the Lord were here physically, would you pray in that way? No, you would stand or prostrate yourself." I was right, but in a childish way. As a child in the Lord I was right. Gradually after many years, I became able to pray at any time, in any place, in any posture. I can pray with the full confidence that nothing is wrong. This is not a degradation; it is a real growth and improvement.

Many years ago my conscience was good, but it was weak. More than thirty years ago, in order to have the peace to open the Bible, study, and pray in the morning, I had to rise, wash my hands and face, and dress. Without washing I was condemned. Once I went to Shanghai to stay with some brothers. I noticed that in the morning they did not wash. They simply put on their robes and read the Bible. I said to myself, "What, are you reading the Bible? How can you pray in this way?" Again, I was right, but in a childish way. This is the weakness of the conscience. With the young believers there is always the weakness of the conscience. We must learn these things; then we will know how to help people. Otherwise, we will damage them.

THE BREACH OF THE CONSCIENCE

If we have condemnation that we never deal with, it becomes an offense. Eventually, this offense causes a breach in our conscience. When we have a breach in our conscience, our fellowship with the Lord is broken. Then we lose our faith, our assurance is gone, and our peace disappears.

In order to deal with our conscience, we must learn all these things—the consciousness of the conscience, the condemnation of the conscience, the offense of the conscience, the keenness of the conscience, the weakness of the conscience, and the breach of the conscience—not only the terms but also the facts.

SATAN'S ACCUSATION ON THE CONSCIENCE

We must differentiate between the condemnation of the conscience itself and the accusation of the enemy on the conscience. Many Christians do not differentiate these two. The condemnation of the conscience is right and normal, but the accusation of the enemy on the conscience is not only abnormal but wrong. As to the condemnation of the conscience itself, we must deal with it, but as to the accusation of Satan on our conscience, we must reject it.

The condemnation of the conscience is always based on a fact. If it is a fact that we have done something wrong, that we are wrong with God, with others, or with ourselves, our conscience will condemn us. The accusation of Satan, however, is mostly without facts. We may have done nothing wrong, and we cannot find that we are wrong in anything, yet there is a certain accusation in our conscience. It is very easy for those who seek the Lord diligently to be attacked by the enemy, to be accused by him in their conscience. Before the enemy comes in to accuse our conscience, he always sends a fog. He makes our feeling foggy with no sunshine and no clarity. Then we do not know what is right or wrong. If we ask a brother how he is, he may say, "I really do not know whether I am right or wrong. I simply don't know." Is he wrong? No, he cannot truly say he is wrong. Then is he right? No, he does not think he is right either. If we are in this condition, we must immediately realize that we are under the accusation of the enemy.

If we do not seek the Lord, we are careless and indifferent Christians, and we do not have the problem of accusation. With so many Christians who are not seeking, every day is bright; they have no problems. However, when we start to seek the Lord, and the more we try to walk in the spirit and fellowship with the Lord, we will have all these problems. Without any fact as the ground, we will have an accusation. We must realize that this kind of accusation is a lie, because it has no basis in fact. We must learn the lesson. If even we ourselves cannot point out how we are wrong, yet we still have an accusation within us, we must conclude that it is something of the enemy and not take it. We must learn to reject it; otherwise, we will be frustrated and bothered day after day, and we will be damaged. There is much danger in letting the accusation be prolonged.

With the accusation of Satan in our conscience, there is never a fact as a ground. There may have been some ground, some fact. We may have been wrong in certain things, but we confessed it and dealt with it. Still the accusation is there. We have to know that this accusation is a lie. After we apply the cleansing of the blood, the ground is gone and the fact is over. The blood solves the problem. However, Satan is subtle, still telling us that we are wrong.

I learned this lesson painfully in 1931. I confessed all my failures, and according to the fact I should have been at peace. First John 1:9 says that if we confess our sins, God is faithful and righteous to forgive us our sins and cleanse us from all unrighteousness. However, even though I confessed and applied the blood, I still had the accusation. At that time I had not learned the lesson, and I did not have anyone to help me, so I confessed again. The more I confessed, the more I was accused. I may have confessed one failure more than fifty times. After confessing I had a little peace, but after five minutes I felt wrong again, so I asked again for forgiveness. We should never repeat our confession. We must tell Satan, "No! The matter is over because the case in the law court is settled by the blood of Jesus. I do not accept this accusation. It is a lie!" Do not repeat your confession. If you confess a second time, you will have to confess the third time. After confessing many times you will even begin to feel nervous. Satan will fool you, and he will fool around with you.

In order to seek the Lord and walk with the Lord in the spirit, we must learn all these matters, because in this spiritual walk there is an enemy. If you do not drive a car, there is no danger, but because we have to drive, we must learn about the dangers. The more you drive, the more dangers there are. I say again, if you are indifferent with the Lord, you will not have these dangers, and I do not need to say these things.

However, we need to seek the Lord. We have to go on, but in our seeking, going on, and following Him, there are dangers, so we must learn about them.

If we accept the accusation of the enemy, the accusations will become attacks. The attacks of the enemy always follow the accusation, just as offense follows condemnation. If we leave the condemnation there, it becomes an offense, and if we accept the accusation of Satan on our conscience, it will become an attack. Therefore, we must learn how to reject accusations and thus not be attacked in our conscience. Here we need to know the efficacy of the blood. We must always apply the blood to our conscience. However, we should not apply it in a wrong, foolish way, saying, "Maybe I am wrong, so I apply the blood." We must be clear with the enemy Satan. If we are not wrong, we must be bold to tell the enemy, "Satan, I am not wrong." But if we are wrong, we should say, "Lord, I am wrong in this matter. Forgive me. I apply the blood," and to Satan we say, "Yes, I am wrong, but I have the blood." Then we must reject any kind of accusation.

Recently I met a dear, lovely sister, who was under the attack of the enemy in this way. All the time she was wrong in her feeling. That was not based on truth; it was a lie, but she could not be helped. She had been under the attack of the enemy for so long that it had produced a kind of illness.

On the one hand, we have to learn to deal with our conscience, but when we go to deal with our conscience, we have to know how to use the "medicine." Do not accept any kind of accusation from Satan. If you are wrong, you know you are wrong. Then confess and apply the blood. But if you are not wrong, yet there is an accusation within you, do not accept it. Do not be humble before Satan. The enemy always tries to pull us to one end or the other. He would never leave us in a normal, proper state. When you are careless about your situation before the Lord, he pulls you to one end; he would never allow you to have a troubled feeling about yourself. Then when the grace of the Lord comes to you, you realize you are wrong, and you deal with your situation before the Lord,

Satan pulls you to the other end. We have to know the subtle ways of the enemy, and we have to be careful.

I say again, if we are wrong, we will have the condemnation in our conscience. Then we must confess our wrongdoing and apply the blood. That is good, and that is all. If, on the other hand, there is nothing wrong, but we have an accusation, we must be bold to tell the enemy that we do not accept it. Then we will be kept and delivered from his attack.

PREMATURE KNOWLEDGE

We should not give a child of seven years the knowledge of a fifteen-year-old. That is premature knowledge. It does not help, but rather it damages. A new believer may just have been saved last week and was baptized last Saturday. Although he is a dear brother, he still smokes, but at this stage his smoking does not bother him. He can still say, "Praise the Lord! Hallelujah!" I have seen this kind of case. Such a brother may say, "Formerly I lived in sin. Day by day I lived in the place of gambling, but now I have dropped it. Praise the Lord!" This kind of brother is still young. Do not bother him. Do not tell him, "Brother, since you praise the Lord, you should not smoke." To do this is to give him premature knowledge. What then should we do? We have to feed him just as a mother has to feed her children and let them grow. When the child grows to a certain age, then she can give him a certain amount of knowledge.

If a new convert is fed in the church and grows, perhaps after two months he will drop smoking. However, if we give him premature knowledge, we will damage him. This is because, on the one hand, he now knows; just as Adam and Eve took the fruit of the tree of knowledge, his eyes are now clear. On the other hand, this new one does not have the growth of life, the stage and degree of life, to follow up on the knowledge. He will know that he should not smoke, but he will not be able to give it up. In this way we damage his conscience. Before we tell him about smoking, he can praise the Lord with confidence. But now he cannot, and neither can he give up smoking. Then his conscience is condemned, there is a breach in his conscience, and he is shipwrecked. I am not guessing about this; I am speaking something that I have seen in the past.

Never pass on premature knowledge. Rather, help people to grow. If a new believer grows, perhaps after only two weeks he will come and ask, "What is the matter? Whenever I smoke I am not so happy." Even at this point we should be careful. We should simply say, "Brother, bring this matter to the Lord. Pray more. Talk to the Lord. If after you pray, you have the peace to smoke, then just smoke. Smoke by the mercy of the Lord. But after you pray, if you feel it is the Lord's grace that you give up this thing, then give it up by the grace of the Lord." Perhaps after another three days, this brother will come to the meeting and give a testimony. This is the growth of life. Premature knowledge, however, damages. Never set yourself up as a standard, and be careful in the church meetings when you are giving a testimony never to set up your experience as a standard. That is wrong.

THE ADEQUATE KNOWLEDGE FROM THE GROWTH OF LIFE

We should learn to deal with the conscience not according to premature knowledge but according to the adequate knowledge from the growth of life. If, for example, a sister stands up in a fellowship meeting and testifies how the Lord dealt with her way of dressing, she must be careful not to set up her experience as a standard, giving people the impression that all the sisters in the meeting must be like her. If you give this kind of impression, you are not ministering the adequate knowledge from the growth of life. On the other side, the other sisters should not follow the first sister simply because they heard her testimony. They should not say, "She is a spiritual sister. From this day she will never dress like she did before. Therefore, I have to follow her." This also is wrong. The dealing with the conscience must be according to the living knowledge from the growth of life. When we grow in the Lord, we gain an amount of knowledge to realize that we must deal with the Lord about certain things. Then we deal with them. This is right.

THE SUPPLY OF GRACE
WITH THE DEALING OF THE CONSCIENCE

Whenever there is the proper knowledge of the conscience that comes from the enlightenment of the spirit, the supply of grace always follows. Whenever we have the realization in our conscience to deal with certain things, we must know there is always the supply of grace to come.

CHAPTER TWELVE

THE MIND

Scripture Reading: Mark 12:30; 1 Cor. 2:16b; Rom. 12:2a; Eph. 4:22-24a; 2 Cor. 4:4a; 11:3; 10:4; Matt. 16:21-26; Rom. 8:6; Heb. 4:12; James 1:21

Many passages in the Scriptures, especially in the New Testament, deal with the mind. Mark 12:30 shows us that the mind is different from the soul, and the soul is different from the heart. The last part of 1 Corinthians 2:16 says, "But we have the mind of Christ." Can you find a verse that tells us we should have the heart of Christ? Rather, this verse says we have the mind of Christ.

TRANSFORMATION AND THE NEW MAN
BEING RELATED TO THE MIND

Romans 12:2a says, "And do not be fashioned according to this age, but be transformed by the renewing of the mind." This verse speaks of transformation being related to the mind. Ephesians 4:22 through 24a says, "That you put off, as regards your former manner of life, the old man...and that you be renewed in the spirit of your mind and put on the new man." The renewing in the spirit of our mind comes between putting off the old man and putting on the new man. *The spirit of the mind* is a strange term. To be renewed in the spirit of the mind is related to putting off the old man and putting on the new man. Whether or not we can put off the old man and put on the new man depends on the renewing in the spirit of our mind. These verses alone show us how important the mind is in relation to the inner life. In order to know the inner life and be transformed, we must know the mind.

THE BLINDING OF THE THOUGHTS,
THE CORRUPTING OF THE THOUGHTS,
AND THE STRONGHOLD OF THE REASONINGS
AND THE THOUGHTS

Second Corinthians 4:4a says, "In whom the god of this age has blinded the thoughts of the unbelievers." Whenever one does not believe, this means that there is the blinding of the mind. However, the Greek here does not say *mind* in a general way; it says *thoughts* in a detailed way. The mind is the whole, whereas the thoughts are the items, the details, of the mind. Verse 3 of chapter eleven says, "But I fear lest somehow, as the serpent deceived Eve by his craftiness, your thoughts would be corrupted from the simplicity and the purity toward Christ." Again the Greek here says *thoughts* in the plural. Chapter four tells us that the thoughts of the unbelievers are blinded, while chapter eleven tells us that the thoughts of even the believers can be corrupted, confused, from the simplicity toward Christ.

Second Corinthians 10:4 says, "For the weapons of our warfare are not fleshly but powerful before God for the overthrowing of strongholds." What are the strongholds? Verse 5 tells us, "As we overthrow reasonings and every high thing rising up against the knowledge of God, and take captive every thought unto the obedience of Christ." The strongholds here are the reasonings and the thoughts. Reasonings are in the mind; thus, our mind is the stronghold. If we read 2 Corinthians, we can realize that what the apostle Paul intended to do at that time was to pull down, cast down, all those rebellious thoughts, to subdue all those confused, rebellious minds.

THE MIND BEING THE SECRET
TO OUR BEING ONE WITH SATAN OR ONE WITH GOD

Matthew 16:21 says, "From that time Jesus began to show to His disciples that He must go to Jerusalem and suffer many things from the elders and chief priests and scribes and be killed and on the third day be raised." The Lord Jesus told them not only that He was going to be killed but also that He would be raised from the dead. However, it seems that poor Peter did not hear Him. Verses 22 and 23 continue, "And Peter took Him aside and began to rebuke Him, saying, God be merciful to You, Lord! This shall by no means happen to You! But He turned and said to Peter, Get behind Me, Satan! You are a stumbling block to Me, for you are not setting your mind on the things of God, but on the things of men." Instead of addressing him as Peter, the Lord said "Satan." This clearly shows us that when we are in the soul and in the self, we are united with and related to Satan. We are one with Satan. Peter was speaking, but the Lord rebuked Satan. In verse 23 the Lord said, "You are not setting your mind on the things of God." The mind has something to do with the things of God, with God's interests, and it also has something to do with Satan.

Verse 24 continues, "Then Jesus said to His disciples, If anyone wants to come after Me, let him deny himself and take up his cross and follow Me." This verse speaks of the self. Then verses 25 and 26 say, "For whoever wants to save his soul-life shall lose it; but whoever loses his soul-life for My sake shall find it. For what shall a man be profited if he gains the whole world, but forfeits his soul-life? Or what shall a man give in exchange for his soul-life?" In these verses there are four items: Satan, the mind, the self, and the soul. The self is the soul, and the soul is very much related to Satan and is one with Satan. To speak and do things in the soul is to be one with Satan. Here Peter spoke something in his own soul. He thought that it was himself, but the Lord Jesus realized that was not Peter alone but Satan. Therefore, He rebuked Peter, saying, "Satan." Then He added that in order to follow Him Peter had to deny his self and lose his soul. Again, self is the soul, the soul is the self, and the soul, or the self, is related to Satan and is one with Satan. This is the key: Whether we are one with Satan or one with God depends upon where we set our mind. If our mind is set on the side of God, then we are one with God, but if our mind is set on the side of Satan, we are one with Satan. These few verses have very much to show us.

Romans 8:6 says, "For the mind set on the flesh is death, but the mind set on the spirit is life and peace." This speaks again about setting the mind either on the spirit or on the flesh, either on the Lord Himself or on something other than the Lord Himself. By this we can see that the mind is the secret and the key.

OUR SOUL WITH THE MIND NEEDING TO BE SAVED

Hebrews 4:12 says, "For the word of God is living and operative and sharper than any two-edged sword, and piercing even to the dividing of soul and spirit and of joints and marrow, and able to discern the thoughts and intentions of the heart." The soul and spirit must be separated, divided, by the living word of God. James 1:21 says, "Therefore putting away all filthiness and the abundance of malice, receive in meekness the implanted word, which is able to save your souls." The Greek word *implanted* implies a seed planted into us. God's word is a living seed planted into us. It is by receiving this implanted word in meekness that our soul is saved. This verse does not say that our spirit is saved in this way. Verse 18 says, "He brought us forth by the word of truth, purposing that we might be a kind of firstfruits of His creatures." God has already brought us forth, begotten us, that is, regenerated us, with His word. Regeneration took place in our spirit, but after we are regenerated, we need to be transformed in our soul. In verse 18 the spirit is regenerated, while in verse 21 the soul is saved. After being regenerated, we still need our soul to be saved.

Some may ask what our soul is saved from. Verse 15 of chapter three says, "This wisdom is not that which descends from above, but is earthly, soulish, demonic." This verse uses three adjectives: *earthly, soulish,* and *demonic.* This indicates that the soul is earthly and demonic, related to the demons. That is why the soul needs to be saved. Our spirit was deadened and dormant, so our spirit needs to be made alive, regenerated. Our soul, however, is fallen, demon-like, and earthly, so it needs to be saved. I would ask you to keep all these verses in your memory. If you will spend more time to read them and pray about them, the Holy Spirit will give you a clear vision of the inner life.

MAN IN THE CONDITION OF THE FALL
BEING TAKEN OVER IN HIS MIND

Fallen Man Having Personified Sin in His Flesh

We all must remember that we are fallen people. To be fallen is not a small matter. The fall was due to Satan; by the fall, Satan worked himself into us. Satan was originally outside of us, but by the fall he worked himself into us, and now he is within us. According to Romans 7, something dwells in the sinful body that is powerful yet evil (vv. 17-20). This is not just sin but personified Sin, with a capital *S*. This Sin reigns like a king and has dominion in us. Verse 20 says, "But if what I do not will, this I do, it is no longer I that work it out but sin that dwells in me." This is similar to Galatians 2:20, which says, "It is no longer I who live, but it is Christ who lives in me." Galatians 2 says that Christ lives in us, but Romans 7 says that Sin dwells in us. Personified Sin is powerful and evilly alive. This is the satanic nature and life, even Satan himself, because by the fall Satan worked himself into human beings.

Most People Being Taken Over by Satan
in Their Mind

However, this is not all. The history of the human race is a history of the fall, but one day, after four thousand years of this history, the Lord Jesus came to man. While He was on the earth, He met many people. What was their situation and condition? According to the four Gospels, these persons were both learned and unlearned, strong and weak, but if we have the view of the Spirit, we can see that they all were under the fall. Therefore, the Lord came to save them from the fall. One day while I was considering the record of the Gospels, the Lord showed me that the thousands of people that the Lord met can be placed into several categories, or classes. One class was the people possessed by demons. This is a matter of the body; people who are possessed by demons are possessed in their body. Another class comprises those whose mind, whose mentality, was taken over by Satan, the evil spirit. Many people that the Lord met were possessed by demons, but most were taken over by Satan in their minds.

The learned ones—the Pharisees, Sadducees, scribes, priests, and lawyers—were all very thoughtful, clever people. They were not possessed by demons in their body. However, they were not free or independent. They were taken over by Satan. In what part of their being were they taken over? It was in their mind. Therefore, when John the Baptist came, the first word he proclaimed was "repent." To repent is to change the mind, or turn the mind. The first step fallen people must take in order to contact God and have a godly, right relationship with Him is to turn their mind.

The situation on the earth is the same today. Almost everyone is either possessed by demons in their body or taken over by Satan in their mind. Many professors, scientists, and holders of doctoral degrees are one hundred percent in the mentality. They think they are the most clever people. They suppose they are free. They are not superstitious and believe that they have nothing to do with God or with any kind of spirit. However, they are not free. Unconsciously, their mind is taken over by the enemy.

The Evil Forces of Satan's Dark Kingdom

Satan is the ruler of this world (John 12:31; 14:30). He is the king of the dark kingdom. In most modern countries there are three forces: the air force, the navy, and the army. To be strong, a nation must have strong forces. Likewise, in Satan's dark kingdom there also are forces. Satan is not a simple king, ruling by himself without any forces. In the four Gospels, for example, there are many demons, even a legion, a camp, of demons. Then the Epistles, especially those written by the apostle Paul, tell us that in the air there are principalities, powers, and dominions—that is, the wicked spirits. If we read the New Testament carefully, we can see that in the dark kingdom of the ruler of this world there are at least three forces: the demons in the water, the wicked spirits in the air, and the fallen people on the land, the earth.

The Demons Possessing the Body

The demons like to take over bodies. If they cannot take over human bodies, they will take over even the bodies of swine. Moreover, they like to dwell in the water. In Matthew 12:43 through 45 the Lord said that when an unclean spirit is cast out from a man, it roams through waterless places, seeking rest, and when it does not find it, it returns to the man. By this we can realize that the demons like either to take over a body or to stay in the water. Those who have experience in casting out demons know that a symptom of demon possession is that the possessed person is always thirsty, drinking day and night.

On the second day of creation God did not say that His work was good (Gen. 1:6-8). God saw that His work on the first, third, fourth, and fifth days was good (vv. 4, 10, 12, 18, 21, 25). Moreover, His work on the sixth day was very good because on the sixth day God created man, and man in the eyes of God was very good (v. 31). On the second day, however, God did not say that His work was good, because His work on that day was to separate the waters below the expanse from the waters above the expanse, knowing that in the water there were the demons and in the air there were the evil spirits.

Once when the Lord was crossing the sea, a storm suddenly came. There were waves in the water and winds in the air (Matt. 8:23-27). We may have thought that this was something natural, but this is not so. If it were natural, there would have been no need for the Lord to rebuke the winds and the sea. The Lord rose up and rebuked the winds and the sea, because in the wind were the wicked spirits and in the sea were the demons. The demons who possess bodies are the dark kingdom's force in the water.

The Evil Spirits Taking Over the Mind
through the "Darts"

On the other hand, the evil spirits, the wicked spirits in the air, like to take over the mind. They do this by sending thoughts as the "darts" (Eph. 6:16). Every thought from the evil spirits is a dart full of poison. Satan's intention is not merely to cause us to fall. His intention is to take us over. From the time he caused man to fall, he has used his forces—the demons to possess the body, if possible, and the wicked spirits in the air to constantly take over the mind. Man can avoid being possessed by demons, but he cannot avoid being taken over by the evil spirits in the mind. Today in America not many people are possessed by demons, but sorry to say, perhaps more than ninety percent are taken over by evil spirits in their minds. The darts are there in their minds. This is why we need the helmet of salvation. We need a covering for our head, that is, for our mind, our mentality.

Satan constantly sends the darts. Being taken over in this way is very subtle. No one is ever conscious that he is being taken over by the evil spirits. A person always thinks and considers that it is he himself who has so many thoughts. These thoughts, however, whether they are good or evil, come not from within but from without as the darts.

I do not like to speak much about demons and evil spirits; this is not my ministry. However, we need a strong spirit to stand against the evil forces of darkness. Today the evil forces of darkness are still trying to take over the body or the mind. Sane and sound human beings do not want to be possessed by demons in their body, but they can still unconsciously be taken over by the evil spirits in their mind. All the Pharisees, Sadducees, and other thoughtful people believed they were very clever. They did not know that they were taken over by the evil spirits in their minds.

It is easy to cast out a demon, but it is hard to deal with the stronghold in the mind. In a case of demon possession, it is easy to cast out the demon in a short time by strong prayer. It is very hard, however, to deal with a person who is taken over in his mind by the evil spirits with all kinds of thoughts and doctrine. In China the most difficult people to deal with in gospel preaching were those learned ones who followed the teachings of Confucius. Those teachings were good teachings, but Satan utilized those thoughts to take over the minds of those learned people. Satan blinded their thoughts by the teachings of Confucius. Those teachings became the veil over

their mind, so that the light of the gospel of the glory of
Christ could not shine into their hearts.

Today I am burdened that we would be clear to no longer
trust in our mind, for two reasons. First, we are fallen.
Second, the subtle one knows that he cannot possess us by his
demons in our body, but he can do one thing subtly and easily:
He can take over our mind by sending in many thoughts. Just
today, from the morning to the evening, how much of the time
have you been free from your thinking? Day by day and hour
by hour all kinds of thoughts are sent in. All of a sudden I may
consider something about one brother, and suddenly I consider
something about another brother. This is dark. It seems that
the darts are not poisonous, but sometimes they are very
poisonous. Darts are being sent in all the time. That is why
we need the helmet, the covering, of the Lord's salvation. We
need the protection.

I first experienced this almost thirty-five years ago. In
1931 for more than half the year I went to a mountain to pray
day by day. Almost every morning after my prayer, while I
was coming down from the mountain, the thoughts would
come. Many times I shook my head and said, "I do not want
these thoughts." Later I read a book that said that others
would shake their head in the same way and say the same
thing. Brother Watchman Nee once said that if you do not
want a thought, but it keeps coming, that proves that it is
not your thought. It is not something of yourself but from
someone else.

THE BATTLE BETWEEN SATAN AND GOD
BEING IN OUR MIND

I hope I can make it clear that the battlefield within us
between Satan and God is the mind. Our mind is the battlefield for Satan to fight with God. It is not easy for Satan's
forces to possess human bodies. Even the unbelievers, if they
are sound and sane, do not allow demon possession. However,
Satan is subtle, and it is very easy to take over people—both
unbelievers and believers—in their mind. As we have seen,
2 Corinthians 4:4 says that the thoughts of the unbelievers

are blinded, while 11:3 says that the thoughts of the believers can be corrupted. This is why we have to fight the battle.

Sooner or later we all have to experience this. The more we go on with the Lord, the more we will be attacked in our mind. It is very dangerous to open and expose our mind to the air. We need to pray, "Lord, cover us with the helmet of Your salvation. Cover us with Yourself, and cover us with Your blood." Our mind needs to be covered. We should not expose our mind to the enemy. Even brothers who are very faithful to the Lord cannot withstand the attacks if they expose their mind to the air. I can testify that if I expose my mind to the evil spirits without any covering, my Christian life will immediately be wrecked. Someone who does this may even doubt that there is a God. We need the covering for our mentality, our mind. The shield of faith quenches all the flaming darts, and the helmet of salvation keeps away all the thoughts. We need this covering.

When we preach the gospel, many people like to argue. If we argue with them, we fall into a snare. We can never help a person to be saved through our arguments. Satan always likes to challenge us, to ask something, in order to get us into the snare of arguing, because the more we argue, the more we are in the mind, the more we are under the attack of the enemy, and the more God is gone. This is why we try to help people to pray, because when they pray, they turn their mind to God. Day by day we are under the attack of the enemy. Where is the attack? It is in the mind. Therefore, we need the covering of the blood and the helmet of God's salvation.

REPENTING BY TURNING OUR MIND
BACK TO THE LORD

We need to learn always to turn our mind to the Lord. This is clear not only in the New Testament but also in principle in the Old Testament. Isaiah 26:3 says, "You will keep the steadfast of mind / In perfect peace / Because he trusts in You." This verse speaks of one whose mind is steadfastly on the Lord. Today the Lord is in our spirit. Our spirit is the very organ, the very center, for us to contact the Lord and for the

Lord to contact us. Therefore, Romans 8:6 says that the mind set on the spirit is life and peace.

The enemy's attack today is on our mind. It is very hard for our mind to be focused on the Lord. The proper direction for the mind is to be toward the Lord, but the enemy entices our mind to be directed toward something other than the Lord. Whether that thing is good or evil, it is the same. When our mind is set on something other than the Lord, we are under the attack. Therefore, we all must learn to repent, which in the spiritual language means to turn the mind.

I have observed that after a husband and wife have a honeymoon, what often follows is a "vinegar moon." Even a Christian husband may become disgusted with his wife the more he considers about her. The more he considers in this way, the more Satan does his best to attack his mind and turn it to something other than the Lord. Sometimes Satan would attack the mind of a husband toward his wife, or he may attack his mind concerning another brother or other matters. I say again, whenever our mind is set on something other than Christ, we are under the attack already. If we know the secret, we will repent right away. When we are considering something about our wife, we should right away say, "Lord, forgive me. I just turn my mind to You." This is to repent.

It is the same with the sisters. The more many Christian wives consider their husbands, the more bitter they are. If a sister learns the lesson, then whenever she has a thought like this about her husband, she will immediately repent; that is, she will turn her mind from her husband to the Lord. Then she will be covered, and she will be saved.

I hope the Lord will make you clear that the mind is the battlefield and that we need to take the responsibility always to repent, to turn our mind to the Lord. Even when we go to the department store, Satan will utilize many things to attract our mind. Right away, then, we have to repent, to turn our mind to the Lord. This is the principle that we must apply to our daily life. To repent, to turn our mind to the Lord, is a significant step in constantly being saved. We must learn this. If you would ask me what is the most practical lesson I have learned in all these years, I would say that it is to turn my mind to the Lord all the time. Much "information" may come to us, with criticism, opposition, and many matters. All these things just attack and distract us from the Lord. We must learn always to turn our mind to the Lord. In the morning we must repent, at noon we must repent, and in the evening we must repent again. We must repent all the time, and to repent means to turn our mind to the Lord.

We must learn the lesson always to set our mind on the Lord. We should not argue, and we should not discuss. The more we argue and discuss, the more we are distracted from the Lord. We should simply turn our mind to the Lord. Someone may come to us asking us to explain this or that. If we have learned the lesson, we would never answer. We would simply say, "Brother, let us pray." Sometimes the subtle enemy would lead the person to say, "I know that it is your way to tell me to pray. What does it mean to pray?" If we try to explain the meaning of prayer, we are caught. Rather, we should learn to turn our mind to the Lord and help others to turn their mind to the Lord.

The more we quarrel, the more we have to quarrel. We can quarrel until this time tomorrow. I and some brothers once had a ten-hour talk with one person. What did we accomplish? Later I regretted this to the Lord and to myself. I was foolish to waste the time. I should have just gone to sleep. There is no need to talk, argue, and discuss. It only brings in more opinions, more attacks, more poison, and more death.

We all have to learn this basic, practical lesson: always to turn our mind to the Lord. Then when our mind is turned to the Lord, it will be renewed. Consider our repentance when we were saved. How much renewing we received just through that one repentance! The more we repent, the more our mind is renewed; that is, the more we are transformed. We should forget all the thoughts, arguments, and reasonings. These come from without, from the enemy. We must learn to turn our mind inwardly to the Lord. Then we will meet the Lord; spontaneously our mind will be renewed, and gradually our whole being, our soul, will be transformed.

It is in this way that our soul will be saved. Our soul today is fallen, earthly, demonic, and devilish. It is mingled with the devil; therefore, our soul needs purification. First Peter 1:22a says, "Since you have purified your souls by your obedience to the truth." The only proper way for our soul to be saved and purified from Satan is to turn our mind to the Lord. In this way our soul will be saved from mixture with the enemy Satan, and it will be transformed.

James 3:8 says, "But the tongue no one among men is able to tame; it is a restless evil, full of deadly poison." Darby's New Translation says, "Full of death-bringing poison." Why can the tongue not be tamed and bridled? It is because the mind has too many thoughts. When the mind is full of thoughts, the tongue exercises to express something. The thoughts are like electricity, and the tongue is like the blades of a fan. When the electricity is flowing, the blades turn. The tongue is full of death-bringing poison because the tongue passes on the thoughts like poison darts. Many times when people talk with me—both believers and unbelievers—I just look to the Lord, saying, "Lord, cover me." I do not want to have thoughts as darts coming into me. That brings the poison of death.

We must learn the lesson that in order to control our tongue, we have to turn our mind to the Lord. We cannot control our tongue unless we turn our mind to the Lord. When we have a real repentance, our tongue is "cut off"; it is circumcised. We may exercise much effort to control our tongue; without a real repentance, however, even if we control it in the morning, it will explode in the afternoon. When we have a real repentance, turning our mind to the Lord, this turning of the mind will silence our tongue.

This is not a mere doctrine; I am speaking something of experience. The more we turn our mind to the Lord, the more we will be persons of fewer words. We will not have much to say. If we have something to say, it will be something of the Lord, something bringing life rather than death, something full of life, not death. But when we are taken over in our mind by the enemy, then we cannot control our mouth. We need repentance. We can all agree from our experience that the more we turn our mind to the Lord, the more silent we are. We can only speak praises to the Lord and testify of His grace and mercy. We have nothing to say, however, about any other person. When we turn our mind to the Lord, we are silent in speaking but very powerful in praying.

All of the above matters are related to the mind. I am limited in my language and expression, but I look to the Lord to make this clear to you. This is a part of the spiritual warfare. In order to fight the battle in a better way, we must know that the mind is the battlefield today, and that we have no other way to protect and cover the mind but to turn it to the Lord all the time. We do not care about anything other than the Lord, good or evil. We simply care for one thing: the Lord Himself. Therefore, we turn our mind to Him. Then we are protected. In addition, we are renewed in the mind, and our soul is transformed. Spontaneously we will be circumcised in our mouth, and we will be silent. The tongue will be absolutely controlled, because the source is gone. The "electricity" is cut off at the source, so the "fan" stops turning. We must learn this lesson. Then we will be powerful in the spirit.

Remember that our soul is fallen, demon-like, and devilish. Therefore, our soul needs to be saved by our turning our mind—the leading part of the soul—to the Lord. We always must turn our mind inwardly to the Lord. Then our mind will be renewed, and the entire soul will be influenced; that is, it will be transformed, and our soul will be saved. Why must we read the word? It is because the implanted word, the word planted into us, helps us to divide the soul from the spirit, and the more the soul is divided from the spirit, the more it is saved. We should never let our spirit stay mixed with the soul.

CONTACTING THE LORD
BY READING THE WORD AND PRAYING

Scripture Reading: 2 Tim. 3:16a; John 6:63; Col. 3:16; Eph.
5:18-19; Matt. 4:4; Jer. 15:16a; John 5:39-40

Recently the brothers and sisters have been practicing a
time of morning watch to learn how to contact the Lord by
reading the word and praying. In this message I do not want to
give you more knowledge. Rather, I would like to stress this
practice and confirm that it is right. Reading the word and
praying is absolutely necessary in our spiritual life.

THE WORD BEING THE BREATH OF GOD

Many passages in the Bible show us what the word of God
is, what the proper way is to appropriate it, and how to take
the word and apply it to ourselves. Second Timothy 3:16a
says, "All Scripture is God-breathed." *God-breathed* is the
literal translation of the Greek word in this verse. All
Scripture is the breath of God and is something breathed
out of God Himself. We all know that God is Spirit. Whatever is breathed out of God as Spirit must be spirit; this
is logical. Therefore, we have John 6:63, which says, "It is
the Spirit who gives life; the flesh profits nothing; the
words which I have spoken to you are spirit and are life."
The words He speaks are spirit because He is the Spirit.
The words He speaks are something breathed out of Him,
and anything breathed out of Him must be spirit. All
Scripture is the breath of God. In Greek, *pneuma,* the word
for spirit, is the same word for *breath* and *air.* This is very
meaningful. By 2 Timothy 3:16 and John 6:63 we can realize

that the word of God is simply the breathing of God as the Spirit.

THE WORD AND THE SPIRIT BEING ONE

All the words spoken by God in the Scriptures are spirit. Two more passages prove that the word and the Spirit are really one. Colossians 3:16 says, "Let the word of Christ dwell in you richly in all wisdom, teaching and admonishing one another with psalms and hymns and spiritual songs, singing with grace in your hearts to God." Ephesians and Colossians are two sister books; many things in them are the same. Ephesians 5:18 and 19 say, "And do not be drunk with wine, in which is dissoluteness, but be filled in spirit, speaking to one another in psalms and hymns and spiritual songs, singing and psalming with your heart to the Lord." Colossians says that we sing psalms, hymns, and spiritual songs by the word of Christ richly dwelling in our heart, while Ephesians says that we sing psalms, hymns, and spiritual songs by being filled in spirit. By comparing these two passages we can realize that the word is the Spirit. To be filled with the word properly means that we are filled in spirit. It is wrong to have the mere knowledge of the word but not be filled in spirit. To have the word dwelling in us requires that we be filled in spirit, because the word is the Spirit.

How do we know that we are filled in spirit when we have the word? If we keep the word only in our mind, we will not sing, but when we have the word as the Spirit filling us, we will spontaneously sing psalms, hymns, and spiritual songs. Psalms are long poems. We should not say that we have too many long hymns. I am still not satisfied with the length of our hymns. I would like to write one with more than one hundred verses, like a psalm. Psalm 119 has one hundred seventy-six verses, consisting of twenty-two paragraphs of eight verses each. In general, though, hymns are not too long and not too short, while spiritual songs are short, like a chorus. When we have the word as spirit filling us, spontaneously we will sing psalms, hymns, and spiritual songs. When we sing hymns, do we exercise our mind or our spirit? To memorize the word is to exercise the mind, but to sing hymns from the word is to exercise the spirit. We should learn to sing and not just to memorize.

THE WORD BEING
GOD HIMSELF AS OUR FOOD

Matthew 4:4 says, "But He answered and said, It is written, 'Man shall not live on bread alone, but on every word that proceeds out through the mouth of God.'" According to this verse, the word spoken by God is not only the breath of God but also bread as food to feed us. Because we have a body, we need physical food, but besides the body we also have a spirit, so we need spiritual food. The spiritual food is God Himself, and the way to appropriate God Himself is by His word. God is Spirit, and the word spoken by Him is the Spirit as His breath. Moreover, God is in this word as food to us. Therefore, we need to take the word of God, not as mere knowledge, instruction, or teachings, but as food, not as the "menu" but as the "dinner." When we go to a restaurant, we do not go for the menu or pay the most attention to the menu. Regrettably, though, many times we come to the Bible for the "menu," not for the food. We have to learn to come to the Lord to read His word for the food, not for the knowledge.

Jeremiah 15:16a says, "Your words were found and I ate them, / And Your word became to me / The gladness and joy of my heart." If we do not know how to eat the word, how can we enjoy it; how can we have the gladness and joy in our heart for the word and with the word? We have to know how to eat the word. When we find the Lord's words, we should not only know them but eat them, so that they become both the gladness and the joy. Gladness and joy imply singing; we have joy within and singing as our rejoicing without.

In the first stage of my Christian life, for about seven years, I was taught very much not only to study but also to search and research the word by exercising my mentality to take the knowledge in letter from the word. I was not taught how to eat the word and apply it by exercising my spirit, and I never heard of people doing this. After this stage, by the mercy of the Lord, I came to know a different way to deal with the word. It is to exercise the spirit to apply the word in our spirit, that is, to eat the word.

THE BIBLE BEING
A BOOK OF KNOWLEDGE TO BRING DEATH
OR A BOOK OF LIFE TO GIVE LIFE

Many people have been reading and studying the word for years, but I am not speaking about the old way of taking the word. What I am speaking is a new way that the brothers and sisters among us have been helped to realize. Some of us, though, may not know it very well, or we may know it partly but not in an adequate way. I would like to make this clear to you so that we can be brought into the proper way to apply the word of the Lord daily. In the garden of Eden there were two trees, the tree of life and the tree of the knowledge of good and evil. Without the revelation of the Scriptures we could never realize that the tree of the knowledge of good and evil is something negative, bringing death to us. However, the Bible tells us clearly that this tree brings death. This is confirmed by 2 Corinthians 3:6, which says that the letter kills. The letter here is mere knowledge, the knowledge in letters. The letter kills, but the Spirit gives life. When we take the tree of life, we have life, but when we touch the tree of knowledge, we find death. The one Bible can be two kinds of books to us, a book of knowledge or a book of life. If it is a book of knowledge to us, it will kill us; it will bring death.

How can this book be a book of knowledge, and how can it be a book of life? I will tell you the secret. If we take this book merely by exercising our mentality to read, study, memorize, and keep it in our mind, it is one hundred percent a book of knowledge to us. But there is another way to contact this book and apply it. It is not only to exercise our mind but even more to exercise our spirit. Of course, we have to read it. We have to use our eyes, that is, our body. When we exercise our eyes as members of our body to read the word, spontaneously the mind of the soul understands it. However, this is not all. After this, we have to exercise our spirit. When we exercise our spirit to contact the word and apply it, the Bible becomes a book of life. Whether this Bible is a book of knowledge or a book of life to us depends on whether we exercise our mind or our spirit to contact it. If we exercise only our mind, this book becomes a book of knowledge. Then it will not help us; on the contrary, it will kill us. However, if we exercise our spirit to contact the Bible, spontaneously it will be a book of life to constantly nourish us.

John 5:39 and 40 says, "You search the Scriptures, because you think that in them you have eternal life; and it is these that testify concerning Me. Yet you are not willing to come to Me that you may have life." The Jews, especially the scribes and Pharisees, spent much time to research the Scriptures. However, they would not come to the Lord Jesus. This means that they contacted only the written word by exercising their mind to understand it; they would not exercise their spirit to come to contact the Lord. Therefore, the Scriptures became a book of knowledge to kill them. The Jewish scribes and Pharisees knew the Scriptures, but they were killed by the Scriptures. They did not have life to constantly nourish them because they were using the wrong organ. They used only their mentality without exercising their spirit.

Let us apply this principle. Whenever we come to read the word, we first must realize that the Bible must be a book of life, not a book of knowledge. It must not be knowledge but spiritual food. Second, when we come to read the Bible we should not have the intention to get mere knowledge. Rather, we must have the intention to get some spiritual food. Yes, the Bible is written and printed in black and white. Yet, we must realize that it is not an ordinary writing; it is something breathed out of God Himself. It is the breath of God as the Spirit to be food to us. Therefore, we come to the Bible not with the intention to gain some knowledge but with the desire to be fed. We should not say that we already know these things. We may know them, but we may not practice them. We must thoroughly, clearly realize that the Bible is food to us rather than knowledge, so we come to it not for knowledge but to be fed.

PRAYING OVER WHAT WE UNDERSTAND IN THE WORD

Because the Bible is written in black and white, we have

to read it. Praise the Lord, He created two eyes to read with and a mind to understand! Whenever we read, therefore, we spontaneously understand something. Some may say that many times they do not understand what they read. This is true, but still we understand something. We may not understand all the passages we read, but we understand some. Out of eighteen verses, we may understand one verse, or at least one phrase. We should not deal with what we do not understand. We should take care of what we do understand and not be tempted to exercise our mind to understand more. If we simply read the word, spontaneously we will understand something. We may illustrate this with eating chicken. When we eat a chicken, we do not care for the bones. Rather, we care for the tender parts. If we simply eat the delicious, tender parts, we can enjoy the chicken and forget about the bones. Then we will be nourished. No one is so foolish as to try to eat the bones. Whoever does will end up tired and hungry.

With any chapter, any passage, or any portion of the Bible, we simply should read it, understand what we understand, and not try to understand any more. Then we should not wait. Right away we should transform what we understand into prayer, the more the better. By praying about and with what we understand, we will eat the word. We will feed on the Lord through the word by exercising our spirit. We must learn to pray in this way.

We may use any chapter to illustrate the way to feed on the Lord through His word. It is easy to use a chapter such as 1 John 1, so for our illustration we can select a more difficult chapter, such as Titus 2. A new believer, a sister, may come to the book of Titus, even though she did not formerly know where Titus is. She may turn to chapter two and read verse 1: "But you, speak the things which are fitting to the healthy teaching." She does not know what the healthy teaching is, so she continues with verse 2, which says, "Exhort older men to be temperate, grave, of a sober mind, healthy in faith, in love, in endurance." She also does not know what these words mean, although she knows a little about love. She reads verses 3 and 4: "Older women likewise to be in demeanor as befits those who engage in sacred things, not slanderers, nor enslaved by much wine, teachers of what is good, that they may train the young women to love their husbands, to love their children." At this point the sister understands something. She is impressed concerning loving her husband and her children, so right away she puts these two items into prayer. She prays, "Lord, You know that I cannot love my husband. We have been married for many years, but we always fight. I cannot make it." In this way she prays and opens herself to the Lord. Then while she is praying, the Lord as the Spirit within her imparts something into her. Even though she has never heard such a prayer before, she can still say, "Lord, I have no love, but You are this love. You are the love by which I can love my husband. Lord, fill me. When You fill me, I will be filled with love, and spontaneously I will love my husband through You, by You, with You, and in You."

When we learn to pray in this way, the Holy Spirit will teach us many good prayers. In this way we will pray ourselves into the Lord, and we will pray the Lord into us. In the illustration above, we may go on to pray about the second point concerning loving our children. At this point we will open to the Lord, and we will exercise our spirit to contact Him. There is no need to spend the time to exercise our mind to read and understand. We need to stop the exercise of the mind and open ourselves by exercising our spirit. This opens the gate, paves the way, and gives the opportunity to the Lord to come in more and more as the Spirit. Moreover, we will learn to pray in a wonderful way, in the way of life.

We do not need to hurry to read a certain number of verses. We should simply pray about the points we understand until we feel the burden is gone. Then we can say, "Lord, now I have to go." We may stop our prayer, but we will have received something.

TAKING THE COMMANDMENTS IN THE WORD
AS THE LORD HIMSELF

I have been a Christian for more than forty years. Even up until now, I do not know the proper language to express what I have learned. However, I may illustrate it in this way. All the commandments of the Scriptures, both in the Old and New

Testaments, are the Lord Himself. To love your husband is a commandment, but this commandment is the Lord Himself. If it is not the Lord Himself but merely a commandment in letters, it will kill and condemn. This never helps or nourishes us. We should tell the Lord, "Lord, this commandment to love my husband must be Yourself. So Lord, I will not take this word apart from You. I must take You as this word, and I must take this word with You. Lord, if You do not come into me, if You do not impart Yourself into me, then even if I seem to keep this word, I still cannot love my husband. The love which I need for my husband must be You, Lord. You must come into me. I am not taking merely this commandment; I am taking You as this commandment." How can we take the Lord as the commandment? It is by praying about what we understand. While we pray in this way, we will absorb the Lord into us.

We should not deal with the word alone. Rather, while we are dealing with the word, we have to deal with the Lord. When we deal with any commandment, we must deal with the Lord at the same time to make the Lord one with His word. As we have illustrated, a wife may have fought with her husband for many years, but then she becomes a Christian. She loves the Lord to a certain degree, and she knows that she should read the word. When she reads in Titus 2 that she should love her husband and her children, she is inspired by this word. However, it is not good enough that she keeps this word in her mind and makes the decision to keep the Lord's word from that day onward. If she does only this, she has a kind of religion, not a salvation. Even the teachings of Confucius among the Chinese are almost the same as this. This is the wrong way.

The right way is that when we read this word, we realize that the Lord can never be separated from His word. Every word of the Lord is something breathed out of Himself. It is the breath of the living Lord. All the commandments must be the Lord Himself. Therefore, we take this word to the Lord to pray with and about this word. We contact the Lord through this word and spend time with the Lord by taking this word, praying, praising, thanking, and looking to Him. In this way, it seems that we are taking the word into our mind, but even the more we are absorbing the Lord into us. There is no need to make up our mind to love our husband. If we simply read by praying to the Lord about what we understand, we will absorb Him into us. Eventually the Lord will fill us, and we will love our husband spontaneously and unconsciously. We will love him because we are absorbing the Lord and being filled with Him. If we pray for twenty minutes in the morning about, for example, loving our husband and our children, we will be filled not only with the word of the Lord but with the Lord Himself. Then the Lord Himself in His word will be our love.

PRAYING BEING THE REVOLUTIONIZING WAY TO READ THE WORD

The revolutionizing way to read the word is to pray. Pray about every word you understand. If you do not understand something, then forget about that part. The Bible is too rich. Some friends brought me into an American supermarket and said, "Brother Lee, do you see how rich America is? See how big the supermarket is with so many items." I tell you, the Bible is bigger than the supermarket and richer than America. There are so many items in it. I have been laboring on this book for more than forty years, but today I still do not understand many things. Many items are new to me day by day. Therefore, there is no need to be tempted to know more. The supermarkets in America are not poor. There is no need to search for things. There are plenty of items; just pick something. In the same way, simply come to any corner of the "supermarket" of the Bible and stretch out your hand, and you will get something.

We should not read the word only to read the word. The right way to read the word is that as soon as we understand something, we should put it into prayer. We should not spend more time in reading than in prayer. Rather, we should pray more than read. We must learn to change our way.

Some may say that they do not understand much about the Bible. Praise the Lord that you do not understand much. I am afraid that many people seem to know the Bible too much.

I can assure you that by taking the word with prayer the Bible will be very open to you after only five years. You will know this book in a living way. The first time you read it you may not understand much; still you understand something. The second time, however, you will understand more, and the third time even more. Even so, I would advise you not to try to understand more. Rather, always try to pray more.

HAVING A TIME OF READING AND PRAYING IN THE MORNING

There is a real need, especially for the new and young believers who have not been built up in this way, to daily spend some time with the Lord, at least half an hour a day. I would recommend that you have a morning time, but if that is not convenient, you can use other times. The best time, however, is the morning. If possible, you must build up such a habit to spend at least half an hour to be with the Lord every day. Make this your top regulation. During this time simply read the word, understanding it spontaneously, but mostly spending your time in prayer. Do not try to read too much, and do not try to understand too much. Rather, always spend more and more time in prayer. I do not mean that you should bring many items to the Lord. Instead, simply pray according to what you understand. As to your needs, leave that to the Lord's care. We have the promise that if we seek first His kingdom and His righteousness, our Father will take care of whatever we need (Matt. 6:33). You have to stand on this promise. Simply seek the Lord Himself; seek His kingdom, and seek His righteousness. Then forget about your need, or rather, leave your need to His care.

We need to spend time to read, to understand, and to pray over the word. By doing this, we will absorb the Lord into us and apply the word to ourselves in a living way. Then we will be nourished by the Lord Himself. The commandment that we receive will be the Lord Himself, and it will be an easy thing for us to do. To love our husband will be easy. It will be spontaneous. It will not be a burden or a mere commandment; it will be an enjoyment. We will enjoy the Lord to love our husband. It will not be we but the Lord who loves our husband through us.

We must learn to change our way to read the word. Fifteen years ago I did not dare to tell this to people. Today, however, I have the full assurance that this is the right way. Do not say this is too slow or that it will take twenty years to finish the whole Bible. Leave that to the Lord. With this way, we will know the word better and more deeply, and we will enjoy it in a richer and more living way. When will we finish reading the Bible? Leave this to the Lord. Simply come to the word day by day. Do not ask, "When will I exhaust all the riches of America?" We cannot finish eating all the riches. They are too rich. Simply take care of your nourishment. Be nourished that you may grow and be strong. In the same principle, learn to spend at least half an hour with the Lord daily. During this half hour, do not pray for something else, such as the church, the gospel, the work, or the service. Forget about everything else. We need to first feed on the Lord through the word, taking the word as life and food. We need to learn how to practice reading in this living way.

I have no assurance that we all practice this. Therefore, I am still concerned. Would you promise yourself and the Lord that from today you will practice this kind of reading, spending half an hour every day with the Lord to open His word, read, understand something, and put it into prayer, the more the better? If we are open to the Lord in this way, the Holy Spirit will inspire us to pray, and He will give us the living utterance to pray. Then whatever we pray will be our nourishment. It is by this kind of prayer that we will absorb the Lord into us and apply the word as our spiritual nourishment that enables us to grow.

SINGING HYMNS THAT FIT THE SCRIPTURES

Sometimes we need to sing something. This is why we need the hymns. For the proper Christian life, there is the need not only for the Bible but for a hymnal. That is why we have spent much time in the preparation of our hymnal with one thousand eighty hymns. I would encourage the church to learn one or two new hymns in every meeting. Then we should spend time to sing them, privately or with two to six others. Every time after reading and praying, it is right to sing the hymns. We should sing them not merely in a musical way according to the regulations of singing, but from our spirit. We should sing the hymns spiritually. If we learn the hymns, we can select those that fit the meaning of certain Scriptures. Then we can use a proper hymn to fit our situation. To sing in this way will stir up our spirit. Therefore, I am in much anticipation for the completion of our hymnal. It will be a great help to us.

I would encourage the brothers and sisters to practice two things, which strictly speaking are one. First, we should spend half an hour with the Lord daily, not to pray for our needs, the church, the gospel, or the work, but to feed on His word. Then second, every time we feed on the word we should sing a proper hymn that matches our prayer, our understanding, and our feeding. We should practice these two things daily.

CARING THE MOST FOR THE EXERCISE OF THE SPIRIT

In this message we have clearly seen that the word of God is the breath of God as food and drink to us. We have to learn how to take the breath of God by exercising our spirit. The way to exercise our spirit is to transform what we understand from our reading into prayer. Then as we are open to the Holy Spirit, He will grant us many new experiences and new utterances. Many times when we pray in this way, it is easy to be filled with the Holy Spirit. If we do this, we will have a feast, a rich nourishment. If we have the time, we can try this a second time in the day and have another meal. However, we should at least have one meal a day. Forget the old way to read the word. Take this new way of practice. Do not care for your concordance; just take the word in a simple way. Open the Bible. Go book by book, chapter by chapter, and verse by verse without skipping. Just keep reading. Then when you understand something, put it into prayer. Do not care for how long it will take. Simply pray and let the Holy Spirit have the free way to get into you. Do not make a regulation that you must understand a certain number of items each morning.

Simply open yourself very much to the Lord and leave the understanding to Him. Try to learn this way.

Concerning whether or not we should pray aloud, I would not make a regulation. What we do depends on two things, the Holy Spirit within and the environment without. If the Holy Spirit leads us to jump, we have to jump. If the Holy Spirit leads us to shout, we have to shout, if the environment allows. If we shout too loudly, though, we may be thrown out of our apartment. That is not right.

With everything in the universe, however, there is a principle, a natural law. In principle, it is hard for a person to pray with no voice. It is hard to maintain a silent prayer. At least it is hard for me; I have to utter something with my voice. In order to keep ourselves in prayer, we may have to utter something. I say again, however, do not make a regulation. It depends on the Holy Spirit. If we are open to the Lord, the Holy Spirit will lead us to release our spirit, and if the environment permits, He will lead us to pray loudly. The most important thing, though, is to read, understand something, and pray.

We have three parts: a body, a soul, and a spirit. Especially in reading, we must exercise all three parts. We use our body with our eyes to read, our soul with the mind to understand, and our spirit to pray. Most Christians only go so far as to read and understand. Eventually they are killed, and they kill others. Because they know so much, they are condemned, and they condemn others. The more we read the Bible in this way, the more we know how to condemn others. Because we receive the fruit of the tree of the knowledge of good and evil, our eyes are opened. This is good for killing others, condemning others, and criticizing others. When we come to the message meeting and a brother turns to Genesis 2, we may say, "I know. He will talk about the two trees." This is because we have the knowledge. Then we will listen with a criticizing spirit; we will be killed, we will kill others, and we will spread much death. We have to break through this limitation. We have to get into the spirit, not merely to read and understand but to pray.

We should exercise our eyes a little to read the black and

white letters. Spontaneously there will be no need to exercise our mind. Our mind is too exercised already; it is too active. Even when we sleep, our mind is still working in our many dreams. We are good dreamers who exercise our mind too much. There is no need to exercise our mind, because when we read, we will spontaneously understand something. However, we must pay our full attention to the exercise of the spirit though prayer.

Learn this new way. Then the Bible will be living to you. It will be a book of life and the real tree of life. Day by day we will sit under the shadow of this tree and enjoy all its fruits. We will not be killed, and we will not kill others. Neither will we be condemned, nor will we condemn others. Rather, we will be nourished, so we will be able to nourish others. Learn to read the word in this way. If we all would practice this kind of reading, the church will be very enriched, strengthened, and built up. We will be so rich to nourish others. We will have the life nourishment without the dead knowledge of letters. May the Lord be merciful to us and deliver us from seeking the knowledge of letters, that we may take the word as the nourishment of life. I would ask you to take this and put it into practice.

BEING BALANCED IN THE WORD AND PRAYER

Scripture Reading: 2 Tim. 3:15; 2:2; Col. 3:16; 4:16; Psa. 119:147-148

The verses in the Scripture Reading above show us how to deal with the word in a balanced way. Psalm 119:147 speaks of rising in the morning, saying, "I anticipated the dawn and cried out; / I hoped in Your words." Simpler translations, such as the New American Standard Version, render the first phrase as, "I rise before dawn."

THE NEED TO BE BALANCED

There are two kinds of reactions to the message in the previous chapter concerning reading the Lord's word by exercising our spirit to take it as food. This is because there are at least two categories of people among us. One reaction is to say, "Hallelujah, praise the Lord! This is a release from burden and bondage." Another reaction, however, is to be bothered by that message. Those who are bothered may not say anything, but their mentality is turning, and they ask, "Is there no need to know the word? Is there no need to understand the Scriptures?" I sympathize with both kinds of brothers and sisters.

Consider how many ears we have. We have two ears, one on each of the two sides of our head. Is one bigger and the other smaller? No, they are of equal size. Likewise, we have two eyes of equal size and two nostrils of the same size. We also have two shoulders, two arms, and two hands, each on two sides. They are all balanced. We stand solidly and strongly because we have two legs and two feet. If we were made with one leg and one foot, we could not stand for long and we would be shakable. We are not shakable, though, because we are balanced on two legs, not one. We can apply this principle to almost all things. In almost everything in the universe there is the principle of two for balance.

In contacting the Lord by reading the word and by prayer there is also the balance. Some say that the morning is the best time to come to the word and pray, while some say that the evening is better. In this also there is a balance; we need the evening to balance the morning and the morning to balance the evening. In the previous message I stressed that we should not exercise the mind but exercise the spirit to pray about what we understand in the word. I did this because people in Christianity have gone too far in one direction in an unbalanced way. That is why we must first do our best to bring people back.

Many brothers and sisters have gone too far in one direction in dealing with the word of the Lord. In Christianity many are careless about the word of God, so they are dead. A small number of Christians, however, care for the word so much that they are unbalanced. In their Bibles there are many notes and marks in different colors. I too have a number of Bibles like this. In a sense this is good, but in another sense it is not so good. Many have been spoiled by coming to the Bible in this way. Hosea 7:8 says, "Ephraim is a cake / Not turned." The sisters who cook know they must turn a cake. To cook the cake is good, but too much cooking on one side spoils it. Some younger believers are proud of the marks and notes in their Bible and are willing to show them off. Those notes, however, simply show that they are cooked too much on one side. They exercise their mind too much in reading and understanding the word, and that spoils them.

Cooking is necessary, but it must be proper. Too much on one side spoils the cake. Have you realized that you may be cooked too much on one side? You may read much, but you do not pray much. You know the word so much, but you do not pray much about the word. You may read the word, understand it, study it, and search, even research, it much by exercising your mind, but you may not pray much by exercising your spirit. Therefore, you are unbalanced. There is too much cooking on one side with respect to the word.

Some Christians give up the Bible and leave it on the shelf. They do not touch it or even bring it to the meeting. They are unbalanced in this way. The Bibles of certain persons, however, especially of those who have a background of one-sided cooking, may have many notes and marks. They think, consider, and meditate on the verses. They are unbalanced in another way, and they may need to exchange their Bible for a new, clean one with no notes and marks. I say again, to cook a cake is not only right but necessary, but to cook it too much on one side is wrong. This is a "cake not turned."

How many hours have we spent in reading, studying, searching, and researching the word? And how many hours have we spent in prayer? If in our Christian life we have spent ten thousand hours in reading, studying, searching, and researching the word but only one hundred hours in prayer, we are in debt. We have a credit on one side and a debit on the other side, and the balance is wrong. If someone would say that he has spent ten thousand hours for reading and eleven thousand hours for prayer, I would praise the Lord for that. This is a small imbalance, but it is a credit, not a debit, of only one thousand hours. Some brothers, though, have no desire, no burden, and no "bondage." They are one hundred percent "released" and "free." They have a blank account with no credit and no debit. They say that it is too much to carry both a Bible and a hymnal, but they themselves carry neither a Bible nor a hymnal.

TWO WAYS TO DEAL WITH THE WORD

If we mean business with the Lord, if we seek Him, love Him, and desire to know Him, we need two ways to deal with His word, and we need two ways to pray. The first way to deal with the word is to come to feed on it, to take it as food. This is a basic, important matter. We may illustrate reading and feeding in this way: In order to eat, we must first go to the supermarket, buy the food, and then cook it. Then we have to sit down and eat it. To buy groceries is one thing, but to eat is another. Which is more important, to buy the food or to eat it? On the one hand, if we do not buy it, we will not have anything to eat; on the other hand, there is no point in buying it but not eating. Just as our two ears are equally important, both buying the food and eating it are just as important.

Why then did I stress eating the word in the previous message? It is because of the unbalanced situation in today's Christianity, and perhaps among us also. We have been too much on one side, just "buying the groceries" and not eating them. In this message, however, I would like to stress buying and preparing the food. In order to have the proper eating, we have to do the shopping and the cooking. In other words, all the brothers and sisters need to learn how to read and study the word.

The Need for Two Times Daily to Deal with the Word

A proper Christian who intends to lead a proper Christian life needs two times daily to deal with the word, one for eating and the other for studying and learning. The first time is in the morning to eat the word. The other time may be at noon, in the evening, or late at night. This is especially true for a young Christian, a new convert who has just started to seek the Lord. More than thirty years ago I received the help that I needed to have two Bibles, a clean one without notes, marks, or diagrams, and another one with marks. In the morning when we come to contact the Lord by eating the word, we should use the clean Bible, while at the other time, when we come to study the word, we should use the one with notes, marks, and diagrams.

In the Bible there are the passages concerning the first way of coming to the word. As we saw in the previous message, some verses show us that the word of God is food for our spirit. Jeremiah 15:16a says, "Your words were found and I ate them," and 2 Timothy 3:16a says, "All Scripture is God-breathed." This is one side. On the other side, there are the verses in the Scripture Reading at the beginning of this message. Second Timothy 3:15 says, "And that from a babe you have known the sacred writings, which are able to make you wise unto salvation through the faith which is in Christ

Jesus." In Colossians 3:16 the apostle tells us to let the word of Christ dwell in us richly, and in 4:16 he encouraged the church to read his epistles and to cause others also to read them. On this side, we must learn to study the word.

Reading the Entire Bible Once a Year

In order to better study the word, we should arrange a way to finish reading the entire Bible once a year. This requires that we read three chapters in the Old Testament and one in the New Testament each day. On the Lord's Day, however, we can skip the reading of the chapter in the New Testament and just review what we read in the past six days. This is because there are three hundred sixty-five days in a year but only a little more than two hundred chapters in the New Testament. This is not a hard task. If we desire to do it, we will be able to. It takes about five minutes to read one chapter, eight minutes at most. You can test this by reading Genesis 1; five minutes is enough to read the whole chapter. This means that it will take only half an hour to read the four chapters. I would suggest that the young brothers and sisters obtain a pocket-sized Bible, or if that is too thick, buy a Bible and take it apart to separate the books. You may, for example, carry only the book of Genesis in your pocket, and while you are waiting for someone, open it and read a few chapters. This will save you time.

If we have the heart to do this, I assure you that we will be able. We should not say we are too busy. We are not too busy. Some brothers put a chapter in front of them and enjoy it while they are eating. That does not hurt their digestion; that helps it. We have the way to work it out. If a young believer were under my training, I would require him to read the Bible in a year.

Every day we should spend about half an hour in the morning to feed on the word. At this time we should not read too much. We simply should read and pray according to our understanding. This is the way to eat the word. Then every day we need another half hour to read three chapters of the Old Testament and one chapter of the New, using a few minutes on the Lord's Day to review what we read throughout the past week. Even in this kind of reading, we should stay in balance and not try to know too much. If we read three chapters in the Old Testament and one in the New, we should not be tempted to do more. To be tempted to do more does not help; it only causes us to be cooked too much on one side—to be burned on one side and raw on the other. Rather, we should keep the rule of reading three chapters plus one.

When we take five to eight minutes for each chapter, we will learn something. Here again we can apply the principle that if there is something we do not understand, we can just let it go. If we understand something, we understand it, but if we do not, we do not; we should leave it and not spend too much time there. However, I am sure we will understand something. We can spontaneously keep in mind what we understand and remember it. By reading a chapter we will get the general idea, the general thought, of it. Then we can also keep that in mind. In the same principle, we should not try to remember more than we are able. If we simply read, spontaneously we will remember something. Over the long term, this will help us. If we practice these two kinds of reading—the reading to feed on the word and the reading to understand something—we will be wonderful Christians after only one year. We will have the proper and genuine knowledge with the adequate growth in life. This is the balanced way to deal with the word.

Some may still say that they are too busy. I sympathize with them. I admit that some are busy, but they still have vacations. In their vacation time they can try their best to make up their account of the three chapters plus one daily. If someone is too busy for one week and has no time to read anything, then he loses twenty-seven chapters, but if he has a day of vacation on the following week, he can read these chapters. This will be easy. I am older than many of you, so the experience of my age allows me to say this. Many dear ones spend more time in reading secular writings, such as newspapers and magazines, than the holy Scriptures. Therefore, to say that we have no time is a lie. If we have the heart, we can do this. If we will, we can. Do we not have even twenty minutes? We do have it.

Gaining the Proper Understanding
over the Long Term

If possible, we should buy Strong's *Exhaustive Concordance of the Bible* or Young's *Analytical Concordance to the Bible*. We should also buy one of the better Bible dictionaries and a Greek text with an interlinear translation. We need these. However, we should not lose the time for reading the four chapters. We need to keep this account daily. If we do not finish the four chapters, we will lose something. Sometimes in the four chapters there may be some special terminology, such as *reconciliation*. There is no need to go to the dictionary right away; that will waste our time. We simply should keep the word in mind. Then at the end of the week we can go to the concordance or the dictionary to find the meaning. To gain understanding is for the long term; we cannot make it within a day. We do not need to drive ninety miles an hour; we simply should drive a few miles an hour over the long term. Eventually we will arrive at the goal, but those who try to go too fast will not advance properly.

Over the long run we will grow in life, and we will have the capacity to know more. While we are growing, our capacity will increase. All the time we will be learning something, feeding on something, and growing in what we learn and in what we feed on. Again I say, this is a matter for the long term. We must learn to read and study the word in this way. Then after a year's time we will see the difference. We will be "cooked" on both sides adequately, properly, and in a balanced way, not like those who read the word in an unbalanced, over-cooked way. I hope that the churches will be built up in such a good condition that whenever new converts come in, we can immediately help them to deal with the word in this way.

This way to deal with the word is like walking with both feet, the right and the left foot one after the other. It is not like walking only on the right foot or only on the left. If we walk properly little by little, we will walk straightly and successfully. If we learn to deal with the word in this way, just consider what kind of marvelous, wonderful Christians we will be. There is no need to go to the seminary. That is to put ourselves into the oven to be overcooked in an unbalanced way. There is no need to be in a hurry to know the word. Rather, we must know the word in a proper way.

Helping the New Ones
to Properly Deal with the Word

We should train the new converts by fellowshipping with them about the proper way to deal with the word. We can tell them that starting on the following day they should eat the word, beginning, for example, with the Gospel of John. In addition, they should start reading three chapters of the Old Testament, beginning from Genesis 1, and one from the New Testament, beginning from Matthew 1. We can ask them to give us a report of their progress, if not monthly then at least quarterly. They should also stand in the meeting to give a testimony of how they have been feeding on the word and how they have been reading. They can tell people what chapters they have read and what chapters they have fed on. If we bring the new converts into this way, they will grow quickly.

There is no need to recommend a synopsis or exposition for the new ones. We can forget about that at first. Perhaps after half a year a few will come to say that there are many terms, phrases, and names in the Bible that they do not understand. Then we can tell them, "Do not try to understand too much. Simply read four chapters a day and feed on the Lord in the word every morning. Then understand whatever you understand." In addition, though, we can give them Strong's *Concordance* as a gift, and after another half year we can give them Young's *Concordance*. In this way we will care for them gradually, just as a mother takes care of her family. Then one by one they will grow. A mother does not put all the food she has into the mouth of her small child. Rather, she gives him the proper proportion daily, and after one, two, and eventually eighteen years, he grows up. This is the right way for the church as a family, a home, to bring up the new converts. Regrettably though, after many of us were saved, we did not have a proper home and family to take care of us. If we all learn this proper way, we will lay a foundation for the proper church life. Just as a sister who is trained under her mother knows how to care for her children, we also will be able to care properly for the new ones who are brought in among us.

How poor today's Christianity is. Almost nothing proper has been built up there. People establish seminaries and Bible colleges, and some attend them to learn a trade, a profession. However, I have no intention to criticize. My intention is that we learn the proper way to deal with the word. The way we have fellowshipped here is the proper way. All the responsible brothers and sisters who take the lead need to practice this way. On the one hand, they need to learn this, and on the other hand, they need to set up an example.

The proper way is that we first feed on the word so our spirit will be nourished. Then we study, we learn the word, that our mind may be renewed and enlightened. We are not beings who are only spirit, like the angels. We are persons with a spirit and a mind. For our spirit we need nourishment, and for our mind we need enlightenment, teaching, and education. We should not be unbalanced. We have to be balanced. In this way our mind will be enlightened day by day by learning the word, and also our spirit will be nourished day by day by feeding on the word. We need to practice these two sides.

TWO WAYS TO PRAY

Contacting the Lord to Breathe Him In

Likewise, there are two ways to pray. One way is to breathe in the Lord. In this kind of prayer we should care not for affairs or business but for breathing. We can pray in this way at the same time that we feed on the word. As we have said, to feed on the word requires much prayer, contacting the Lord by thanking, praising, and praying with what we understand from the word. This "hits two birds with one stone"; on the one hand, we feed on the word, and on the other hand, we breathe in the Lord. Every morning we should not pray for affairs, burdens, or needs; we simply leave those to the Lord. Rather, early in the morning we need to contact the Lord by breathing Him in. We read His word, understand something, and put it into prayer to digest what we read by prayer. This kind of digestion is both to feed on the word and to breathe in the Lord.

In our morning watch, it is better not to pray for affairs, business, or needs. We simply pray to breathe in the Lord, look unto Him, contact Him, praise Him, thank Him, and have a talk with Him. We should learn to forget about our needs and simply praise Him for His kindness, goodness, greatness, and for so many other aspects.

Telling the Lord of Our Needs and Burdens

We also need another kind of prayer. Before or after noon, in the evening, or even at night we need a time to bring all our burdens to the Lord. This is the time to pray for affairs, business, and needs, to discharge our burdens, to pray to tell the Lord whatever is on our heart or in our environment. If possible, we should do this daily. In whatever we do or need, we must speak with the Lord first; we have to tell the Lord. Sometimes we have to thank Him for His answers, and sometimes we have to remind Him of His promises. This is easy to teach, but it requires our entire lifetime to practice.

If we are a proper Christian, then even when we go to buy a pair of shoes, we have to tell the Lord. On the one hand, the Lord will take care of everything we need. On the other hand, though, in everything we need and do it is better to tell the Lord first. This will not only bring many answers from the Lord and many blessings, but it will also help us to grow.

We need to put all these things into practice. We should keep the rule of spending twenty to thirty minutes with the Lord every morning, forgetting about and not caring for our needs, but simply praising Him, thanking Him, contacting Him, and digesting the word by praying about what we understand from our reading, in order to fellowship with Him. Then later in the day we must find a time to tell the Lord. Some may say that here again is the problem of time. Again I say, if we will to do this, we can. While we are driving, we can say, "Lord, I need a pair of shoes." Simply tell the Lord in this way. You may say, "Lord, next week I will go north to visit some people. Please prepare their hearts." This is easy. The Lord is not a judge, so we do not have to go to court with prepared phrases, sentences, and terminology. There is no need to do this. We can talk with the Lord in any place, under any kind of circumstances, and with any kinds of terms, expressions, and utterances. We must learn to pray in this way. If possible, of course, it is good to find a time to be alone with the Lord, but often time does not allow us to do this; however, we can still pray.

BEING BALANCED IN ALL WAYS

We need the morning, and we also need the evening. In the morning we have to contact the Lord, and in the evening we also have to do something with the Lord. This is the balance. The proper Christian life is a life to contact the Lord in the morning and spend time with Him in the evening.

There is another need for balance. We need to pray privately, and we also need to pray publicly. If we can only pray privately but not publicly, we cannot grow adequately. Some brothers like to pray only publicly. They say that they cannot pray by themselves. This is to be lazy. They must also practice to pray privately. However, some, especially sisters, do not pray publicly. If their voices are never heard in the public meetings, they are a "cake not turned." Some Chinese brothers and sisters make the excuse that they cannot express themselves in a foreign language. In this case, I would suggest that they pray in their own language. No one will be bothered. In Taiwan we sometimes had prayers in Japanese, Mandarin, and other dialects. In Taipei we can hear many dialects during the prayer. We need to utter something publicly.

We need all of the above balances: the balance in reading the word, the balance in prayer, the balance in our morning and evening, and the balance in public and private prayer. If we have the proper balance, we will grow. I am not giving you more doctrines. Rather, if you will take this word as an instruction and put it into practice, you will see wonderful progress within only one month. This will be a great help for our times together; it will prepare us very well and even change us. I would ask you to earnestly promise to do this. Try to read the word and pray, spend time in the morning and the evening, and have the proper Christian activity in private and in public in a balanced way.

MAKING A DECISION TO PRACTICE IN THIS WAY

I do not like to be legalistic, but it helps to make a decision. It would be good to make the decision to spend at least twenty to thirty minutes to contact the Lord by feeding on His word, to read three chapters plus one daily, to pray publicly once a week, and to give a testimony in the church once a month. This would be very helpful. Make a decision with the Lord to practice this way. Then we will see the growth, and we will drop the excuses. I am not criticizing or condemning, but I am sorry to say that week after week and month after month we can never hear certain ones' voices in prayer or in testimony. Therefore, we need this kind of encouragement. Try to make these four decisions: every morning to feed on the word to contact the Lord, every day to read four chapters, every week to pray one public prayer, and every month to give a testimony in the meeting. Then you will see the change.

Sometimes in our trainings we have helped the young brothers and sisters to keep a record of how many times a day they are under the regulation of the inner law and to record how many times they have the inner anointing. In 1949 when we started the work in Taiwan, we printed forms related to these matters and gave them to the new converts to fill out. This practice truly helps people; otherwise, we are too loose. Still I do not like to be legalistic. I like to give people the freedom. However, I hope you will be a little strict with yourselves. Then you will receive the help and bring in the blessing.

CHAPTER FIFTEEN

LIFE, GROWTH, AND BUILDING

Scripture Reading: Gen. 2:8-9; 1 Cor. 1:9, 24, 30; 2:2; Matt. 13:3-8, 19-23, 44-46; Rom. 12:1-2; 2 Cor. 3:17-18; 1 Cor. 3:6, 9-12; 1 Pet. 1:23; 2:2, 5

The central thought of God is that He desires to work Himself into us. The only way for God to accomplish this is to be life to us. There is no other way for God to work Himself into us. For anything to become a part of us, it has to be eaten and digested by us, and it even has to be mingled with us. Nothing can be wrought into us as much as the food we have eaten. By the evening, the breakfast and lunch we ate earlier in the day already have become a part of us.

GOD'S INTENTION TO BE LIFE TO US

After we read the first part of Genesis about God's creation, especially the record of God's creation of man, we may ask what God's purpose with this created man is. We find the answer right away in the second chapter of Genesis. Immediately after God's creation of man, He did not give many commandments to man, telling him to do this and not to do that. It is not a matter of doing or not doing. God simply put man in front of the tree of life with the intention that man would eat of this tree (Gen. 2:8-9). By studying the whole Bible, we can realize that this tree of life signifies God Himself in Christ as the Holy Spirit to be life to us in the form of food. Therefore, God put man in front of the tree of life to eat God Himself, to receive something of God into himself as his life. The record of the picture in Genesis 2 is very clear; there is no other way for God to be life to us other than by being food to us.

The New Testament tells us clearly that man was made of clay to be a vessel (Rom. 9:20-23; 2 Cor. 4:7). Vessels are containers to contain something. What does man contain? Clearly, it is the tree of life, that is, the riches of God in Christ as the Holy Spirit.

In the New Testament we see that the Lord Jesus, who is the Word of God and God Himself, was one day incarnated to be a man. People thought that He was a great prophet or a great king. According to the Gospel of John, however, the Lord Jesus made it very clear that He came that we may have life and may have it abundantly (John 10:10b). He came to be the bread of life for us to eat, saying, "As the living Father has sent Me and I live because of the Father, so he who eats Me, he also shall live because of Me" (6:57). In the twenty-one chapters of John, the Lord Jesus did not tell us many things to do or not to do. He simply reminds us to receive Him, love Him, and abide in Him—to feed on Him day by day as the small pieces of manna. By feeding on Him and drinking Him, we have Christ in us, and we become His multiplication, His increase, the many grains that come into existence from the one grain, and the many branches of the one vine (3:30; 12:24; 15:4-5). All these items give us a very clear picture of God's intention to come into us in Christ His Son as the Spirit to be our life, that we may have life and have it abundantly.

THE VEILS THAT COVER THE MATTER OF LIFE

Although I believe that we are all very clear about this, I have the deep burden to share this with you again. Throughout all the generations and especially today, there have been too many things—good things, even the best things—that distract, frustrate, hinder, and veil people from life. I almost cannot express the burden in my heart. What I am speaking did not come from a dream; I speak out of the realization I have received through my recent visits. In the past two and a half years I have visited more than sixty cities in the United States, from the west to the east and in the southern, northern, and middle parts of the country. I have visited different groups and have met different situations. Just in a recent period of about two weeks, we encountered more than five different kinds of Christian meetings. Through all this I have realized something concerning God's intention and the enemy's activity.

God created the earth and the heavens with billions of items so that man can exist on the earth in order to fulfill God's purpose. And what is God's purpose? It is that God wants to put Himself into man as his content and reality, so that man will become His expression. The enemy, however, has utilized all these material things to distract people from the central purpose of God. Millions of people on the earth have been and are still distracted. Some, for example, are distracted even by loving a car. They just do not pay any attention to God's central purpose. Rather, they pay attention to having a better living.

Why did God create so many items for us? It is simply because we need to exist in order to fulfill the purpose of God. We need food, drink, housing, and many other things for our existence for God's purpose. However, Satan came in, and he is still doing his best to utilize what God created to distract us from God's purpose. Food and marriage are for God's central purpose, but Satan utilizes these things to distract people away from this purpose.

In the Old Testament time God came in to give His people the law. The Old Testament was given, revealed, and inspired in order to help God's people to understand His central purpose, but the enemy Satan utilized even the Old Testament to distract people from Christ. Satan could use even the Old Testament to distract God's people to pay attention to something other than Christ and which is contrary to Christ. In the four Gospels we can see clearly how the enemy used the Old Testament to distract the Jews from Christ. In John 5:39 and 40 the Lord said, "You search the Scriptures, because you think that in them you have eternal life; and it is these that testify concerning Me. Yet you are not willing to come to Me that you may have life." It was too hard to turn the Pharisees from the outward Scriptures.

In the New Testament we have knowledge and the gifts. Today many Christians are still being distracted by knowledge, such as doctrines concerning the dispensations, and they are also distracted by gifts. The New Testament is for the central purpose of God, but Satan utilizes even this to distract people from Christ. Many people talk only about dispensations, doctrines, and the gifts. Satan has covered up God's central purpose. Perhaps even some of you are still under the covering. These covers include all the material things and even the Old and New Testaments with the teachings of dispensations, gifts, tongues, and healings. All these can become the covering, veiling elements. Some may make the excuse that they are standing for sound doctrine and contending for the teachings from God, without realizing that they are under a veil which keeps them from seeing properly.

This matter troubles my heart. I have contacted many dear saints in this country. Sometimes I am very happy because I can see God's move, the Lord's work in people. But many times my heart is rent. They are dear saints with seeking hearts toward the Lord, but they are blinded. We may speak concerning life, but even for the word *life* they have various interpretations; the word is the same, but their dictionary is different. When we speak of life, they nod their heads, but after the meeting we find out that they were nodding about something else. They are under a veil.

CHRIST AS LIFE IN 1 CORINTHIANS

The book of 1 Corinthians deals with the matter of gifts by showing us that Christ is our portion. Christ is all in all to us; He is God's power and God's wisdom, and He became wisdom to us from God, both righteousness and sanctification and redemption (1:9, 24, 30). In chapter one of this book, Christ is everything to us. Then chapter two tells us that the apostle did not determine to know anything among them except Jesus Christ, and this One crucified (v. 2). If we had only chapters one and two, however, we may have mere doctrine. We would not know how Christ can be our portion and our all. God's intention is to give Christ to us as our portion that we may enjoy Him, partake of Him, and share Him. He is our portion, our wisdom, and our righteousness, sanctification, and redemption. But this is the problem: How can we enjoy this Christ in a practical way? When we go on to chapter three, we see that Christ has to be planted in us. Verse 6a says, "I planted." What did Paul plant? He planted Christ. After planting, there must be watering. Therefore, verse 6 continues by saying that Apollos watered and God caused the growth. We must be fully clear that the seed Paul planted was Christ.

LIFE AND THE FRUSTRATIONS TO LIFE IN THE PARABLES IN MATTHEW 13

Now we can understand the parables in Matthew 13. We should not care for the great tree in Matthew 13:31 and 32; that is too negative. Rather, we should pay our attention to life, which is the central thought in Matthew 13.

Sowing the Seed of Life

We may use one word for each parable in this chapter. In the first parable the word is *seed* (vv. 4, 37). A sower went forth to sow the seed into the earth, signifying humanity, the human heart. The sower is Christ, the Son of God, who came to sow the seed of life into humanity. Moreover, the seed is also Christ. He Himself is the sower and the seed. Christ comes as the sower to sow Himself as the seed into us. He did not come to teach or to be a great rabbi. When Nicodemus came to the Lord Jesus, he called Him Rabbi. The Lord right away responded, "Truly, truly, I say to you, Unless one is born anew, he cannot see the kingdom of God" (John 3:3). The Lord seemed to be saying, "I am not coming to be a great rabbi to teach you. I am coming to be a seed sown into you that you may be born anew. I came to sow Myself into you as the seed of life."

The first parable in Matthew 13 has four aspects because it speaks of four kinds of hearts as the growing soil. In the first aspect, the enemy of God came as the birds of the air to snatch away the seed. This indicates a frustration. God's way is to sow His Christ into us, but Satan's way is to snatch the seed away. However, regardless of how much the enemy can snatch away, something is still left. Then in the second aspect there is the stony ground. The stones make a person superficial. Someone may be glad about God's testimony, God's message concerning Christ as life, but he is actually shallow. Underneath, he is full of stones; he is the stony ground. Farmers know that almost nothing can grow in this kind of soil. In the third aspect, the cares of this life, the lusts, and many worldly things become the thorns that choke the growth of the wheat. In this aspect also, there is almost no growth.

Due to the snatching away, the superficiality, and the choking, the seed is almost all gone. But praise the Lord, He is eventually victorious! He will fulfill His purpose. The enemy can only delay God's purpose, but His purpose can never be nullified. So eventually, there is the fourth aspect in which the seed is sown, it grows up, and it bears fruit thirtyfold, sixtyfold, and a hundredfold. This is a brief, clear picture of life.

We must answer before God: Has Christ been sown into us? Yes, praise the Lord, He has been. However, are we in the first, second, third, or fourth aspect? Christ has been sown into us, but is there growth, or is the growth choked?

The Seed Growing into Wheat

In the second parable of Matthew 13, the descriptive word is not *tares;* we do not want to pay attention to the negative things. The word is *wheat* (v. 25). The seed has become wheat. Do you think that the enemy, having done as much as he did to spoil seventy-five percent of the seed, will now go to sleep? We may sleep, but the enemy never sleeps. While people sleep, the one who does not sleep comes in to sow the tares, the false, imitation wheat. The intention of the enemy in sowing tares is to frustrate the growth of the wheat. Satan adds many false Christians with the intention of frustrating the growth of the real Christians. Look at today's Christianity. There is a great mixture. Some may say that it is all right to have the false ones among us, but sooner or later we will be affected. We may illustrate the effect of the mixture in this way: I may wear a dirty, blackened coat, while you stand next to me wearing a white coat. Can your white coat make mine white? No, but eventually my dirty coat will blacken your white coat. I can blacken you, but you cannot whiten me. How many worldly things have been brought into today's church by the imitating, false Christians to frustrate the real growth of the genuine believers! This is the subtlety of the enemy.

Can you trace the subtlety of the enemy? First he snatches away, second he causes us to be stony, and third he chokes. Eventually, God has some wheat, but Satan comes in to plant the tares to frustrate the growth.

Christ as Life Being Small to Us

The descriptive word in the third parable is *mustard* (v. 31). These are parables, figurative records that we must understand in a figurative way. We must learn to read the figures. Seed grows into wheat, and wheat is good for eating. What is grown in Matthew 13, then, is good for eating. In the third parable we still have a seed, a mustard seed. A mustard seed is very small but good to eat. The mustard seed is Christ, who is small to us in order to be life to us. We have a hymn that says, "So subjective is my Christ to me! / Real in me, and rich and sweet!" (*Hymns*, #537). Originally, we sang the second line as, "Small in me, and rich and sweet!" However, some said that if we sing it in this way, simple people will not be able to understand. To think this way is the mentality of Christianity.

In a good sense, are we bigger, or is Christ bigger? Some people may eat turkey for dinner. Is the turkey bigger, or are we bigger? I say to you, we are bigger than anything we eat. Anything we eat must be smaller than we are. If it is bigger, we can never swallow it. Rather, it may swallow us. If it is bigger than we are, we have to cut it into smaller pieces in order for it to be food to us. Christ is so small to us. Praise Him! Many times I worship Him, saying, "Lord, I worship You for Your smallness. Because You are so small, I can feed on You." Christ is fine and small, like the mustard seed that is good to grow into something for people to feed on. Mustard is not a building material; we cannot build a house with mustard, because it can bear no weight. It is good only for eating.

In Matthew 13 the enemy changed the little mustard seed in its form and image to become a great tree. This is against the principle of God's creation in Genesis 1, which says that living things should be "according to their kind" (Gen. 1:11-12). A mustard plant must be after the kind of mustard, but the mustard in Matthew 13 is not according to its kind. It changed in nature and in form, which breaks the principle set up for God's creation. The mustard seed changed into a tree, which is good not for eating but as lodging for the birds, which signify Satan's evil spirits with the evil persons and things motivated by them. Today's Christianity is mostly good for lodging. If you travel throughout the whole world to find mustard good for eating, you will see that there is almost none. If you go to almost any kind of so-called church, you will get no food. You will only find a place good for lodging in the evil sense. This is the frustrating and damaging work of the enemy.

The Meal for Bread to Satisfy God and Man

Still, the Lord is victorious. Some wheat has produced grain, and the grain has been made into fine flour. According to the Scriptures, wheat is for making bread to offer to God as food to satisfy God and man. From the seed comes the wheat, from the wheat comes the grain, and from the grain comes the fine flour to make bread to satisfy God and to satisfy man. Therefore, in the fourth parable in Matthew 13 the characteristic word is *meal* (v. 33). Even at this point, however, the enemy is not satisfied. He still comes in to frustrate by bringing in the leaven to corrupt the meal. We have the seed sown, the wheat grown up, and the fine flour produced to make bread to satisfy God and man. This is God's intention. However, there are still the negative things.

This should not be a mere message; we have to check ourselves according to this message. Consider Christ as the seed of life within us. Is it snatched away? Are we the stony ground? Is something within us always choking the seed? Have we been frustrated by false Christians, either by our friendship with them or by following them in certain worldly ways? Are we growing now? Is the fine flour, the meal, produced in us, or is there the leaven? All these four parables reveal life and growth. Without life we cannot have the meal to make the bread to offer to God. Even if we have life, without the growth we still cannot have the meal. We need life, and we need growth.

The Precious Stones and the Pearl
for God's Building

In the fifth and sixth parables in Matthew 13 we have a treasure and a pearl (vv. 44-46). The treasure hidden in the field must be gold or precious stones. Both the precious stones and the pearl are transformed items. After the growth in life there is transformation. If we read the Bible carefully, we can see that both precious stones and pearls are good for God's building. The New Jerusalem is built with precious stones and pearls (Rev. 21:19-21).

A GREAT STRUGGLE RELATED TO LIFE AND GROWTH

Since Christ has been sown into us as life, there has been a great struggle between the Lord and the enemy, both around us and within us. We should not think that the negative items in Matthew 13 are only there and not within us. Within us are the same matters mentioned in this chapter. The enemy may have snatched away the words and messages we received concerning Christ. In the past two and a half years many messages about Christ as life have been ministered to you, but nearly every bit may have been snatched away by the enemy. You may listen to message after message, but after listening nothing may be left remaining in you. Or perhaps the seed sown remains, but you may be a shallow, superficial person full of rocks and stones beneath. If this is the case, can Christ grow within you?

You may say, "Praise the Lord, I am not too shallow. I am a deeper person." However, is there something choking you within? Are there the cares of this life, lusts, the love of money; is there the desire to be rich, to better your life, and to uplift your standard of living? I do not like to say these things, and I am not happy to say them, but I feel the burden to do so. All these things choke, so after two and a half years, where is the growth? In addition, you may have friendships with imitation, artificial Christians, which may frustrate you from growing. The inner life is working within you, yet there may be an influence without that causes a struggle. By your experiences, you know what I am saying.

Moreover, there may be leaven. In addition, the principle of the great tree is always within us. In these days the church in Los Angeles is looking for a meeting place. Whenever we touch this matter, there is the temptation to have a bigger, more beautiful building. We may say, "Our current building cannot attract people. This kind of building is for the poorer, lower class. The bank managers and people with doctorate degrees will not come here." To speak in this way is the principle of the great tree. If we say that the "poor Jesus" is not good enough to attract people, we must be careful. The principle of the great tree is still in our nature. We still like to be big, to have magnificent, attractive material things. We do not have enough money for those things, but even if we did, we should not care for them. We need to keep the principle of the mustard seed—to be little, temporary, and transient. If you feel that to sit in a nicer chair when we meet is very good, you are still in the great tree. When the Lord Jesus was on the earth, what kind of meeting place did He have? He met on the mountainside and on the seashore. Of course, I am not legalistic, but I do not like anything with the principle of the great tree.

In Shanghai, mostly under my hand, we built a meeting hall that could accommodate three thousand people inside and two thousand outside. The brothers brought the architect to me. He asked, "Mr. Lee, what kind of design do you want for your church?" I explained it to him again and again, but he simply could not understand me. We were both speaking Chinese, but he could not understand. He said, "I have learned architecture. I know how to build a law court, a restaurant, and a church, but I do not understand what kind of church you want to build." His thought contained the principle of the great tree. I told him to let me draw the rough design, and he could just fit it to the city codes. By cooperating in this way, we were able to do it. However, we did not build a "church." We simply built a big "warehouse."

When we came to Taiwan, we built the first meeting hall in Taipei, hall one, in 1952. The same thing happened again.

The architects could not understand what we wanted to build. Again, I drew the rough design and told them to do their best to meet the requirements of the city codes. When the inspector from the housing department came, he said, "Is this your church? It is just a warehouse." I do not feel shameful about this; I feel glorious. This is the principle of the mustard seed.

TRANSFORMATION NEEDED FOR THE BUILDING

To have the church is a matter not only of growth but of transformation. In order to build the church we must be transformed. Human beings were made from clay. Originally, Peter was a piece of clay, but when he received Jesus Christ as the Son of God, the Lord immediately changed his name to Peter, a stone (John 1:42). The clay was transformed into stone. In Revelation 21 we see that Peter becomes not only a stone but a precious stone. The name of Peter is written on the foundation of precious stone (vv. 14, 19). When we are regenerated, we are first transformed from a piece of clay into a piece of stone. After this we are transformed in our soul, and eventually at the Lord's coming we will be transfigured in our body. Then we will be precious stone. Even a pearl is something that has been transformed. We need transformation.

I did not make up the word *transformation*. In Romans 12, before the apostle brings us into the reality of the Body life, he tells us to do two things. The first is to offer ourselves bodily for the Body, and the other is to be transformed by the renewing of the mind (vv. 1-2). Our spirit has been regenerated, but our soul still remains old. We must have our soul transformed by the renewing of the mind. In these two verses we can see that the building of the church depends on our real consecration and the transformation of the soul. We can never be built up as pieces of clay. Even if we are stone within, the stone is still covered by clay; as such, we cannot be built together. Therefore, we need transformation.

The same word for *transformation* is in 2 Corinthians 3:18. Verse 17 says, "And the Lord is the Spirit; and where the Spirit of the Lord is, there is freedom." Then verse 18 says that we are being "transformed into the same image from glory to glory, even as from the Lord Spirit."

As we have seen, in the parables of Matthew 13 there is the view of life, growth, and transformation to produce the building materials. In 1 Corinthians 3, the apostle has the same thought that the Lord Jesus had in Matthew 13. Paul says that we are the cultivated land of God, that we need the seed to be planted and to grow (1 Cor. 3:6, 9a). Then on the other hand, he says we are the building of God, built with precious stones (vv. 9b, 12a). Therefore in Matthew 13 and 1 Corinthians 3 we can see the consistency of the divine thought: Life is sown into us to grow and to cause transformation.

THE PRACTICAL NEED TO PLANT AND WATER FOR THE BUILDING

Now I must speak something practical. As a local church, we must have Christ planted into people as the seed. I do not oppose teachings and gifts; I simply care for how much of Christ has been sown into us. How much of Christ has been planted? We need the sowing of Christ as the seed of life into us. There must be the planting of Christ. The apostle Paul said, "I planted, Apollos watered, but God caused the growth" (1 Cor. 3:6). Do we have the watering and the growth?

Mothers know that after they have a baby, they must feed the baby. In the first week, she feeds the baby one way; then in the second week, second month, and second half year she still knows the right way to feed the baby. A mother knows how to feed a baby to make him grow, but in the church today do we know how to help people to grow? Do we ourselves know how to grow? I have learned much by visiting many places where there were many seeking ones coming together. In the first year of their coming together, the situation among them was not clear, but after two or three years everything was exposed and brought to the surface. In all these meetings almost no one has any idea or knowledge of how to grow. We praise the Lord, however, that He has brought many of these people to the point that they realize they need something.

There are only two ways to build up a church, or a so-called church. One way is to organize; this is the organizing system. All the denominations, including the Roman Catholic Church, depend on the organizing system. As long as they have the best organizing regulations and a strong, proper character for organizing, this so-called church will flourish. It will be built up not by life but by organizing. This is the wrong way; it is the worldly, human way. The proper and spiritual way is to build up the church by life and the growth in life. This requires us to know how to sow Christ into people and know how to grow in Christ and how to help others to grow in Christ.

The real situation, however, is that many meetings in different places drop the organization. They do not like to have the organizing system, but after two or three years they become a vacuum. They have neither the organizing nor the adequate knowledge and understanding of life, so they become empty. They do not know how to grow in life or how to help others to grow in life. They do not have the way of life and the way of growth in life. This is the very reason for the weakness of so many local meetings.

First Peter 1:23 says that we have been "regenerated not of corruptible seed but of incorruptible, through the living and abiding word of God." Then in chapter two he says that as newborn babes we need to grow, and by this growth we become living stones to be built up as a spiritual house (vv. 2, 5). Therefore, in Peter's writings we again see life, growth, and building. Building comes from life and growth. We must have life, and we must have the growth in life. Then by the growth, with the growth, and in the growth we have transformation. We can be transformed only by growing; the more we grow, the more we are transformed. This transformation is for producing the materials good for the building.

The apostle Paul said, "I planted, Apollos watered, but God caused the growth." Do we know how to water? Do we know how to help people to grow? Some may say we need the gifts. In a sense, I admit this is true, but in what way do the gifts help? Have we seen the growth in those people who pay attention to the gifts? For the most part, I have not seen the growth among them. They exercise the gifts very much, but there is almost no growth in life. It is not a matter of exercising the gifts; it is a matter of growing in life. People always desire something miraculous. However, miracles are miracles, and the growth in life is the growth in life. These are absolutely two different categories. What we need is not the miraculous things but the growth of life.

In 1 Corinthians 3:9 Paul says, "You are God's cultivated land, God's building." We are not only planters and waterers but also builders. Do we know how to build, and do we know how to be built up? When we talk about gifts and tongues, people can understand, but they may not understand when we talk about growth in life and building. I was very much impressed with this during my recent visits to other places. I told myself that when I returned to Los Angeles I would once again stress one thing: that the eyes of the dear ones would be opened concerning planting, watering, and building, as Paul said, "I planted, Apollos watered....As a wise master builder I have laid a foundation, and another builds upon it. But let each man take heed how he builds upon it...gold, silver, precious stones" (vv. 6, 10, 12). The problem is, do we know how to be built up, and do we know how to build others up? Let us pray for this in these days. If we do not see the way to grow, to water others to help them to grow, to be built up, and to build up others, we have only doctrines. Chapters one and two of 1 Corinthians speak concerning Christ as our portion and everything to us, but if we do not know how to experience Christ to such an extent, if we do not know how to sow Christ, grow in life, be built up, and build up others, those chapters are only doctrines to us.

In my recent contacts with people, I spoke almost entirely on the line of life and building. After the meetings, however, it was very difficult to talk with them. So many people are just covered by the old concept, understanding, and mentality. It is hard to take away the covering and open them to the Word. It was by these difficult talks that I realized what the need is today and what the enemy's subtlety is to distract people from these matters. This was not only a realization in my understanding; in my spirit I had a certain insight about the situation. The distraction is very subtle, not only among us but even the more within us. There is something within us of the enemy distracting us from life, growth, and building.

CHRIST AS THE TREASURE
HIDDEN WITHIN THE EARTHEN VESSEL

There is nothing miraculous about life, growth, and building to attract us. Is there something attractive about a seed sown into the ground? After perhaps ten days a little shoot comes up and starts to grow. Next week it looks the same as this week, but after three months we can see something small growing. Is there anything attractive, miraculous, or powerful about this process? It is powerful, but not in an apparent way. It is something precious but hidden. If something is not hidden, it is not precious. All the artificial things are superficial; all real treasures are hidden. Only those who have spiritual discernment—those who know a certain brother in Christ not according to the flesh but according to the spirit, not according to outward appearance but according to the inward reality—can realize that with him there is something precious. The inward working of Christ in a brother is the hidden treasure.

In this matter there is no outward show. We, however, may like the outward show. We may like to see that all the ones in the church are like angels. Tell me, though, what have you actually seen? If you say that everyone is wonderful and better than the angels, you are not mentally sound. There is not such a thing on this earth. Someone else may say that they have seen nothing good; everyone is still just flesh. This is marvelous. A certain brother is still that certain brother. The earth is still here, but there is a treasure hidden within him. We are not angels. You may be a Southern Californian, and I am a Chinese. You may be "white earth," and I may be "black earth." However, you must realize that there is a measure of Christ within us. The treasure is hidden under the earth.

I treasure a brother not because he is that brother but because Christ is within him. This is the precious stone; the poor earthen vessel means nothing. Those who handle precious stones buy ones that for the most part look ugly outwardly. This is because they discern through the ugliness the precious stone that is within. If we take nice looking stones to these experts, they may not want them. We should not present ourselves to the "experts" in a nice looking way. The more we show ourselves to be nice, the more the experts will say there is nothing precious within; it is all a show. The experts can see through the show and realize something. The more ugly one is outwardly, the more precious he may be inwardly. This is the treasure hidden in the earthen vessel. We must know people today not according to the outward appearance, not according to the flesh, but according to the inward spiritual preciousness. This is something of Christ worked into us, and this is transformation.

This is a small sketch, a small hint, that we may see what we need today. We do not need an outward show in which everyone looks better than the angels. Instead, we need Christ sown into us, and we need to grow in Christ in a normal, ordinary way, with nothing that is miraculously attractive. We need to grow in Christ and be transformed with Him that we may truly have the fine flour that is good for bread to offer to God to satisfy His desire and to feed others, that they may be transformed to be good material for God's building. This is the proper way. If we know how to sow, grow, build, and be built up, then we can experience the very Christ revealed in the first two chapters of 1 Corinthians. The secret of experiencing Christ is in the third chapter: to have Christ planted into us, to grow in Him, and to be built up in Him. Pray for these things, that they may become real to us in these days.

CHAPTER SIXTEEN

THE WAY TO GROW

Scripture Reading: Eph. 4:15-16; 1 Tim. 1:14; John 21:15-17; 1 Cor. 16:22-23

Ephesians 4:15 and 16 say, "But holding to truth in love, we may grow up into Him in all things, who is the Head, Christ, out from whom all the Body, being joined together and being knit together through every joint of the rich supply and through the operation in the measure of each one part, causes the growth of the Body unto the building up of itself in love." In these two verses we clearly see growth and building together. One is the cause, and the other is the effect; there is growth, and then there is the building. We need to learn how to grow and how to help others to grow.

The intention in sowing a seed into the earth is that the seed will grow up and bring forth something through its growth. Therefore, we all must be very clear that God's intention is to put Christ as the seed of life into us in order to grow within us. This is very clear in the New Testament. However, when many of us Christians come to the Word of God, it is difficult for us to see this simple point. In my youth I listened to preachers, teachers, and pastors speak about Matthew 13 many times, but I was very puzzled by those parables. As a young Christian I tried my best to understand the whole Bible, and I spent all I had at that time to buy expositions. My intention was to buy sixty-six expositions, one for each book from Genesis to the end of the Bible, and I was able to acquire many of these. I thought they would help me know the Bible. The more I read the expositions, however, the more I was confused. It became more and more difficult to understand the Word. Matthew 13 contains seven parables. I spent much time to understand this chapter, and I read many articles, but not one of those articles speaks concerning the growth in life. People always try to give a certain kind of exposition and interpretation of those parables, but they neglect the simple thing.

We need to be very clear that the Lord Jesus came to sow Himself into the human heart. He is the sower and the seed. He sows Himself into our heart with the expectation that we would give Him the ground, the opportunity, to grow in us; then we grow by Him, with Him, and in Him. In addition, Matthew 13 shows us—as do several passages of the New Testament—that out of the growth comes transformation. In the parables in this chapter, there is first the sowing of the seed, then the growth of this life, and immediately there is transformation, which produces materials that are good for God's building. Therefore, three things are basically important: the birth of life, the growth of life, and the maturity of life, from which we have transformation. Then from this transformation we have the precious materials which are good for God's building.

The same thought is in 1 Corinthians 3. On the one hand, the apostle Paul says that we are co-workers with God doing the work of planting, so that God's cultivated land, God's harvest, may grow. Then on the other hand, we are builders to build God's house with the material produced from the growth of life (1 Cor. 3:6, 9, 12). This is also what is revealed in Matthew 13. However, we need the vision; otherwise, we can read this chapter time and again and still not see the birth of life, the growth of life, and transformation to produce the materials for the building of God.

The same thought is in 1 Peter 2. First we are the newborn babes who need to grow; then by this growth we are transformed into precious stones to be built up as a spiritual house (1 Pet. 2:2, 5). God's intention is to have a spiritual house, a building as His corporate expression. How can God accomplish this building? It is by sowing His Son Christ into us that He may grow in us and we may grow in Him and with Him in order to be transformed, changed in nature and in form, to be

THE WAY TO GROW

the precious materials for God's building. As Christians we
need to be very clear about this.

THE FIRST WAY TO GROW BEING TO LOVE THE LORD

There is no one passage that tells us all the things necessary for our growth. From the New Testament teaching and
revelation, the way to grow is comprised of four main items. If
we practice these, then not only are we in life but we are on
the way of growth, and we also will know how to help others
to grow. In Matthew 13 we are first told that after the seed is
sown, the enemy, signified by the birds in the air, comes to
snatch it away. Then even with the seed that is not snatched
away, the seed that remains, there is no growth because the
heart is superficial, shallow; there is the stony condition
beneath the ground. This means that apparently someone
receives the word, but in actuality there is no depth in his
heart. In the third kind of earth the seed begins to grow, but it
cannot grow up because it is choked by the cares of this age,
the anxiety of life, the deceitfulness of riches, and the matter
of living; that is, it is choked by the world.

If we spend time to study these cases, we can see that the
lack of growth is due to one thing: After a person is saved by
the divine seed sown into him, he may not love the Lord. If we
study our history and compare it with the New Testament,
we will find that the first step, the first main thing needed,
for a believer to grow is to love the Lord. If we do not have a
love for the Lord, we are superficial; our heart is either stony
or things other than the Lord Himself choke the seed in it. We
need a love for the Lord.

Faith comes first; then love must follow. Paul said that
"the grace of our Lord superabounded with faith and love in
Christ Jesus" (1 Tim. 1:14). Faith alone does not work. Having
faith without love is like walking on one foot. We can walk a
little bit on one foot, but we cannot walk all day like that; we
need two feet. Love must come to accompany faith. We should
read the whole Gospel of John. It tells us that the Lord Jesus
only demands that we first believe in Him and then love Him.
The last story in this Gospel is a story of love. After twenty
chapters of John there is chapter twenty-one, which contains

only one story. The Lord Jesus appeals to Peter, saying, "Simon, son of John, do you love Me?" (vv. 15-17).

I say again, if we do not have love for the Lord, our heart will be either full of stones or choked by many things. There is no other way besides love. If we want the Lord to grow within us, our heart has to be dug. With what can our heart be dug? Do not think it is by something that seems prevailing; rather, it is by one thing—love. In my whole Christian life I never saw one person whose heart was dealt with by the Lord before he loved the Lord. No one and nothing can take away the hidden stones in our heart. This requires a love toward the Lord. If we do not love the Lord, it is very hard for any of us not to be choked. The enemy is subtle and skillful. He is waiting to utilize everything to choke the seed in our heart. Do not think there are only one or two items that can choke the seed; everything can be utilized by the enemy. There is only one way to escape the choking of the enemy; that is to love the Lord.

If we simply pray, "Lord, be merciful to me. Grant me a love for You," our stony heart will be dealt with. It will be dug and made deep. There will be a digging within not by anything else, but by love. In order to grow, we must go to the Lord to pray definitely and purposely that He will grant us a love for Him. I know one person who prayed this one thing for a long time, day by day, that is, that the Lord would grant him this love. I believe and I can testify that if we pray in this way, one day the Lord will reveal this love to us. This is not a matter of doctrine; it is a matter of inspiration. We can talk about the love of the Lord, but we still may not truly have the sense, the consciousness, of it. One day, however, when the Holy Spirit reveals the love of Christ to us, we will have the tender consciousness, the sense, of the love of the Lord. Then this love will do much work to get rid of all the stones within us. It is this love that is so capable of delivering us from all the choking elements. The more we try, exercise, and endeavor by ourselves to overcome all the things that choke, the more we will be defeated. The only thing that can deliver us from any kind of choking is love. Therefore, we must learn to pray that the Lord would grant us such a love.

This is absolutely different from any religion. Not one leader of a religion demanded that his followers love him. Only the Lord Jesus demands this. He asks us to believe in Him and to love Him. We must have faith in Him, and we must have love toward Him. It may be good that we pray for a few weeks, even when we come together for the prayer meeting: "Lord, show us this love, and grant us such a love." We must learn to love the Lord. Then we will see that we are starting to grow. When we start to love the Lord, we start to grow. There is no other way. The only way for Christians to begin growing is by firstly knowing how to love the Lord.

First Corinthians speaks much about growth. If we read the whole book, we will realize that it is a book of growth. Eventually at the end it says, "If anyone does not love the Lord, let him be accursed! The Lord comes!" (16:22). Then the next verse says, "The grace of the Lord Jesus be with you" (v. 23). If the grace of the Lord is with us, then we will surely love the Lord. Together these two verses mean that the grace of the Lord is with us that we may love Him. There is no other way to grow.

A real revival is a revival full of the Lord's love. Therefore, we ourselves must experience it. Then when we contact others, when we help others, we will know where to start. If we have never learned the lesson to experience the love, not only of the Lord but for and toward the Lord, it is very hard to grow, and we simply do not know how to help others to grow. If we do learn the lesson and we have this experience, then when we contact people, we will know where they are, and we will have an influence on them. We will realize who is in the light of such a love, and those whom we contact will be influenced to love the Lord. This is the beginning of growth. We cannot merely go to the brothers and say, "Oh, we have to grow." To speak in this way is like speaking to the wall, "Wall, you have to grow." We can talk in this way day and night, year after year, with no effect.

We need to pray that the Lord would touch the hearts of many saints. Among us we need this love. The seven epistles in Revelation 2 and 3, dealing with the fall of the church, show us that the source, the origin, of the fall of the church is the loss of the first love (2:4). When the love toward the Lord is lost, regardless of what we do for Him, the life eventually is gone. To receive life requires believing, having faith, but to have the growth in life requires love. Faith is for life, while love is for the growth of life. If we do not have love, it is hard for us to grow. Therefore, we ourselves must have this experience; then we will know how to help others.

If we do love the Lord, we will spontaneously offer ourselves to Him. When we love the Lord, there is no need for others to tell us that we have to consecrate ourselves. Of the sixty-six books of the Bible, there is only one that deals entirely with the matter of growth, that is, the Song of Songs. This book is a book of growth. Brother Watchman Nee's study of the Song of Songs shows us all the steps for growth. The Song of Songs tells us that after a person is saved, she realizes the Lord's love; this is the start. Then at the end of the book we can see maturity and building up. This shows us that growth starts with love, and when we have love, we spontaneously offer ourselves to the Lord. Therefore, I will not tell you that you have to consecrate yourselves, because consecration is included in our love for the Lord. If we do not have love, regardless of how much we consecrate ourselves, we still have not truly consecrated ourselves. The real consecration comes from love and goes with love. If we do not have such a love, our consecration is not real. This is the first main way to grow.

CONFESSION AND CLEARANCE

The second main item we must have is confession, or clearance. After we begin to love the Lord, we must have a clear dealing with ourselves in order to have the real growth in life. We must have a clearance and make a thorough confession before the Lord. In other words, we must deal with our conscience. Then we will have a pure, good conscience without accusation, a conscience void of offense and so much at peace. We have seen how important the conscience is regarding spiritual things. We need a pure conscience, and one who has a pure conscience is one who has thoroughly confessed all the sinful things, dirtiness, failures, and trespasses. We must go to the Lord to have such a dealing. Sometimes we need three days for this. I do not believe you can finish your confession within only one or two hours. If we mean business with the Lord, we will need a longer time to have a thorough dealing. This is not something legal; it is a principle.

Why are many Christians not spiritually healthy? It is simply because their conscience is not purged. Within their conscience are many accusations and offenses. Some even realize this, but they are not willing to make a confession, so to one degree or another they are frustrated. This brings us back to the first point above: If we are not willing to confess, it is because we do not love the Lord. The more we love the Lord, the more we sense our failures, shortcomings, weaknesses, and wrongdoings. Perhaps at this time you do not feel that you are wrong in anything, but when you start to love the Lord, you will realize how wrong you are in many things, with people and with the Lord. You will sense the need to confess to the Lord.

All these matters cannot remain as mere doctrine. I have no intention to give you more doctrine. Rather, if we do not put all these things into practice, they mean nothing. If we put them into practice, we will see that they truly help us. We need to pray that the Lord would grant us a love for Him. Then we must be faithful to make a thorough dealing with the Lord. Do not argue with this, and do not care for mere theology.

More than twenty years ago, when I was in northern China, I learned all these lessons from the Lord and with the Lord; this is how I now know them. At that time some people opposed this very much. They said, "There is no need for us to deal with our conscience, because the blood is good enough. The blood covers and cleanses us." There is no need to argue with people in the way of doctrine and theology. The best way to defeat the opposing ones is to touch their conscience. If we touch their conscience, there is no need to argue; rather, help them to check their experience. Do not take these matters in the way of doctrine. If you come to argue with me, I cannot answer you in a doctrinal way. I know the problem with people, especially with those who study theology, but if you would put these things into practice, you will see they are right. I am not here taking care of doctrine; I am here trying to help people to have the proper practice.

KNOWING AND EXERCISING THE SPIRIT

After loving the Lord and having a thorough confession, we right away have to know the spirit. When we say *spirit* in this way, we mean our human spirit, not the Holy Spirit. This is a difficult matter among Christians today. It is not so hard, however, with new believers. A certain older brother had been a Christian for many years. He studied at Bible institutes and was a preacher for years, preaching, teaching, reading, and listening. After I delivered some messages about the exercise of the spirit, this brother came to me and said, "Brother Lee, what do you mean by the exercise of the spirit? Do you mean to have a whole heart?" I found out that it is difficult to speak concerning the spirit to people with old concepts.

However, I can assure you that if we do not know how to discern our spirit from our soul, we may know the entire Bible in a doctrinal way, but we will not have an inch of the growth in life. We may also experience many so-called spiritual things, but we still will not have the growth. Spiritual growth is a matter absolutely in the spirit. This is why the phrase *in the spirit,* or *in spirit,* is so important and is mentioned so often in the New Testament.

We ourselves must learn how to discern the spirit and exercise the spirit. Then we will know how to help others. I believe that we all know something about the discernment of the spirit, but we still do not know much. In the past few days a brother and his wife stayed in my home, and we had many talks. If you would ask me what I learned from all these talks, I would have to testify that I learned only one thing: I did not exercise my spirit enough. I exercised some, but not adequately; that was my failure.

We may illustrate how we do not exercise our spirit adequately in the following way. I may come to two brothers and say, "Brothers, do you know Matthew 13? Tell me a little about it." This will put them on the test, because it will be very easy for them to be tempted not to exercise their spirit when they answer. They may explain at length, saying, "We have heard a message that tells us that the parables in Matthew 13 are composed of six plus one, and also four plus three. The first four are of one kind, and the last three are of another kind." They may speak for two or three hours, but their talk may be miserable. If we learn the lesson adequately, then when someone asks a question, we will not care for the question. Rather, we will care for contacting the Lord. While we are being asked, we will right away contact the Lord, saying, "Lord, what will you have me to say?" We will not exercise our mind to consider six plus one or four plus three. Instead, we will see something from our spirit and from the Holy Spirit.

It is easy to be tempted to talk about many things. After my many talks with the brother in my home, I had to ask for the Lord's forgiveness. I talked about many right things, but I did not exercise my spirit adequately. The only way to minister life to others is to exercise our spirit. If we are not in the spirit, regardless of how much we speak, we can help people only in their mentality; we can never minister life to them. This is a real lesson. I have been practicing this for more than thirty years, but concerning this matter I may not have graduated from "high school." To say, "Exercise the spirit!" is easy, but the entire, proper Christian life depends on this one matter.

If we do not have a love for the Lord, we cannot exercise our spirit. Likewise, if we constantly have something accusing us in our conscience, we are finished with the exercise of the spirit. To exercise the spirit requires a love for the Lord and a pure conscience. After we have love and a pure conscience, we must learn the lesson of always exercising our spirit. To be soulish is easier than to be sinful. It is not easy for you to induce me to be sinful, but it may be very easy to induce me to be soulish. For many seeking Christians it is not easy to be sinful—it is not easy, for example, to tell a lie—but it is very easy to be soulish, to say things in the soul, to do things in the soul, to contact people in the soul, and to deal with things in the soul. If we do not exercise the spirit, we are merely in the soul.

If we are about to argue with someone and we say to ourselves, "I must try not to argue with people," that will not work. The more we try not to argue, the more we will argue. Everyone who makes up his mind not to argue, argues all the more. We should forget about arguing and learn to always exercise our spirit. When we exercise our spirit, all the arguments are gone. The only way for us to be delivered from arguing, or from anything in the soul, is to forget about the soul, forget about all things related to the soul, and learn to exercise the spirit. Then when we meet a brother, we will not need to tell ourselves not to argue; we will know only to exercise our spirit to contact the Lord. Then we will have the growth.

I can assure you that regardless of how many messages we have heard, how many books we have read, and how many times we have read the whole Bible, if we do not start to exercise our spirit, we will not have real growth. We will have only the growth of knowledge in our mentality. We may know more Bible teachings and more of Christianity, and we may have a certain kind of increase and growth, but we do not have the growth in life until we know how to exercise our spirit.

To know the spirit in this way is to be strengthened into the inner man. Ephesians 3:16 says, "That He would grant you, according to the riches of His glory, to be strengthened with power through His Spirit into the inner man." The inner man, that is, the spirit, needs to be strengthened. We all have to learn to exercise the spirit. All weaknesses, problems, confusions, and disturbances come from the soul. There is no need to deal with all these things. Simply forget about the soul and learn to exercise the spirit. Then all the problems will be resolved. Try this, and put it into practice; then you will see that this is exactly true. We are short of this today. I have been in Los Angeles, ministering something of the spirit at least one or two hundred times, but I do not have the confidence that many of us practice this daily. If we practice this, there will be the real growth.

ALWAYS STAYING IN CONTACT WITH THE LORD

We also must always stay in contact with the Lord. Any time we are not in contact with the Lord, we are in degradation, not in growth.

BEING SIMPLE TO HAVE THE GROWTH IN LIFE

What I told people many years ago about the way to grow was not this simple. Even ten years ago what I said was not very simple. Today, however, if you ask me how to grow, I will tell you something simple but very practical. The simpler something is, the more practical it is. But even though it is simple, if we do not practice it, it will not work. From my own learning and experiences, I have come to realize that the simplest way for Christians to grow is the above four matters: love the Lord, deal with Him thoroughly, learn to exercise the spirit, and keep in contact with Him. If we do these things, we will see the growth. Then because we are in the growth of life, we will know the right way to read the Word, the right and simple way to listen to messages, and the right and proper way to get help and profit from reading a book. We will not care for anything but one matter: the growth of life in the spirit.

The more we grow in the spirit with life, the simpler we become. Suppose there is a brother who does not grow. He meets, listens, learns, reads, and studies, but without growth. Such a brother will become the most troublesome one. When we grow in life, we are so simple. There is a simplicity with all the matters related to life.

In these recent days, through many contacts in my visits, I learned that there is only one way to have the church life, which is by the growth in life. We brothers and sisters must pay our full attention to the growth of life. Certain other things are helpful, even helpful for the growth, but they are not the growth itself. We must be simple, not considering that we know many things. I would beg you not to consider that you know anything. Forget about the old knowledge. As Christians we had all those old things for years, but we had no growth. We are too foolish if we would still keep the old things. However, it is hard to drop the old things to become simple.

Some may ask what I mean by being simple. We may illustrate it in this way. When we come to hear a message, we may come to listen by exercising our spirit and receiving the nourishment from it. This means that we are simple. However, because we have been Christians for many years, when we hear one sentence or one point, we may have more than ten points to consider in our mind. We may say, "This is right, but..." or "This is good, yet...." If we do this, it means we are old. If we learn how not to say "but" or "yet," we are blessed. I am the same as you are, so I also had to learn this. This is the fallen human nature, but we may not realize that it is fallen.

The more we grow, the more we become simple, and we just receive the nourishment for life. Then we will grow, and we will be those who always spontaneously minister life to others. We will have only one thing to share with others, that is, life. Some brothers may say that we also need fellowship, because the fellowship gives us help. However, many times what we have is not fellowship that helps but something else that damages.

We Christians need to be as children. We should not be childish, but we have to be childlike, simple like little children. We need to forget about the old things, old knowledge, and old learning. Regardless of how much we know, we still may not have a love for the Lord. We need such a love. We also need to have a thorough dealing with the Lord and to be thoroughly dealt with by Him. Then we need to know how to exercise our spirit to contact the Lord, live by Him, live in Him, and live with Him. We should not know anything else.

In my earlier ministry and service, whenever anyone came to me, I always had much to say. I would talk about Matthew, John, Romans, Corinthians, Timothy, Peter, and Revelation, and then I would go back around to Genesis. Today, however, many brothers do not like to talk with me because I seem not to know anything. They know that there is no need to come to me; if they come to me, I will have only one answer: "Learn to exercise your spirit." I have been in this line of "business" for more than thirty years. I know that everything else wastes our own and others' time. Only one thing avails: learn to love the Lord, deal with Him thoroughly, exercise your spirit, and contact Him. Then you will grow. This solves all the problems. There is no other answer as prevailing as this. This is the most efficient course.

The church here needs this. We have to pray for this. Then we will be brought into the reality of growth. It is not a matter of knowledge, not a matter of learning the messages; it is a matter of the real growth in life. There is no other way. In our prayer meeting we should pray for this. We should pray, "Lord, cause us to love You. Reveal Your love to us, and grant us an inner love for You." This is wonderful. I know what I am speaking; when the Lord reveals His love to us, we can choose no other way but to love Him. It is by this love that the ties with the worldly things are cut. Worldly ties can be cut only by the tie of love. Nothing else is prevailing to cut the ties. May the whole church be granted to love the Lord.

Moreover, we must know how to be dealt with by Him, to have a pure conscience not only cleansed and purged by the blood but also dealt with by the Holy Spirit. Then we will have a pure, transparent conscience, and we will be strong in exercising the spirit and contacting the Lord. Then, I say again, we will see the growth, and many things in the church will change. In actuality, the things will be the same, but our eyes will be changed. We will have another kind of sight, an insight and foresight. We will see things thoroughly and truly, because we will have the growth of life. In addition, all our problems with others will be spontaneously solved by this growth of life, and we will be built with others. We need the growth, which comes from the aforementioned four items.

If we take this message as a mere doctrine, it will mean nothing; it will be no message at all. This message is just like a map to give directions. If we put these things into practice, we will be led into boundless riches, a boundless realm of spiritual riches. Then we will be built up. We will hold to truth, to reality, in love that we may grow up into Him in all things. We as members will receive something from the Head to share with others. Something of the Head will be transmitted through us into others. Then the Body will be built up.

This is the only way for the building up of the Body life. In other words, the genuine church life depends on this growth. There is no other way to realize this growth except by loving the Lord, dealing with and being dealt with by Him, and learning to exercise. That is why in many places I not only told the saints, I even begged them, "Do not try to learn doctrine. Rather, pray that the Lord will grant you the real growth. Learn to be simple. Simply love Him, deal with Him, be dealt with by Him, and exercise your spirit to contact Him."

CHAPTER SEVENTEEN

THE PROPER SPEECH
FOR THE BUILDING UP OF THE CHURCH

Scripture Reading: Col. 4:6; Matt. 12:36; James 3:6, 8

The messages in this book should be considered as lessons of a training. We have a training in addition to the church meetings because in the past we learned that most believers who attend a church meeting only listen to the message and do not practice it. We should take the lessons presented here, put them into practice, and have further study. Then we will gain the real profit.

In the previous chapter we considered the way to grow in a simple but practical way. First, we must love the Lord. In order to grow in the Lord, we can never neglect our love toward the Lord. If there is no love, there is no growth in life. Second, we must make a thorough confession. Along with our real love toward the Lord, our conscience needs to be exercised. We have to confess all our failures, weaknesses, and trespasses to make a thorough clearance of the past before the Lord. Third, we need to exercise our spirit, and fourth, we need to always contact the Lord.

THE PRACTICAL NEED FOR BUILDING

If we read the New Testament carefully, we can see that the real growth in life eventually brings us to the point that we are built together with others. Growth in life is for building. As we have pointed out concerning the spiritual life, we first have birth, then growth, and finally maturity. Maturity in life is practically equivalent to building. If we are not built together with others as a corporate Body, we will never arrive at the maturity of life; we will be more or less childish in certain aspects. Regardless of how much we may consider ourselves to be mature, we will not actually be mature, because real maturity equals building. Whether or not we are mature depends on one thing—the building.

In the Gospels the Lord Jesus Himself clearly mentioned building (Matt. 16:18). In the Epistles, the apostle Paul was very strong concerning the building. However, I am sorry to say that many Christians today study the book of Ephesians, and many teachers use the things in Ephesians, but it is hard to find one that speaks about the building in this book. The building is the ultimate point of Ephesians.

Without the building, how can we have the church life? How can we have the church in a practical way, and where is the church? We may have many building materials, but this does not mean that we have the building. Many people argue that as long as we are Christians, we are the church. However, we cannot say that as long as there are materials, there is a house. We may have only a pile of materials, but that is not the building. We still have to deal with the materials in order to build them together. The meeting hall we are in has many materials, but the materials are built up, not piled up. In the same way, the church is not a "lumber yard"; it is a building.

A large group of Christians may only be the piled up materials. This is why I have stressed many times that to meet together is one thing, but to have the building is another. We may meet year after year and still be a meeting, not a building. Strictly speaking, if we are not a building, we are not a church in practice; we are only a church in name with meetings. We do not have the reality of the church, because the reality of the church is the building. We cannot say that since we have many pieces of good, wonderful, beautiful materials, we have a building, a house. No, the house is something that is built up with the materials.

At this time we are speaking much about the church life. I have to testify to you in fellowship that if it were not for the church life, there would be no need for us to meet together. If it were not for the church, I would say that you should go to whichever so-called Christian "body" you think is good. There

is no need for us to come together to meet if we do not intend
to have the church life. Why are we coming together here?
Why among so many so-called Christian churches, groups,
and meetings today, do we meet in this way? If it is not for
the purpose of having the church life, there is no reason for us
to have this kind of meeting. We had better go back to those
so-called churches. However, we realize that the present testimony of the Lord is the recovery of the church life. The church
life is the only goal, the only reason, for us to meet together.

We further need to realize that if we are not built up, we
cannot have the church life; we will have the church in term
only, not in practice. The church life in practice depends on
the building, and the building depends on the growth. I say
again, therefore, that if there is no growth, there is no possibility for the building up of the church. We need to grow.

SPEECH WITH GRACE, SEASONED WITH SALT

Colossians is a sister book to Ephesians. The book of Ephesians deals with the Body, while Colossians deals with the
Head. Since it deals with the Head, though, it has something
to do with the Body, because the Head is always related to the
Body and is for the Body. Therefore, it is hard to not see
the Body in Colossians, a book on the Head. One verse in this
book pertains both to the Head and the Body. It seems that
it is only a small verse, but it is very practical concerning the
church life. Many of us may not have paid attention to this
small verse. Colossians 4:6 says, "Let your speech be always
with grace, seasoned with salt, that you may know how you
ought to answer each one." This verse mentions grace. What
is grace? What does it mean that our word, speech, talk, or
conversation should be seasoned? And what kind of salt is
this? Moreover, why did the apostle Paul put this verse in this
book? Some may say that it is because Colossians reveals
Christ as the Head, and a person's speech comes from his
head. However, the Lord Jesus told us that speech comes from
the heart. Matthew 12:34 says, "For out of the abundance of
the heart the mouth speaks." Why, then, did the apostle put
such a verse in a book that deals with the Head, including
the Body?

More than thirty years ago, in 1933 or 1934, I spent much time to study this verse, because three words bothered me: *grace, seasoned,* and *salt.* At that time I did not get the answer, even though I looked into many books to get the definitions of these words. After a long time, I learned from experience to know the meaning of these words, and in these recent days I have been helped by the Lord to know why verse 6 is in Colossians 4. The reason is that what is mentioned in this verse has much to do with the church life. The building up of the church depends greatly on the matter of speech, conversation, or speaking.

By the Lord's mercy, we are here constantly trying our best to build up the church. The enemy of God, however, hates this. He would do everything he can to frustrate, even to damage, the building. I must point out that we are all too careless in the matter of speech, or conversation. I may come to you, or you may come to me, and we may talk for two hours, but many times the enemy utilizes our talk not to build up the church but to tear it down. I have always noticed in my experience, and I am still noticing, that Satan very much uses the careless talk of the dear brothers and sisters to tear down the building. It seems that the builders spend much time and energy to lay one stone upon another, but the enemy uses the careless talk of certain ones to tear it down again. The builders spend much time to set a brother in the right place, but due alone to the fact that others are so careless in talking, this brother is torn down. This is why in the last chapter of Colossians, the apostle Paul points out this one matter: that our conversation, talk, speech, and words must be always with grace, seasoned with salt.

According to the entire New Testament, grace is Christ gained by us and enjoyed by us. We enjoy Christ as our life, power, wisdom, and everything we need. Christ is the real grace to us. This means that to have our speech always with grace is to have our speech always with Christ. We must have Christ in our words, talk, speech, and conversation.

KNOWING A PERSON'S SPIRIT BY HIS SPEECH

This is a real check to prove where we are and what we

are. Nothing can expose us so much as our speech. The most
clever person is one who never speaks much. A wise man
never speaks, but a foolish man is always talkative. The more
we talk, the more we prove we are foolish, because we expose
ourselves more and sell ourselves cheaply. On the night that
the Lord Jesus was betrayed, Peter was put on the spot. A
servant girl came to him and said, "You also were with Jesus
the Galilean," but Peter denied it before all, saying, "I do not
know what you are talking about!" A third time, some came
to him and said, "Surely you also are one of them, for your
speech also makes it clear that you are" (Matt. 26:69-70, 73).
Peter's speech made it clear what he was. A Texan's speech
also makes it clear what he is, because he says "y'all" with a
Texan accent and tone. In a similar way, if you do not speak
one word, I do not know how much you have experienced and
gained Christ and what the measure of the stature of Christ
is within you, but if you speak for only five minutes, I will
know.

One who learns not to talk much seems to be wise, because
he stays hidden and does not expose himself. Watchman Nee
once told me that the best way to know a person's spirit is to
ask him questions and give him the chance to say something.
If we are unwise, we will do all the talking and keep the other
person from talking. This just makes him "wise." If we want
to know him, however, we should give him a chance to speak.
The more he speaks, the more he exposes himself, and the
more we know where he is in the spirit. We may illustrate
this with a diagram of a person with a head, heart, and spirit,
each part being progressively deeper within him. The first
two minutes he talks, he talks only from his head. After ten
minutes, though, he gets down to his heart, but after half an
hour, what he speaks is from his spirit. The more we talk, the
more we expose what we are in our spirit.

All the talk from our head is just superficial and polite,
not genuine. Someone may say, "How are you? Fine, thank
you. Do you know this brother? He's a good brother." If we ask
this person about the brother, though, such as when he met
him and how he got to know him, he will gradually get down
to his heart, and he will speak something more real about the

brother he knows. Then after half an hour, he will pour out what is in his spirit about the brother. At that point we will know what is in his spirit. We may find out, for example, that there is a big problem between him and the brother. According to only the head and the mouth, there is no problem between them, but when we give him the chance to keep talking, he will utter something from his spirit. That is not polite speech; it is genuine speech.

SEASONED BY THE KILLING ELEMENT OF THE CROSS

We must learn to have our speech, word, and conversation with others full of Christ. In addition, our speech must be seasoned with salt. The sisters know how to season the things they cook; most foods are prepared with seasoning. To season is to temper something. To season our speech properly is always to control or check it. As a member of the church, as one who is learning the lesson of being built up, we must have our speech and conversation always tempered, seasoned, controlled, and checked in whatever we say. Our speech should not be "cooked" without being "seasoned."

The meaning of salt is very deep. To understand this requires our experience and the proper, adequate knowledge of the Bible. The meal offering of the Old Testament was made of fine flour with three things: oil, frankincense, and salt. The meal offering needed to be seasoned with salt, but it was never to have honey. In typology, oil signifies the Holy Spirit, frankincense signifies the sweet resurrection life of Christ, and salt typifies the death, the killing element, of the cross. Salt does not give a sweet taste; rather, it kills germs. By our experience, we know that all our speech and conversation must be salted by the killing element of the cross. They must be seasoned by the cross, that is, checked and controlled by the cross. To have our words seasoned with salt is to have them always checked by the cross.

Checking the Motive of Our Speech

From my experience I have learned that there are three all-inclusive ways to apply the cross to our speech. First, whenever we are about to say something, we first must check our motive. Our motive must be pure and even purified. If we would check our motive in speaking, we will see where we are; then we will see the need of the cross. Immediately this application of the cross will kill the intention and motivation behind our talk. Then we may drop what we were going to speak because we realize that our motive was not pure; it needs to be purified. This purification will kill our intention to speak, and we will have nothing to say.

I learned the lesson to deal with my mouth in 1933 and 1934. I found out that it is very hard to be right and proper in our talking. If we would learn to be careful in this matter, we will see that the best way is to keep our mouth shut. At that time I found that after I spoke, I always had to confess that I was wrong. Almost every time I wrote a letter, I had to write it at least two or three times. Sometimes after writing it, I would realize that a certain sentence did not have a pure motive behind it. The motive may have been to glorify myself, condemn others, or expose their weaknesses. Oh, the motive! If we would check our motive and reconsider our writing, we will have to throw it into the wastebasket. We will realize that our motives are not pure.

The Lord Jesus said, "And I say to you that every idle word which men shall speak, they will render an account concerning it in the day of judgment" (Matt. 12:36). An idle word is a word that is not necessary. All such idle words which we speak will have to be dealt with in the day of judgment. I found out that it is not easy to keep silent, and it is even harder not to speak anything wrongly. If we take this word and put it into practice, we will see our problem; we will see our motive. Then if we all learn the lesson, it will be easy to have the building up of the church.

However, if we do not learn the lesson but rather speak carelessly, then day by day by our foolish talk we will unconsciously tear down the church, not build it up. Please allow me to say that even though you have come here to carry out the building up of the church, you do not know how much you have already torn it down by your foolish talk. I have seen this for the past thirty years in many places, and I have seen the same thing happen here. This is why my burden is to point this out to you in the way of training. Some may say that their talk is fellowship, but in actuality it is careless talk. Fellowship is right and necessary, but we are too careless in our talk. To say *careless* is conservative; strictly speaking, if we would check our talk, we will see that we are not only careless but wrong and impure in motive. Our motive needs to be purified.

We are sons of light, so we must stay in the light to check the motive of our speech. Then we will see that it is not a matter of having something right or wrong to speak. What we speak may be one hundred percent right, but our motive may be wrong. This means that our speech has not been seasoned with salt, the killing of the cross. It is full of damaging germs. James 3:8 says that the tongue is full of "deadly poison." According to the Greek, this phrase means a "death-bringing poison." Because our speech is not pure in motive, it sometimes has a poison that brings death into the church life. Therefore, we must check our speech and conversation for its motive: What is our motive in talking in this way; what is our motive in telling people certain things? We should not check ourselves according to the things we say. To check according to the things themselves gives us an excuse and a pretense. This will not help us; it will damage us. Rather, we must check our speech by our motive.

Checking the Source of Our Speech

In order to apply the cross, we must also know the source of our speech. Is the Lord in our spirit the source of our talk? Are we speaking from the Lord as the source through our spirit, or are we speaking something out of ourselves, out of the flesh or the self? We may speak something very good in a right way, but the source of our speaking may be wrong. The motive is one thing, but we also have to check the source. Our motive may be very pure; there may be nothing wrong with our motive, but what about the source? Are we speaking out of ourselves, or are we speaking something from the Lord in our spirit?

In these messages we have been fellowshipping about loving the Lord, seeking the Lord, and practicing the church life. These are the real lessons for us to learn. Before giving this message, I was very much with the Lord. Apparently I was just doing a few things, such as reading and answering letters and studying the Word. The Lord can testify, however, that I was very much with Him concerning this message. I do not want to be here indoctrinating you with more doctrine. I do not believe this is my responsibility. Rather, I feel the responsibility to have some real fellowship with you. I do not want to waste your time week after week and evening after evening, spending almost three hours in a meeting. I want you to get something real. This may not be a good, formal message, but if you do mean business to seek the Lord and practice the church life, then this is a practical lesson with many practical points. We need to put these things into practice to learn the lessons. Even when we talk with our wife, husband, parents, children, and relatives, we must check our motive and ask if we are speaking something from the Lord's Spirit or merely from ourselves.

Checking Our Position in Our Speech

We also have to check our position. Are we in a proper position, appointed and ordained by God to speak a word, or are we speaking out of our own position? Many times we are out of our position. If I stay in a brother's home, I may see something wrong with his son, but I must realize that I have no position to say anything; I am a guest and not the father. In my own home I have the full position to say something to my children, because I have the position of the father, but in someone else's home I do not have the position.

God has His sovereign position. In addition, a man has the man's position, and a woman has the woman's position. A father has the father's position, and the children have the children's position. Moreover, a wife has the wife's position, and a husband has the husband's position. The New Testament clearly indicates that we have to learn our position. Consider a building; every piece in it has a position. One piece of wood has a position in one place, and another piece of wood has a position in another place. The window has a position, and the door has a position. In the building of God, do we realize that we have our positions? You have your position, and I have mine. Therefore, I have to speak in my position, and you have to speak in yours. We all must learn our limit, and we must be limited by our position. At times I may not be in a position to say anything.

Whenever we are going to say anything, we have to check our position: Where are we? What is our position? On what ground are we speaking? Do we have the ground to say something? Are we in the right position? I say again, I am not giving you a mere lecture. My burden is to fellowship with you to learn the practical lessons in the house of God.

Do not say to me, "Brother Lee, you are from the Far East. You speak about keeping your position because that is the way of the Chinese." Forget about this. Even in a so-called American home there is still a certain order. Can a son chastise a father? Would we like to see a son over the father? I have stayed in American homes quite often in the past two and a half years, and I never saw a son be over the father. I appreciate the good order in American homes; in this respect they are no different from the Chinese homes.

I have been in many countries. In 1938 alone I traveled to a number of countries. I never found a country with as good an order as the United States. It is a democratic nation, but it has the best order in the entire world. Everyone keeps the order; if someone does not, he loses his benefit in this country. The more one keeps the order here, the more he is profited, because this is a country of law, and a country of law is a country of order. America is so strong because it has the best order. This means that all the people here keep their position. I do things in my position. I cannot say certain things, because I am not the mayor of this city. Neither am I a police officer, so I do not have the position to criticize the police. America is a democracy, but all the people in a democracy do not have the same position. For people to have the same position is not a real democracy; rather, it is a mess.

In a similar way, we must keep the order and keep our position in order to have a strong church life. Do not be offended by this, and do not interpret it in a wrong way. We simply have to realize that in order to have a proper church life and be built up together, each one of us must learn to keep his position. We are out of position mostly by our speaking. We often speak out of our position. We may not have the position, yet we speak as if we did. This creates many problems, and it causes damage.

Even in our home and family life, we have to check our speaking by the above three things: the motive, the source, and the position. I am happy to hear that many young ones among us will soon be married. Some may ask me to give a word at their wedding. I will say the same thing to all of them: "Learn to speak in a proper way at home. Learn always to speak by checking your motive, the source, and your position. As a husband, you must speak things in the position of the husband, and as a wife, you must speak things in the position of the wife. Keep your position, check your source, and check your motive." If a couple does this, I can "sign a policy" to guarantee that there will be no problems. However, if they do not learn this one lesson, they will have many troubles after only three months. Learn to talk with your dear wife in a proper way. Then you will save yourself, save your wife, and save your relatives. This is a lesson not only for the church life. If we learn this lesson in the church, it will be a great help for us on any occasion.

LEARNING THE LESSON OF SPEECH
FOR THE PROPER CHURCH LIFE

We may now return to Colossians 4:6. Why did the apostle put this verse in such a book? It is because this book deals with the Head, including the Body. We are members of the Body. In order to realize the proper church life, we have to learn the lesson of speech. There is no need to speak of a larger number of brothers and sisters; even among one hundred fifty or two hundred, consider what will happen if we do not learn the lesson of how to practice what is taught in Colossians 4:6. The more we come together, the more problems we will have. If this is the case, it is better for the Lord to make us dumb. We all have to learn the lesson to have our speech, our talk, and our conversation full of grace, full of Christ, and to have the words we speak seasoned, checked, by the cross concerning the motive, the source, and the position. May the Lord be merciful to us. If we are all willing to take this lesson, I assure you that after a short time our situation will be uplifted almost to the third heaven. Almost all the germs among us will be killed.

However, at this time the germs are spreading by our careless talk, by our speech that is not according to the lesson we should learn. We are fallen human beings. According to James 3, the hardest thing to bridle is the little tongue. The tongue is hard to control, and it is dangerous, setting on fire the course of life. Our human life, our self, is the match, and this match is set on fire by the tongue as an evil fire from Gehenna (v. 6). Therefore, in the church life, for the building of the Body, we all have to learn the lesson to deal with our speech. If we all learn this lesson, we will see that among us there is only the building up and not the tearing down. Otherwise, we may build up twelve feet one day, and tear down fourteen feet the next day. Simply by our talking we will tear down more than we build up. I believe that this is why the apostle Paul put verse 6 in Colossians 4. In order to have the proper church life, we have to learn this lesson.

LEARNING THIS LESSON BEING NECESSARY FOR GROWTH AND BUILDING

How much we can and will learn this lesson depends on how much we are willing to grow. The more we grow in the Lord, the more we will be careful in our talk. We can know whether or not a brother has truly grown by checking the way he talks. To grow in life does not mean to have more knowledge in our understanding. To grow in life means to be dealt with, controlled, and checked in many matters. According to the lessons I have learned, the first thing we must be checked in is our speech. If we are truly willing to grow, the first thing the Lord must check is our talking, particularly our motive, the source, and our position. Whether or not it is right to say something depends on these three things. If we cannot get through these three points, we should forget about saying anything. We must be pure in motive, right in source, and proper in position; then we can say something. If we cannot get through one of the points, though, we must be checked. We have to "stop the car" and not run ahead.

We all must learn the lesson. Then we will have the real growth. The building depends on growth, and growth is revealed by the way of our conversation. By their way of speaking, many brothers and sisters expose that they are childish, even babes. They prove nothing except that they have not grown any. I simply give you this word, and I would ask you to put it into practice. Even after one day you will see where you are. "Let your speech be always with grace, seasoned with salt, that you may know how you ought to answer each one." May the word we speak always be full of Christ, checked, controlled, and killed by the cross. We must learn this lesson; then we will see the growth, and we will realize the real building among us.

The more we mature, the more we will be careful in our speaking. There is no doubt about this. Even with the worldly people, the more they learn the lesson, the more careful they are in their speech. However, we are not learning the worldly lesson. We are learning the lesson for the building up of the church, the Body. We should always check whether it is profitable for the building of the church that we speak something in a certain way. I am afraid that although we are all here for the church life, we are too careless in speaking. This contradicts our purpose, because much careless talk has done much damage to the church life. Therefore, we all have to learn this lesson that we may grow, so that the real building up of the church might be realized.

THE PRACTICE NEEDED
FOR THE BUILDING UP OF THE CHURCH

Scripture Reading: Eph. 3:16-19; 2 Tim. 2:22

Ephesians 3:16 to 19a says, "That He would grant you, according to the riches of His glory, to be strengthened with power through His Spirit into the inner man, that Christ may make His home in your hearts through faith, that you, being rooted and grounded in love, may be full of strength to apprehend with all the saints what the breadth and length and height and depth are and to know the knowledge-surpassing love of Christ." Verse 8 says, "To me, less than the least of all saints, was this grace given to announce to the Gentiles the unsearchable riches of Christ as the gospel." The unsearchable riches of Christ are in the dimensions of Christ in verse 18: the breadth, length, height, and depth. These four dimensions are unlimited. We do not know how broad is the breadth, how long is the length, how high is the height, and how deep is the depth. They are all immeasurable. This relates to the unsearchable riches of Christ. Paul did not preach mere doctrines. He preached the unsearchable riches of Christ so that the saints together may apprehend the breadth, length, height, and depth. Verse 19b is the result of the foregoing verses: "that you may be filled unto all the fullness of God."

In this portion of the Word, a prevailing prayer by the writer of Ephesians, there are several main points. The first point is that we are strengthened into the inner man. Second, Christ makes His home not only in our spirit but also in our heart, that is, our whole being within our body. Third, we are filled unto all the fullness of God. In addition, we apprehend with all the saints all the dimensions of Christ. It is impossible to apprehend the immeasurable dimensions of Christ by ourselves. We have to do this with all the saints. Second Timothy 2:22 says that we should flee certain things and pursue with those who call on the Lord out of a pure heart.

BEING DISTRACTED FROM GOD'S INTENTION CONCERNING CHRIST

We always need to keep God's eternal purpose close to us. God's intention and central thought is to work Christ into us. This is basic and very important. God's intention is not for us to know many teachings and be taught with many doctrines. God has no intention that we merely learn doctrines. All the doctrines are not for the doctrines; they are for Christ. Doctrines are simply a means to reveal and convey Christ to us, instruct us how to partake of Christ, and give us the proper understanding of Christ. All the teachings are for Christ. However, many dear saints today have been distracted from Christ by doctrines, such as those concerning predestination, sovereign will, absolute grace, eternal security, and others. Today there are many arguments about these matters. Even among us there may be some who care for these things, secretly speaking with others about them.

Over a year ago when I was in San Francisco, a group of young people listened to my speaking. Afterwards, their leader came to me and asked, "What about absolute grace?" I told him, "Brother, if you have Christ, you have grace that is more than absolute. But if you do not have Christ, you have no grace; you have only the doctrine of grace." Then he asked, "What about eternal security?" I said, "Even security is Christ. If you have Christ, you have eternal security. The doctrine of security is not security; Christ is security. What we need is not eternal security in a doctrinal way. What we need is Christ." What then is God's sovereign will? The real will of God is Christ. If we have Christ, we have the sovereign will of God. If we do not have Christ, however, we have only the knowledge of God. Knowledge puffs up, and the letter kills; only Christ, who is the Spirit, gives life (1 Cor. 8:1; 2 Cor. 3:6, 17).

What we need today is nothing other than Christ. All

things are for Christ. The doctrines are for Christ, and the gifts are for Christ. We need certain kinds of forms, such as baptism by immersion and the Lord's table with the emblems. We are not for these forms, however. Rather, the forms are for Christ. I stress this again, because I sense that there is a distracting spirit today, even among us. Not many, but some, are being utilized by the enemy to distract us, particularly the young ones, by their secret talking. We condemn the distracting things. We do not want to talk about mere teachings. We are tired, even sick, of mere teachings. When I was young, I spent more than seven years to study the knowledge of the Bible. I became sick of mere knowledge. I asked myself, "What is the good of that kind of knowledge? Look at yourself. What kind of life do you have? What kind of character do you have? You are sloppy, lazy, and loose."

I am forced to say these things. Do not listen to those distracting teachings. Look at the character of those who speak them. Consider their life. What kind of life do they have? We do not need mere teachings. We need the living, practical Christ. We need the Christ whom we are practicing to experience day by day by the exercise of our spirit. God's intention is to work this Christ into us and to make Christ everything to us.

I am opening my heart to you. I long to see the day when the conversation among us will be nothing but Christ Himself, not teachings or even just the Bible. Please understand me in the right way. Do not think that I do not know the Bible or read it. I spend many hours in this book every day. However, we should not talk about the Bible alone. The Bible is a means to convey Christ to us. When we go to breakfast, we do not pay attention to the silverware. To have good silverware is helpful, but we do not go to breakfast for that. We go to breakfast for nourishment. All the utensils are the means by which we enjoy the nourishment. In the same way, the Bible is a means by which we enjoy Christ. It is a means through which Christ is conveyed and revealed to us. We are not for the Bible; we are for Christ. We are not for teachings; we are for Christ.

I hate to see and hear that among us, even today, some

brothers still talk only about doctrines. I have to fight the battle because of this. I have to shut the door. This is one hundred percent wrong, and it damages the situation here. We have no intention to care for mere doctrines. We are not here for doctrines. We have been made sick, and we are still sick, by doctrines. We do not need that. We need the riches of Christ. We are not even for the knowledge of the riches of Christ; we are for the riches of Christ themselves. We need not only to know the riches of Christ; we need to experience, partake, and share the riches.

BEING FOR NOTHING BUT CHRIST AND THE CHURCH

Based on this word I would ask you, how much of Christ have you enjoyed today? Perhaps twelve hours have passed today, from the morning to the evening. How much of Christ have you enjoyed? If I ask what kind of food you have enjoyed, you can immediately tell me what you had for breakfast, lunch, and dinner. Now, however, I am asking you in a practical way how much of Christ you enjoyed today. Christ is our life and life supply as our food. As our food, we must enjoy Him daily. He is our daily manna. I am afraid that we talk much about doctrines, and perhaps even about Christ, but we neglect the enjoyment of Christ. I would like to see that from now on, by the mercy and help of the Lord, the church will learn how to help the saints in a practical way to enjoy Christ, not only to know Christ, but to partake of Christ.

This time of training from the very beginning to the end is for nothing but Christ, along with His Body. It is for us to enjoy Him as our life and express Him as our Head. I beg you to learn to forget about other things. Do not talk about other matters, and do not listen to this kind of talk. Talk about things other than Christ is distracting. I realize that a number of the young people have been distracted by that talk. This is not right. This is to not be faithful. Our training is not for this. It is for the experience of Christ. I hope that from now on we do not give the young people any kind of mere teachings. Rather, we should give them the adequate instruction that they may know how to contact Christ, deal with Christ, be dealt with by Him, and share Him with others. The leading brothers among the young people have to pray together very much that the Lord would deliver them from anything other than Christ.

We do not know anything else. We just know this one thing, to fellowship one with another about Christ. What we apprehend with all the saints is not knowledge and teachings about absolute grace or sovereign will. That is something of the Lord's recovery of four or five hundred years ago. Today is not the time of Martin Luther. Luther was a great servant of the Lord; there is no doubt about that. But today the teachings of absolute grace and sovereign will are too childish. The Lord's recovery today is Christ Himself as life and His Body as His expression. God's recovery today is Christ and the church. Even the gifts are an item of the Lord's recovery in the previous century. God's recovery today is the full experience of Christ and the practical expression of Christ in each locality. We should never be distracted by anything else, even by the good things. I hate to see that anyone among us would speak only on those other, good things. Those things distract from the very purpose of the church. The church is not for anything else but Christ and His Body. The church should help the saints in a very practical way, not to talk about anything else or even merely to talk about Christ, but to share Christ with one another.

Ephesians 3:18 is Paul's prayer that we would apprehend with all the saints the dimensions and the riches of Christ. In addition, 2 Timothy 2:22 instructs us to flee. At that time there was the need to flee, to escape, and today there is still the need. Flee from the distracting, dissenting, and vain talk. Moreover, we should pursue after righteousness toward others, faith toward God, and love and peace, which are also toward others, with those who call on the Lord out of a pure heart. We must learn to experience Christ in such a way and not know so many other things.

PUTTING WHAT WE HAVE LEARNED INTO PRACTICE

The church must help the saints to experience Christ, partake of Christ, and share Christ with one another. As a rule, the church should not give people much teaching.

Rather, it must give adequate instruction concerning the experience of Christ. Then after giving instruction, the church should help the saints to practice what they have been taught. For instance, we can instruct the saints that Christ is the life-giving Spirit who dwells in our spirit today; therefore, we must walk in our spirit and exercise our spirit to contact Christ and take Him as our life. This much is good enough. Now we have to help the saints to put this into practice, because the messages, teachings, doctrine, and knowledge are not adequate.

Meeting Together to Testify of Our Experience

In order to put this into practice, we need to have the meetings. The most profitable and proper way to meet is to fellowship with one another according to the instruction we have received. Someone may ask a brother, "Do you realize that we have to exercise our spirit to contact Christ, walk in the spirit, and take Christ as our life in a practical way?" Then the brother can testify how he has experienced Christ as the life-giving Spirit by exercising his spirit. This should not be a testimony about what happened twenty years ago. It should be a testimony of the brother's recent experience. Moreover, it should be something real, not mere knowledge. Simply to repeat the points of a message means nothing. We may compare the speaking of knowledge to teaching someone to drive a car. If we only tell a person how to turn the steering wheel, he still will not know how to drive; rather, he needs practice.

We also have seen that in order to experience Christ in a living way, we have to deal with our conscience. Our conscience must be pure, purged, good, and without offenses. This is the instruction of dealing with our conscience. It is brief, because even the apostles did not give long messages in the New Testament. To put this into practice, though, we can ask a brother, "Would you please tell us what your experience is of dealing with your conscience?" The right way is to put the brothers on a little test. Some may say that this will scare people away. That is all right; let them not come. Then whoever comes will come with a sincere heart, not just to listen as a "pew member." What is the good of listening like this even for twenty years?

Much instruction has been given, but I am concerned about the practice. We do not meet together to learn the "menu" and the "recipes." I do not care to learn these; I simply want to eat. Sometimes my little daughter teases me and asks me if I know what I am eating. However, I do not have to exercise my mentality to know; I simply eat to enjoy.

Today too many Christians come to the meetings only to sit and listen. They learn to criticize and say, "Good speaker, marvelous message." After doing this for twenty years, do they have the growth in life? Do they know Christ in a practical way? Rather, after twenty years they are still the same, as far as life is concerned. They are spiritual dwarfs, without a proper stature. We need to grow, and in order to grow we need to eat. We cannot grow without eating. All mothers know that children grow by eating, not by knowledge. The church needs to nourish the saints, and the saints need to be nourished by learning to take Christ and by practicing all the things that we have learned.

I am not without the experience of these things. I experienced the vanity of the mere teachings in Christianity, so I know that today we need the real practice and the real experience of Christ. When we say that we need to deal with our conscience, the church must immediately help the saints to put this instruction into practice, and everyone should practice dealing with his conscience. Then we may ask a brother to give a testimony of dealing with his conscience. This is the proper way. If by the Lord's grace we take this way, then week after week and month after month the saints will grow in life.

We have said that the inner anointing is the heavenly, spiritual, divine "painting." Through this strange language we have received the instruction; however, I am concerned that even after five months not many of us have practiced the inner anointing. This is another example of how the leading ones need the experience to take the right way. It is easy simply to read a certain chapter and a certain verse and speak about a certain subject. To help the brothers and sisters to go on in a practical way, however, requires that we have the real experience. I hope the church will take this way.

Meeting in Small Groups
for Fellowship and Practice

The leading ones in the church should pay attention to those who improve, those among the brothers and sisters who have made some real progress. It is better to divide our meeting into groups of ten or fifteen and let one or two who have some progress in the growth of life take care of each group. Then the ones in the group can share and fellowship with one another, not about other things but about the instruction the church has received from the Lord. Week after week there should be one or two meetings for the saints to come together in this way. This will be very practical and very helpful. All the brothers and sisters will be interested in this kind of meeting; they will have a taste for it, and spontaneously they will bring others into it. This will help the increase in the number of saints meeting. There may be ten or twelve people in a group, but after three months there may be eighteen or twenty. Then more leading ones will be produced. After five or six months, we may have to divide a group into two groups of ten, each with some leading ones. In this way, the saints will constantly learn to grow, and there will be the continual increase of numbers.

In addition, the useful ones will be manifested. We may even say that they will be "exposed." In the church the ones who are truly spiritual and actually know something always like to hide themselves, to make themselves hidden. The fleshly ones, however, always like to make a show of themselves. Therefore, the spiritual ones need to be exposed, that is, manifested.

I say again, it is in this way that the saints will grow in life, our numbers will be increased, and the useful ones, the leading ones, will be produced. Then spontaneously all the members will be functioning members. Everyone will learn to function by growth. It will not be like today's Christianity, in which everyone sits while one person speaks. A brother once incorrectly called me a "pastor." I told him, "Brother, if I am a pastor, you must be the pastor of the pastor." We are all functioning brothers. I have my function, and you have yours. I have my ministry, and you have yours. I have my responsibility, and you have yours.

To say this is easy, but we must put it into practice. The proper way to practice this is what I have shared with you in this message. Once a week on the Lord's Day morning, some brothers who truly know something of the Lord can give us a message of ministry. However, one message a week is good enough. The rest of the time can be for worship, the remembrance of the Lord and the Father at the Lord's table. We can also have a time to come together to pray, as in our prayer meeting. Then we can come together one or two times a week for practice meetings. In this meeting there are no messages or teachings. We simply practice all the instruction we have received from the messages.

Many of you have studied in college or in graduate school. In college many students spend more time in the lab than in the classroom. Without the lab, the classroom does not mean much. We need to put what we have been instructed with into practice. In addition, we also will help others and practice the outreach to unbelievers or believers. This is very practical. Allow me to speak frankly: If we do not have some brothers with some real ministry, there is no need to have a so-called message meeting for speaking nonsense and wasting time. Do not have the expectation of coming only to listen to more and more doctrines. You have been listening to many doctrines, but what help is it? We have to put all the things we have heard, the things that are necessary for the experience of Christ, into practice, and we should forget about the things that are not necessary.

Helping the Young People to Practice

The whole church, including the young people's work, should take this way. Those who lead the young ones should help them to practice. Do not merely lecture them; just use a short time to give them some instruction. Then put them on the test and help them to practice. In addition, help them to "open the fields" in the universities, colleges, and high schools. Do not say that they are not grown enough. All mothers know that they have to let their children make mistakes. Then they will learn the proper way. We cannot say that since a baby does not know how to walk, we should not let him walk. This is foolish. Let him walk; then he will know how to walk. Let them make mistakes. However, we must check their motive. If a child does something wrong with a wrong motive, he should be reproved. But if he does something wrong with a good motive, he should be encouraged. Let all the young ones practice and learn from mistakes. If you do not know how to do this, you are wrong.

Do not let the young ones become the old ones. Do not let the grandchildren become the grandfathers. I live in a small, quiet apartment. The neighbors do not have the energy to make noise. Most of them are retired and too old to make noise; they spend the day on the sofa or in bed. I, my wife, and my little daughter are the most active persons there, with the most energy to make noise. Do we expect all the young people in the church to be old ones who do not have the energy to make noise? We must help the young ones to "make noise." There are a number of universities and colleges in this area. If we have the proper practice, it will be easy to have three or four hundred young people in these schools to open all the "fields" in the campuses and dormitories. We have to help all the saints to practice. When we went to Taiwan in 1949, we had only a handful of young people, about ten or twelve. After less than a year, however, we had over one hundred college students. We have to put the young ones on the test; we must help them to practice and learn the lessons. I say again, though, that we must have a pure motive. It is not serious to make mistakes; our motive is the most important thing. What the church needs today is the real practice.

Learning to Pray in a Living Way and Read the Word to Feed on the Lord

One very necessary matter is that all the saints must learn how to pray in a living way and how to read the Word to feed on the Lord in the spirit. All the saints must learn the lesson to rise up a little earlier to have a time with the Lord, to pray in a living way, and to read the Word to feed on the Lord. We should check ourselves concerning these things. Do not listen to vain talk about doctrines, sovereign will, and absolute grace. Rather, check concerning people's living. At what time does someone rise in the morning? What is he doing at 6:00 A.M.? If a brother or sister does not know how to rise early in the morning to contact the Lord with living prayer and living reading of the Word, yet this one speaks much doctrine, we should not listen. Rather, this one should be reproved. We may say, "Brother, I do not care for your talk. I would check you by your living, not by your talk. I advise you to rise early in the morning. Do not love your bed more than you love the Lord." However, I do not see those who speak much about doctrine come often to morning watch.

CARING FOR PRACTICAL LIVING
AND NOT FOR VAIN TALK

I do not believe in vain talk. Rather, we must have a practical living. All the dear brothers and sisters must be helped to practice the normal, practical Christian living. We are children of God. Therefore, day by day we need to contact the Lord in a living way. We need to know how to pray to Him and how to read His Word. We need to have a living contact with Him day by day. Then based on this, we need to deal with our motive, intention, desire, conscience, and relationships with others. This is practical. Whether or not we know what sovereign will is means nothing. What is truly sovereign is that we learn how to have a practical living and bear a burden for young ones, for spiritual children, caring for them and feeding them all the time. We should always be bearing a responsibility for two or three, or five or six, unbelievers, praying for them, bringing their names into the presence of the Lord, watching for them, crying to the Lord for them, and finding a time to bring them to the Lord and to help them to know the Lord. These are the necessary things.

Do not stay in your sitting rooms to have vain talk. Whenever the church has a meeting, come to the meeting. I am sorry to see that some do not come to our prayer meeting. Where are they? Are they sitting in their living room talking about vain things? Come to the church meeting to function, to build up others and to be built up by others. These are the practical things. Forgive me if this offends you. I am a frank brother, and I cannot stand to see the saints going astray. I like to see them going on in the proper way.

We need something practical and real. If we still have the distracting things, there is no need to meet together here. There are many Christian "bodies." You can go there to talk with them, because they are for the teachings. We, however, are not for the teachings. We are here for a practical life to experience Christ and to come together to express Him. We do not care for the doctrines. We look to the Lord to rescue us from going astray, to deliver us from the distracting elements.

I exercise my heart and my spirit much to look to the Lord that from now on the church will go on in a very practical way to help the saints, not to gain more knowledge but to put all the instruction we have received into practice, to deal with all these things, not to criticize or condemn but to fellowship with one another, to help others, and to be willing to be helped. Then we can go on in a practical way, and we will have the real growth. We will see the glory of the Lord among us, and His glory will fill us. Then we will render help to many others; that is, we will minister Christ to them. Whenever people come into our meetings, they will not sense teachings or something else, but the anointing and the gracious presence of the Lord. Many people will be saved in the way of life, and we will help them to know Christ in the way of life. This is what the Lord is seeking after today. This is our burden, and we all have to pray and plan for this. I beg you, not that you would cooperate with me—I am nothing—but that you would cooperate with the dear Lord for His recovery. I assure you that if we go on in this way, we will see His blessing on us. On the other hand, however, I must warn you that if you are doing something against this recovery, I am concerned for you. Some vindication may come from the Lord.

ABOUT THE AUTHOR

Witness Lee was born in 1905 in northern China and raised in a Christian family. At age 19 he was fully captured for Christ and immediately consecrated himself to preach the gospel for the rest of his life. Early in his service, he met Watchman Nee, a renowned preacher, teacher, and writer. Witness Lee labored together with Watchman Nee under his direction. In 1934 Watchman Nee entrusted Witness Lee with the responsibility for his publication operation, called the Shanghai Gospel Bookroom.

Prior to the Communist takeover in 1949, Witness Lee was sent by Watchman Nee and his other co-workers to Taiwan to ensure that the things delivered to them by the Lord would not be lost. Watchman Nee instructed Witness Lee to continue the former's publishing operation abroad as the Taiwan Gospel Bookroom, which has been publicly recognized as the publisher of Watchman Nee's works outside China. Witness Lee's work in Taiwan manifested the Lord's abundant blessing. From a mere 350 believers, newly fled from the mainland, the churches in Taiwan grew to 20,000 in five years.

In 1962 Witness Lee felt led of the Lord to come to the United States, settling in California. During his 35 years of service in the U.S., he ministered in weekly meetings and weekend conferences, delivering several thousand spoken messages. Much of his speaking has since been published as over 400 titles. Many of these have been translated into over fourteen languages. He gave his last public conference in February 1997 at the age of 91.

He leaves behind a prolific presentation of the truth in the Bible. His major work, *Life-study of the Bible,* comprises over 25,000 pages of commentary on every book of the Bible from the perspective of the believers' enjoyment and experience of God's divine life in Christ through the Holy Spirit. Witness Lee was the chief editor of a new translation of the New Testament into Chinese called the Recovery Version and directed the translation of the same into English. The Recovery Version also appears in a number of other languages. He provided an extensive body of footnotes, outlines, and spiritual cross references. A radio broadcast of his messages can be heard on Christian radio stations in the United States. In 1965 Witness Lee founded Living Stream Ministry, a non-profit corporation, located in Anaheim, California, which officially presents his and Watchman Nee's ministry.

Witness Lee's ministry emphasizes the experience of Christ as life and the practical oneness of the believers as the Body of Christ. Stressing the importance of attending to both these matters, he led the churches under his care to grow in Christian life and function. He was unbending in his conviction that God's goal is not narrow sectarianism but the Body of Christ. In time, believers began to meet simply as the church in their localities in response to this conviction. In recent years a number of new churches have been raised up in Russia and in many eastern European countries.